KT-177-416

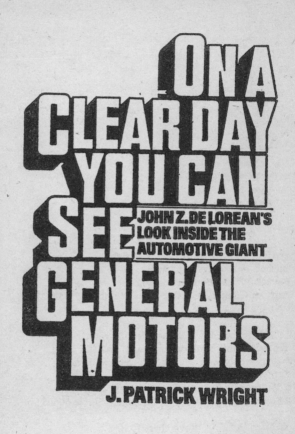

ON A CLEAR DAY YOU CAN SEE GENERAL MOTORS

JOHN Z. DE LOREAN'S LOOK INSIDE THE AUTOMOTIVE GIANT

J. PATRICK WRIGHT

 AVON
PUBLISHERS OF BARD, CAMELOT AND DISCUS BOOKS

AVON BOOKS
A division of
The Hearst Corporation
959 Eighth Avenue
New York, New York 10019

Copyright © 1979 by J. Patrick Wright
Published by arrangement with
J. Patrick Wright Enterprises, Inc.
Library of Congress Catalog Card Number: 79-56627
ISBN: 0-380-51722-1

First Avon Printing, November, 1980

AVON TRADEMARK REG. U.S. PAT. OFF. AND IN
OTHER COUNTRIES, MARCA REGISTRADA,
HECHO EN U.S.A.

Printed in the U.S.A.

To Mary Ann, Patrick and Molly—three important reasons why I've pursued this project to its completion.

Acknowledgments

Many people in many ways had a hand in this work. For some their involvement was simply in the encouragement they gave to me when the project seemed hopeless. For others, it was in their continuing interest in this book, which bolstered my own conviction that it must be published. Thank you to all of you.

There are, in addition, a number of people who had a direct role in this effort. They merit not only special mention, but also my very special thanks.

At the top of the list is John H. Niebler, a long-time friend and trusted counselor, whose persistence and unfailing, positive outlook kept this project alive and moving forward during its many dark moments over the past four years.

Five top-flight professionals read and edited the manuscript at various stages of the book's development. They are Mike Sheldrick, Terry Bormann, Pat Reardon, Tim Trainor and Bill Bruce. Each was very instrumental in the outcome of this project.

Along the way, the advice and perspective of Jim Dunne, John Garr, Bill Hampton and Dan Wright were eagerly sought and gladly received.

Special recognition must be given to John J. T. Shinners and Shinners Publications, Inc. for having the courage to print this work when many about them were shrinking from the formidable task.

During five years work on this book, there were many people whose deft typing skills were essential to this final product. They are Patience Peterson, Nancy Trainor, Kathy Hunwick, Sue Garr, Rita McKay, Diane Simmons, Sister Rosemary Sam, Kathy Conway, Vicki Binkowski, Margaret Kemp and Mary Kaliordos.

Three books were very helpful in providing historical perspective to the General Motors Corporation. Two works by the late Alfred P. Sloan, Jr., *Adventures of a White Collar Man* (Doubleday, Doran & Company, Inc. 1941), and *My Years With General Motors* (Doubleday & Company, Inc. 1964), contributed valuable insight to the formation of GM as an industrial giant. And Lawrence R. Gustin's book, *BILLY DURANT Creator of General Motors* (Eerdmans Publishing Co. 1973), helped supply details of the life of GM's founder.

I am especially indebted to two people for helping me acquire the time necessary to put this book into production. First is my wife, Mary Ann, who willingly returned to work full-time to support our family during the past year while I finished this project. Second is Jane Hastings, a loving grandmother and a mother-in-law without peer, who gladly looked after Patrick and Molly when their parents were tied up with their work.

A final acknowledgment must go to John Z. De Lorean, a controversial and talented executive whose candor is this story. Today he is working diligently on a unique sports car, the DMC-12, which he plans to introduce sometime in 1980. Good luck, John.

J.P.W.

Foreword

> *Pat has done a fantastic job. . . . This book is what
> should be said about American Business. . . .*
> —John Z. De Lorean,
> February 6, 1976

In February of 1974, John Z. De Lorean asked me to write a "no nonsense, no bullshit book" with him about his life and experiences at the General Motors Corporation. The work would "open up the board room from the inside," he said, adding, "I know you have to name names and talk about specific decisions."

His proposal was intriguing. De Lorean had built a reputation in the auto industry as a forward thinking, crack executive who often spoke his mind even when his comments were critical of his company and the industry. The book he outlined would be the first of its kind, and a meaningful contribution to business journalism, a field heretofore populated with slick autobiographies that have been sanitized by the public relations department, or boring treatises that are bereft of life and personalities.

In our discussions over the next several months, John reiterated his reasons for wanting to write this book. He felt the country needed an insider's view of how business was actually run that might serve as a vehicle for corporate reform. He was quite specific saying that the book must demonstrate "that somehow we (should) return back to the stockholder and the American public some of the responsibility for the end result that corporations derive from their activities. Many things that happen (in business) are really not good for the public and not good for the country . . ." he said. "The ideal thing, of course, would (be to) have this turn out to be a bible of what's wrong with the way business is done." We agreed on the tone and content of the book and to co-author it.

John handed me a large stack of material which contained personal papers, memos from GM, business analyses he had prepared, rough drafts of several chapters, his handwritten notes about items and sections to be included in the manuscript, and his correspondence with several literary agents and publishers. "Here," he said, "you're the doctor."

We wrote a detailed proposal outlining the book we planned to write. Playboy Press outbid several other publishers for the book with an advance of $45,000. De Lorean and I, as co-authors, signed a contract with Playboy and then began hours of intensive interviewing which was tape-recorded. The comments and analysis which John presented were consistently frank, honest and tough. A title was selected: *On a Clear Day You Can See General Motors.* And a manuscript was prepared, rewritten and submitted to the publisher over the Labor Day weekend in 1975. Playboy was ecstatic.

John De Lorean was not. He refused to let the book be published. His objection as expressed to me was that the book we'd written would anger General Motors executives who he said would make it difficult, if not impossible, to build and market an "ethical sports car" which he was developing. He admitted that this consideration was a latter-day influence on his plans for the book and was not a part of our original discussions or agreement on the project.

Despite his objection to publishing the book, he praised it on several occasions, including one time during a meeting in New York called by Bill Adler, executive editor of Playboy Press, to try to resolve the book crisis. It was February 6, 1976 and John said flatly to Adler, Philip Spitzer, our agent, and me: "Pat has done a fantastic job . . . The book is what should be said about American business. The book is what should be published. It really is the only book." But he also reiterated his fear of reprisals from GM if the book was printed. A month later he added, "I've got to play with the system for another 18 months. Then I can say this stuff."

Despite his praise and professed willingness to publish the book at a later date, De Lorean embarked on a four-year pattern of vacillation on the book. At times, he said he was eager to get the book published. At other times, he was adamantly opposed to it. And at still other times he offered to help me do my own book about General Motors, provided I leave him out of it.

Playboy touted the book as a "major property," said that tens of thousands of advanced orders had been received from bookstores around the country and that it wanted dearly to publish the book. Nevertheless, it seemed willing to let the project drag on. When Playboy did make efforts to get the manuscript into print, it could not get John's cooperation.

My position remained the same. Playboy had the book which was proposed, contracted for and delivered. John had admitted this. Therefore, it should be published. In addition, I told both John and Playboy that if they did not publish the book, I would find another publisher or publish it myself.

Still there was no action on the book. Twice, De Lorean indicated he would repay the advance and cancel the contract if that was Playboy's wish. However, when Playboy submitted a cancellation agreement he refused to sign it.

Before terminating the Playboy contract he first wanted me to sign an agreement with him not to publish the book on my own, or write anything about him without his permission. He also wanted me to turn over to him all of the documents, notes and tapes used in writing the book. In return, he would give me $5,000 and 20 percent of the author's revenue of any "De Lorean/General Motors book" that he might write. This proposal was unacceptable to me and thus the book remained tied up into 1979.

I decided that the only way to get this book published was to do it myself. My reasons for doing so are these:

• Despite John's vacillations on the book for the past four years, one constant fact is apparent from our discussions: He believes the manuscript submitted to Playboy to be a factual representation of his thoughts and analysis of General Motors and American business.

• He also believes that this story should be told, and that the book submitted to Playboy is the book we agreed to write, did write and delivered to the publisher.

• John De Lorean's story is vitally important to providing a better understanding of the process of big business. It provides a never-before-seen insight into the process of management at the highest levels in the world's largest industrial corporation.

• Great care was taken in preparing the final manuscript to reflect many of the changes, deletions and alterations that John said he wanted on various occasions.

• Much of the factual content, anecdotes, tenor and tone of the book has been confirmed by my own outside reporting.

Bear in mind while reading this book that it was essentially written in 1974-75. The content is supported by the materials, documents and notes which John gave to me, as well as his own spoken words.

Make no mistake. What follows is John Zachary De Lorean's own story. It is not a dispassionate overview of an industrial giant. It is one man's heartfelt story about the business world about him as he worked his way toward the summit, and then found that the climb was not worth the reward. In this case, that man is one of the most successful and talented executives in the post-World War II automobile industry.

J. PATRICK WRIGHT

Grosse Pointe, Michigan
September 1979

Contents

CHAPTER ONE

Why I Quit General Motors

It was Sunday night, April 1, 1973. I was arriving in New York City to resign from the General Motors Corporation. The next morning I would sign the official letter of resignation in the office of Chairman Richard C. Gerstenberg. In the afternoon the Board of Directors was expected to accept the resignation at its regular monthly meeting.

My action was not hasty. It was rational and planned. What was going to take place the next day was the culmination of a growing conflict I had with the methods of management of General Motors Corporation.

At the time, I was GM's fastest-moving executive. As group executive for the Car and Truck Group, I had reporting to me the heart of the corporation's business—the five American car divisions: Chevrolet, Buick, Oldsmobile, Pontiac and Cadillac; the GMC Truck and Coach Division and the Canadian car and truck operations. The combined sales of these seven divisions were over $25 billion a year. In total, these operations alone were larger than all but a handful of companies in the world. This job paid up to $650,000 a year in salary and bonus, making it one of the highest-paid executive positions in the United States, or the world for that matter.

By most conventional measures of business success, I had it made. In less than 17 years I had risen from being a

1

greenhorn engineer at the Pontiac Division to an office on the prestigious Fourteenth Floor in General Motors' World Headquarters in midtown Detroit. Most General Motors executives spend a lifetime, 40 years or more in some cases, chasing an elusive dream of one day moving upstairs to The Fourteenth Floor. At 48, I was there with a better than even-odds chance of one day being president. But I was about to toss all that away. This was the most crucial decision of my life. For the first time in 25 years, I would be without a job in the auto industry, my first and only career love. The decision was mine to make. But it was irrevocable once it was made. When you leave GM you seldom return. There is no prodigal son parable for the GM executive who leaves his corporate home. He is rarely welcomed back. General Motors is a very proud corporation. It places great importance on a history of continual service to the company cause. It stresses the team approach of management for its executives who put in their years working up the corporate ladder. For instance, the annual report for 1974, the year after I left, proudly proclaims the longevity of top management:

Thomas A. Murphy, Chairman, service—37 years;
Elliott M. Estes, President, service—40 years;
Oscar A. Lundin, Vice-Chairman, service—41 years;
Richard L. Terrell, Vice-Chairman, service—37 years.

The implication is obvious: The only way to learn the GM system of management is to put in the years of service. For your continued efforts and time, you reap bountiful rewards in money, perquisites, prestige and financial security. But once you break that string, leave the team, the locker room is closed to you forever. In my mind, I had already left the team. And in recent weeks that had made it difficult to go through the motions of my job, and to accept some of the perks which went with my position. Other perks were not difficult to accept, and I was briefly warmed when a familiar face came out of the crowd at La Guardia Airport. It was Bill Finelli, the long-time Chevrolet Division driver who'd met me at the airport so many times in the past when I was running Chevrolet. He was waiting with a Chevrolet sedan to take me to the Waldorf Towers in midtown Manhattan. We talked intermittently on the trip into the city. And I thought about what I felt was a tragic irony of my resignation: That this mammoth corporation, which was founded by a maverick, Billy Durant, and built into the prototype of the well-run American business by men who were distinct individuals, could not today accept or accommodate an executive who had made his mark in the corporation by being different and individualistic. I never pretended to compare myself with the great founders and shapers of the modern General Motors—Alfred P. Sloan, Jr., the du Pont family, Donaldson Brown and others. But I was a student of their lives and techniques, and it bothered me that I was no longer able to work for the company that they had founded. I had made a substantial contribution to General Motors by using foresight, detailed planning and a broad consciousness of the effect of our business on the outside world, as they had taught. The parts of the corporation under my jurisdiction grew and prospered under my management. My business record, frankly, was better than that of any other GM manager at the time. And yet there was no place for me.

As I reflected on my career, it was easy to recall my first day at GM. A naive, rough-edged engineer from Detroit's near east side when I joined the company's Pontiac Division on September 1, 1956, I came under the tutelage and into the friendship of Semon E. (Bunkie) Knudsen who was head of the Division. He taught me the automobile business as he transformed Pontiac from an old lady's division into the hottest car division of the 1960s. We gave Pontiac a youthful image by producing a whole new range of cars featuring the wide-track look and distinctive, sporty riding and handling characteristics. Creating the 1964 GTO, the industry's first muscle car, etched that image on the public's mind. The momentum begun under Bunkie Knudsen was still at Pontiac four years after he left, when I was named general manager of the division, and a General Motors vice-president.

There followed more product firsts at Pontiac, such as the Grand Prix, a moderately priced personal luxury car which pioneered the booming personal luxury car market. By 1968 Pontiac was selling a record of about 900,000 cars a year, and it had jumped from sixth to third place, behind Chevrolet and Ford, in sales among all of Detroit's car divisions.

From Pontiac, in early 1969, I was promoted to general manager of the Chevrolet Division. Except for corporate insiders, no one knew the depths of the troubles at Chevrolet. The nation's most popular nameplate was heading toward red-ink performances and running totally uncontrolled in its operations. The three-and-a-half years which followed were the most difficult and challenging in my business life. I was able to put together an energetic, young management team which got its arms around this unwieldy giant and developed a sophisticated system of internal management controls which turned Chevrolet around. We improved our sales penetration, but more importantly extracted billions of dollars profit where there had been little from Chevrolet's vast operations. In 1972, the division set an all-time divisional sales record for the industry, 3.1 million cars and trucks. The next year was even better, 3.4 million vehicles. These totals proved our programs for Chevy's recovery to be right.

Those were happy times, and yet I could not relive those happy emotions as I reflected on them. Settling into my room in the Waldorf Towers, I had no emotion because my spirit had been spent months previously when I decided to leave GM. I simply felt numb that Sunday night. This whole ordeal was a downer for me. The final pieces to the puzzle were all ready. I was simply putting them in place, completing the picture by physically going through the formal steps of final separation.

The process of separation had begun long before. As I grew in the corporation, I guess I gradually came into conflict with it. Conflict with the philosophy of business. Conflict with the system of management. And conflict with the people in positions of power.

Sometime in the late 1960s, I cannot remember when, a nagging suspicion about the philosophy of General Motors and the automobile business began to overtake me. It was the kind of feeling that you have and then quickly dismiss. But it comes back again and again. Pretty soon you find that you are thinking differently than you once did. My concern was that there hadn't been an important product innovation in the industry since the automatic transmission and power steering in 1949. That was almost a quarter-century of technical hibernation. In the place of product innovation, the automobile industry went on a two-decade marketing binge which generally offered up the same old product under the guise of something new and useful. There really was nothing essentially new. But year in and year out we were urging Americans to sell their cars and buy new ones because the styling had changed. There really was no reason for them to change from one model to the next, except for the new wrinkles in the sheet metal, which to me weren't sufficient reason. While this was an indictment of myself as well as my fellow auto executives, it was true that each year all we were offering to the customer was a supper warmed over.

It struck me that not only was this management dereliction, but also an unfair, even immoral practice, because the heart of this system was to take some American wage earner who was working his fanny off trying to pay for a car and, just about the day he got it paid off, convince him that he should start the payment process all over again. His 36 months were up. Now he should take his token residual value in this used car and plunk it down on another car. He just starts the whole goddamned procedure over again. He is tied into a new series of payments for another three years. Somehow this didn't seem to be a meaningful contribution to society and business.

If we could give the new-car buyers something really new, such as power steering, power brakes, a more efficient engine or vastly improved durability, then that would be a good reason for him to move from a product without these innovations to one with them. There would be benefit to him because these kinds of innovations make people better drivers, or they make the car safer and easier to drive, more trouble-free, or more economical to operate. This broader view of our business was a marked departure from my outlook earlier in life.

At one time, I was pretty much a typical company man —doing the job I was told to do, never questioning anything further about my work than whether I was doing it the most effective way. As an engineer, my work was uncomplicated. Engineering is a very logical and precise science. The answers are all there in cold mathematics. But as I grew in management, from an engineer to department head to chief engineer to division general manager, my awareness grew also, and I began to recognize the power and responsibility I had in building cars, in terms of the safety of people, providing value to the customer, the security of the economy and the fulfillment of my life. It was then that I began to question the ethics of my business strictly from the perspective of my own involvement.

Soon I found myself questioning a much bigger picture, the morality of the whole GM system. It seemed to me that there was (and is) a cancerous amorality about this system. The undue emphasis on profits and cost control without a wider concern for the effects of GM's business on its many publics seemed too often capable of bringing together, in the corporation, men of sound, personal morality and responsibility who as a group reached business decisions which were irresponsible and of questionable morality.

At General Motors the concern for the effect of our products on our many publics was never discussed except in terms of cost or sales potential. And being a member of the management team meant that you supported your boss's decisions, and the corporation decisions, even if you thought they were wrong. When you opposed your superiors, you were accused of "not being on the team." Charlie Chayne, vice-president of Engineering, along with his staff, took a very strong stand against the Corvair as an unsafe car long before it went on sale in 1959. He was not listened to but instead told in effect, "You're not a member of the team. Shut up or go looking for another job." The car was approved even though serious questions were raised about its engineering. These were not immoral men who were bringing out this car. These were warm, breathing men with families and children who as private individuals would never have approved this project for a minute if they were told, "You are going to kill and injure people with this car." But those same men, in a business atmosphere, where everything is reduced to terms of costs, profit goals and production deadlines, were able as a group to approve a product most of them wouldn't have considered approving as individuals.

When the safety of the car was called into question by Ralph Nader in his book *Unsafe at Any Speed,* the corporate reaction was just as irrational as the approval of the car. Nader was tailed and spied upon, and attempts were made to destroy his reputation by raising questions about the morality of his personal life. They failed and so did the Corvair.

What bothered me was that there was no means to make the changes in our business philosophy and the response to our publics which I felt were paramount to the long-term health and growth of the corporation. In theory, the GM system of business management featured two functions: centralized policymaking and control, and decentralized operations. The latter meant that the operating decisions for the day-to-day running of the business were made at the divisional level. It was here that you smelled the clay in the styling studios; ran the plants where engines were built, body panels stamped out and cars and trucks assembled; created the advertising campaigns; worked with the dealers and managed all of the physical aspects which took a product from design to production to retail sale.

To coordinate all the company's many and varied divisions and operations, and to direct them toward the overall good of the corporation, general policy guidelines and controls were formulated and administered within which the divisions ran their own businesses. This policy and control function was the responsibility of corporate management, and exercised through a series of committees composed generally of men who had made their marks in the divisions. Once "upstairs" on The Fourteenth Floor, the men who sat on these committees were supposed to draw upon their operating experience to plan the growth of the business and control the company. The success of General Motors in the past had come from a finely tuned balance between this centralized control and the decentralized operations.

But I found that the fine tuning had gone out of control. As I progressed in the corporation, I watched GM's operations slowly become centralized. The divisions gradually were stripped of their decision-making power. Operating decisions were more and more being made on The Fourteenth Floor. This is because men rose in power who did not seem to have the capabilities of broad business outlook necessary to manage the business. They had gotten into power because they were part of a management system which for the most part put personal loyalties from one executive to another, and protection of the system above management skills; and put the use of corporate politics in place of sound business leadership. They consequently lost sight of the corporation's management goals of keeping a keen eye on the marketplace and a firm hand on the corporate tiller. They also lost sight of the corporate objective of keeping policymaking and control separate from the day-to-day operations of the business. As The Fourteenth Floor began to run the operations of GM, it had no time or inclination for planning the growth and direction of General Motors. There was no forward planning to speak of at GM. Policymaking was often shallow and insignificant. The group executive's job I held had little real substance. It was a paper-shuffling stopover for executives who were in the running for the company's presidency.

And the committees and subcommittees which were methodically set up during the '20s, '30s and '40s to plan and guide General Motors growth were not doing that. They spent little time looking at the big picture, instead occupying themselves with miniscule matters of the operation which should have been considered and disposed in the divisions or much farther down the corporate management line. A good example of this misdirection was the work of the powerful Engineering Policy Group (EPG), which within the original design of the corporation was charged with recommending broad product policy and new product areas for top management to consider. Instead of operating within that area of responsibility, the EPG was deeply enmeshed in small engineering detail decisions such as the size and design of bumpers for individual car lines or carburetor configurations or the tone of the seat belt buzzer. Practically every operational product decision, no matter how small, had to be brought before the EPG. These were not policy matters. Preoccupied with this minutiae, the EPG often missed the broad trends in product innovation which were sweeping the industry. The small-car boom is one example of a missed trend. Several different small-car programs with which I was associated were presented formally and informally to the EPG during the mid and late 1960s. These programs proposed small, more interchangeable and lighter-weight cars which would lower material and energy consumption and make our products and costs competitive with the fast-selling imported cars. The proposals never were approved, though the market was racing headlong in that direction, because the EPG was too involved with day-to-day operations to see the bigger picture.

Just as the EPG was usurping the engineering prerogatives of the divisions and failing in its much larger responsibility of planning, so too were the other corporate committees and subcommittees missing the mark in their areas of concern—marketing, public relations, personnel, manufacturing, distribution and the rest.

In my group job I could see firsthand the stultifying effect of this centralization. Corporate management was not making the decisions that the needs of GM demanded. The system also was causing long delays in making decisions which cried out for quick action. I complained about this, but I couldn't garner support for change. Usually, when I proposed futuristic programs which would get some measure of control and planning into the domestic automotive business, my bosses said, "Hell, go ahead and do it." But I never got their support or the money I needed to implement the programs.

It was a shocking experience for me "upstairs." After eight years of running car divisions, I suddenly found myself in the fall of 1972 with no direct operating responsibilities and a non-job as a group executive. I had no business to manage directly. Where I had been a quarterback for eight years, I now was watching the game from the sidelines. I still wanted to play in the games. On the field. These feelings of occupational emptiness were complicated by personalities.

At the time in my career when I was just one of the corporate boys spending my working and non-working hours with General Motors people or the company suppliers, I had a tightly knit group of corporate friends, and I obeyed the corporate dictates in behavior and dress. But as I grew it dawned on me that all of us were becoming too inbred. We were losing contact with America. With our customers. In addition, while I enjoyed work, I've always placed enjoying life high on my list of priorities. So I made a habit of widening my circle of friends and broadening my tastes. This awareness precipitated a seemingly endless chain of personality conflicts, the most difficult of which was with Roger M. Kyes, who was my boss while I was running Pontiac and Chevrolet divisions. He made life unbearable for me, and he was dedicated to getting me fired; he told me so, many times. Fortunately, I had the protection of my ability as I ran those two divisions to fend off Kyes. But I remember vividly my conflicts with him, especially when he was irritated by my style of dress. The corporate rule was dark suits, light shirts and muted ties. I followed the rule to the letter, only I wore stylish Italian-cut suits, wide-collared off-white shirts and wide ties.

"Goddamnit, John," he'd yell. "Can't you dress like a businessman? And get your hair cut, too."

My hair was ear length with sideburns. I felt both my clothes and hair style were contemporary but not radical, so I told him:

"General Motors' business—selling annual styling changes—makes this a fashion business. And what the hell do you know about fashion? Most of these guys around here wear narrow-lapelled suits and baggy pants with cuffs that are four inches above their shoes."

The fact that I had been divorced, was a health nut and dated generally younger actresses and models didn't set well with the corporate executives or their wives. And neither did my general disappearance from the corporate social scene. Dollie Cole, the second wife of then President Ed Cole, who himself was divorced, called me up after my second divorce when I was dating my wife Cristina and told me, "They are all shook up on The Fourteenth Floor. God! Don't get married again. You'd better cool it. All you've got to do is lay low and wait them out. Those guys will all be gone in five years. Don't kick away your career now."

Company officials too often called up my friends and asked them, "What's up with John and this girl Cristina Ferrare? They aren't going to get married are they? That would be bad. . . . Why doesn't he have dinner with the other executives? He's not acting like a team player."

I thought all of this was an improper intrusion into my personal life, but I didn't pay much attention to it, which I guess perpetuated the problem. I figured I was loyal and dedicated to GM. I did my job and did it well. The company had a right to know how I was spending my business life, but it had no right to know how I was spending my private and non-business life.

Nevertheless, my clothing and lifestyle were increasingly rattling the cages of my superiors, as was the amount of publicity my personal and business lives were generating. I was being resented because my style of living violated an unwritten but widely revered precept that said no personality could outshine General Motors. The executives were supposed to be just as gray and almost as lifeless as the corporate image.

The resentments toward me festered and grew to great proportions without my knowledge. I knew some people disliked me. But since I didn't play the corporate political game, I was not wired into the underground flow of information which would have given me better knowledge about those who viewed themselves as my corporate enemies. The depth of these resentments became known to me in December 1972 when Dollie Cole told several friends of mine over lunch at the Plaza in New York, "De Lorenzo, Lundin, Terrell are out to get John." She also said they appeared to have a personal vendetta against me, and that they were using every means at their disposal to hurt my credibility.

It was the first I realized there was apparently a concerted campaign within GM to hunt me. Anthony G. De Lorenzo was vice-president of Public Relations. Oscar A. Lundin was executive vice-president of Finance, and Richard L. Terrell was my boss as executive vice-president for Car and Truck, Body and Assembly operations. Each in his own way could make a considerable amount of trouble for me. This revelation provided an explanation of several strange things that had happened to me in the previous years.

One incident occurred while I was at Chevrolet. A firm that builds custom and special order cars was building a limousine for Ford Motor Company, one of which ended up as an official car of the President of the United States. The papers seemed to be talking daily about the "Presidential Lincoln." So I thought, "What a good publicity vehicle for Chevrolet," to get a Chevrolet limousine into the hands of the President or at least some prominent people. I told the division people at the General Motors Tech Center to build a pilot car. I figured, if it was done right, we could sell the idea to a firm like the special order company, which would build the limousine from our regular Chevrolets and sell them through the Chevy dealer network.

Somehow, word got back to the corporation that I was building a private limousine for myself with company money. No one asked me about this. What was I doing? Why was I doing it? They just apparently bought the line from the grapevine that I was doing a limousine for myself. One day I got a call from Kyes.

"Who the hell do you think you are building a special car for yourself! That's company money you are wasting. And we don't like that one damn bit."

His charges infuriated me. I attempted to explain the matter to him but when it was obvious that he wasn't prepared to hear me out, I just listened to his monologue and didn't reply further. Rather than go through a big project of explaining to the corporation what I was up to, wasting time that might better be spent solving the division's serious problems, I simply called up an aide and told him, "Drop the goddamn project." I had never seen the car. It was not a significant thing in the first place. And its existence dropped from my mind in the presence of more compelling business.

Almost a year later, the board of directors was meeting at the GM Proving Grounds to review product programs with the general managers of each division. It was a command performance. That morning I picked up a copy of the Detroit *Free Press,* and there in one of the gossip columns was an item that said, in effect, that I was building a private Chevrolet limousine that cost $60,000—about four times the actual cost. The item was embarrassing as hell to me. All of the directors were talking about it, which destroyed the effectiveness of my presentation. I called up our people at the Tech Center and told them, "Find that goddamn car, if it is still around, and cut it into scrap." If someone was out to get me in the corporation, slipping a phony item like that to a columnist was an effective way of doing it.

On other occasions it bothered me when Tom Murphy,

my boss during my term at Chevrolet, many times said to me, "You know, John, everybody said I was going to have a helluva lot of trouble with you. But I would really have to say that this is untrue. As far as I am concerned you do the best job of running your division of anyone. You keep me informed of the important things. I know what you are doing. Far and away I have less trouble with you than anybody in the divisions."

Those were kind words from Murphy, the only top manager with whom I felt I had a good rapport. However, the warnings he was getting from other members of management that I was "trouble" indicated to me now that my papers were being graded "upstairs" by something other than my test scores. But my support from Murphy suddenly ended. It was a sinister occurrence which terminated it.

In November 1972, the corporation was staging a massive management meeting of the top 700 GM executives in Greenbrier, West Virginia. These were infrequent gatherings, at least three years apart, which were designed to discuss in total all of the corporation's problems and exchange ideas on how to solve them. Many of The Fourteenth Floor executives were given broad subjects on which to address the conference. As a group executive, I was given the topic of "Product Quality." I prepared a tough talk which in essence said the only way we can remain a success and grow is to deliver real value to the customer. I said that I felt the emphasis at General Motors had switched from this goal to one of taking the last nickel out of every part to improve profits in the short run. I singled out specific products and programs for criticism. The talk was both critical and constructive. It was the kind of talk that was for corporate ears and none other.

As is the required practice, we submitted early drafts of our talks to top management through the public relations department. Management then made corrections and generally edited the draft along the lines it felt was proper. In the process, an executive could wind up writing a speech four or five times or more. After each new draft was prepared, all the copies of the previous version were destroyed. My final draft was toned by management and edited to complement the speeches of the other executives.

Just prior to the conference, my Greenbrier talk turned up in the hands of Bob Irvin, automotive writer for the Detroit *News*. And he printed it. It was not the final version which he wrote about. It was one of the earlier drafts. The only people who had copies of that version were myself, the public relations staff and top management. I hadn't leaked it. Nothing in the world could do me more harm personally and internally than to leak this type of a speech. My job was to sell our cars, not criticize them publicly. I was trying, with the talk, to impress people in the corporation with the need for drastic improvement in product quality to counter the growing wave of consumer unrest, fulfill our responsibility to our customers and restore our tarnished image.

The leak destroyed the Greenbrier conference for me and was probably the single thing that hurt me most in the corporation. I could tell that my solid image in Murphy's eyes began to diminish from the day the newspaper story appeared. I was shocked and sick. So was my staff. It was obvious that someone who wanted to give me a good shot to the gut, did.

A short time later, a friend of mine lunching in a downtown Detroit restaurant ran across a private investigator who knew GM's operations and who told him that the speech was leaked by a man on the GM public relations staff.

If I was having my doubts about staying with the corporation, and I was, it was now quite obvious that some people in the corporation were taking steps to see that I couldn't stay.

While I enjoyed my work in the divisions, for the most part, frustrations and other job-related concerns prompted me to ask to leave the corporation twice. The first time was in 1971, when I was with Chevrolet. At that time management prevailed upon me to stay. However, the strongest feeling that I was not destined to stay with GM management came after two incidents in October 1972 just after I moved from Chevrolet to The Fourteenth Floor, and a month before the Greenbrier leak.

I balked at becoming a group executive when the job was first offered to me in September. I refused the promotion, first, because I felt my job at Chevrolet should go to another Chevy executive who deserved it and who would continue the programs I'd started; and, second, because I had a distinct fear that with the personality clashes I had with some of the top management, I would be very vulnerable "upstairs." I also had been told by a number of executives up there that Fourteenth Floor jobs were very boring.

Nevertheless, after two weeks of ceaseless pressure from my bosses, I relented and went upstairs. A non-Chevrolet man was named to the post I was departing. It was not very long before I realized I had made a horrible mistake. On my second day in the new job my boss, Richard Terrell, who succeeded Kyes as executive vice-president for Car and Truck, Body and Assembly, called me into his office. I had heard very little from him when I was running Chevrolet. Not once did we get into a serious discussion about the division's business. I suspect this was his choice since, until he succeeded Kyes, Terrell's entire 36-year GM career was spent in non-automotive businesses, first with Electro-Motive Division and then the Frigidaire Division. He, therefore, knew little directly about GM's automotive operations. This was my first meeting with Terrell in my new capacity. He is moderately tall, with thin gray hair, steel-rimmed glasses, a perpetual smile that looks more like a smirk and a manner that often gives a false sense of authority to what he says.

I walked into his office and sat down in front of his desk. Terrell pushed a button under the cabinet behind his desk which closed the office door, leaned forward in his chair, looked sternly across his desk and said to me in steely tones, "I want you to disappear into the wallpaper up here. I don't want to see you in the newspaper."

Those were not his exact words. He couched his message in terms of "team play," "good of the corporation," and how "no man is above the corporation." But the point of Terrell's message was as obvious to me as the dark suit and white shirt he wore.

"De Lorean, disappear into the boondocks."

I was shocked. And I knew that, while I hadn't heard from Terrell when I was running Chevrolet, I was going to

15

be hearing a lot from him in the secretive quarters of The Fourteenth Floor because I was not protected by my ability and performance as I had been when I ran the car divisions. Up here I had nothing to operate to show that ability. I thought to myself: "Dealing with Terrell is going to be the Kyes situation all over again."

About a week or so later, I was in the office of Elliott M. (Pete) Estes, who was executive vice-president of Operations. I was talking to him about some of my doubts about the business in general and life upstairs, and he said, "I've always told them that it's good for GM to have someone like you in the ranks. It shows how democratic we are."

I am sure Pete didn't realize the impact on me of his comment. He didn't say anything about how well I'd managed my businesses, the people I had developed, or what I'd contributed to the corporation in terms of quality products and substantial profit. All he said was I was sort of a weirdo. Until then, I guess I had deluded myself into thinking I was held in high esteem by my superiors, even if they didn't like me personally, because I was a business success. I had risen faster in the corporation than any of them, and I thought for that reason that I at least had their professional respect.

So I was tragically shocked to realize that this was not the case. Just as the corporation at the time had token blacks, token women and token Chicanos, I was viewed as their token hippie. I just didn't fit in. When I thought over the meetings with Terrell and Estes, I began to realize once again that I could no longer stay with General Motors. I agonized over the prospect of leaving.

The Greenbrier incident made it obvious that someone in the corporation was making an effort to hurt my business reputation. The comments of Dollie Cole to my friends in New York told me there was in fact an active program to force me out. I then began a campaign to leave the corporation which was going to culminate tomorrow morning when I officially resigned. Late Sunday night, I went to sleep.

Monday morning, I awoke at about 6:00 a.m. Dressed. Went downstairs to the coffee shop for my usual breakfast of bacon and eggs, and read The New York *Times*. Afterward, I took a walk around midtown Manhattan, watching the city slowly come alive. At about 9:30 a.m., I arrived at the General Motors Building at 59th Street and Fifth Avenue. A minute or so later I walked into the office of Chairman Richard C. Gerstenberg on the twenty-fourth floor.

In the room were Gerstenberg, Murphy, by now the vice-chairman, and Kenneth C. MacDonald who was secretary of the board's bonus and salary committee. This committee and the full board of directors had to approve my resignation since the official reason I was leaving was to take over a new Cadillac dealership in Lighthouse Point, Florida. This is just about the only way possible for a GM executive to resign and still receive his accrued bonus. I had over $500,000 in bonus coming to me which I had earned, so taking a dealership would let me "earn out" this money as well as provide a good income while I replanned my business life. In addition, it also was agreed that I would run the National Alliance of Businessmen for Gerstenberg, who was chairman of NAB in 1973, for one year at a salary from GM of $200,000.

The atmosphere in Gerstenberg's office was neither friendly nor bitter. It was strictly businesslike. The meeting lasted less than 20 minutes. I signed the document of resignation, effective May 31, 1973, which was prepared by the corporation. We all shook hands, and I left the room and headed for the bank of elevators.

Once on the main floor, I walked out onto Fifth Avenue. For the first time in a quarter of a century I was out of work in the auto industry. There was a slight feeling of relief because the struggle was over. Bill Finelli took me back to La Guardia and a flight to Detroit.

The board met that afternoon and approved my resignation. The public relations department prepared a news release—which was made public later in the month—announcing my resignation in which Gerstenberg praised my contributions to General Motors and wished me well in my new ventures. Once back in Detroit I drove home.

As I ate dinner quietly at home that night with my wife Cristina and my son Zachary, I fully realized I had done what few top executives have ever done in the automobile industry. I had quit General Motors.

CHAPTER TWO

The Fourteenth Floor

In General Motors the words "The Fourteenth Floor" are spoken with reverence. This is Executive Row. I cannot remember when I first visited there. It was probably early in my career at Pontiac. But in the 17 years I was with the company, The Fourteenth Floor did not change much, and neither did the mystique surrounding it.

Executive Row actually occupies only one I-shaped end of The Fourteenth Floor in the giant GM headquarters in Detroit's New Center area. The building itself was built in 1919-20 for $20 million and originally was called the Durant Building after the founder of General Motors, William Crapo Durant. The name was changed after he fell from power. Today, as then, the General Motors Building, where about 7,000 people work, is the most impressive structure in midtown Detroit whether viewed from air, the windows of skyscrapers in downtown Detroit four miles to the south, or the cement channels of the nearby Edsel Ford and John Lodge Freeways. The giant letters "GENERAL MOTORS" atop the building can be seen 20 miles away on a clear night. That name dominates the New Center area as General Motors dominates the auto industry. Two stories below the sign is The Fourteenth Floor where rest the power and future of that dominance.

To most GM employees, rising to The Fourteenth Floor

19

is the final scene in their Horatio Alger dream. The Mt. Olympus of business. The place where the biggest corporate decisions are made. Getting there assures that you'll be a millionaire, if you are not already, because General Motors pays its management better than almost any other company in the world. In a good year the chairman has made almost $1 million in salary and bonus. The vice-chairman and the president have made a little less, and so on down the corporate ladder—executive vice-presidents, group vice presidents (where I fitted in), divisional general managers-vice-presidents, staff vice-presidents. The lowliest vice-president in GM makes well over $200,000 in a good year, which is more than most chief executive officers in American business.

At least 60 percent of a top executive's income in a very profitable year is comprised of his bonus. When sales were depressed as they were in 1974, earnings fell drastically and so did executive salaries. In 1974 General Motors earned only $950 million. Chairman Thomas A. Murphy made only $273,000. President Elliott M. (Pete) Estes made only $236,000, and Vice-Chairmen Richard L. Terrell and Oscar A. Lundin received only $229,000 apiece.

The atmosphere on The Fourteenth Floor is awesomely quiet. The hallways are usually deserted. People speak in hushed voices. The omnipresent quiet projects an aura of great power. The reason it is so quiet must be that General Motors' powerful executives are hard at work in their offices studying problems, analyzing mountains of complicated data, holding meetings and making important, calculated business decisions. There is no room for laughter or casual conversations in the halls. Those are frivolous. There is too much work to be done to be frivolous.

A thick glass door protects the entrance to The Fourteenth Floor. It is electronically locked and is opened by a receptionist who actuates a switch under her desk in a large, plain waiting room outside the door. The door is locked because there is a very great fear on The Fourteenth Floor that someone will burst into Executive Row and do them "great bodily harm"—a radical leftist, an irate customer, or a furloughed blue-collar worker. This fear reaches a peak every three years around the time of labor negotiations when, as I understood, the president and chairman may hire bodyguards. (Actually, GM does such an effective job of keeping a low executive profile, I doubt most people would recognize the chairman or president.) GM executives usually arrive at and leave their offices by a private elevator located just inside Executive Row.

Across from the elevator are several bedrooms used by visiting executives or those too tired to go home. To the right, inside of the entrance, is the executive dining room. Straight ahead, down the shaft of the I, are executive offices opening on either side. They are arranged in order of importance. These first offices are for vice-presidents. At the top of the I to the left are the offices of group vice-presidents, and to the right are the suites for executive vice-presidents and then the top level of corporate management. There is great jealousy among some executives about how close their offices are to the chairman and president. The feeling is that the closer you are to the top officers the more important you are to the corporation. And the better your chances are of promotion. My office was on the top of the I, to the left, about three offices down, which put me pretty high in the corporation.

The decor of The Fourteenth Floor is almost nondescript—blue-green carpeting and beige, faded oak paneling. Some might call it dull, others tasteless. It's both. Seemingly, it was arranged almost as an afterthought. It quite befits a corporation which consciously seeks to play down personality.

The executive offices are arranged in pairs, separated by a central office occupied by a private secretary for each executive (each executive is also assigned a junior executive referred to as "your dog robber"—a servant who picks up dog droppings in a mansion—who is sort of an executive assistant or secretary). Doors on each side of this room open to a single, spacious executive office. All were uniformly decorated in blue carpet, beige walls, faded oak paneling and aged furniture, as I recall, except for those of a few uppermost executives, who could choose their own office decorations. That was a rule.

When I ran the Chevrolet Division twelve floors below, I redecorated the lobby and the executive offices. The dull carpet and paneling were replaced with beige, deep-pile carpeting and freshly sanded and restained paneling. Walls were repainted in brighter colors and modern furniture was purchased. An executive could decorate his office to his own taste, within reasonable bounds and budget. I could get away with all of this at the division, because I ran it. It was my budget. If I wanted the offices redecorated, it would be done.

On The Fourteenth Floor, however, it was quite different. I learned the game the hard way. Shortly after I was promoted, a guy who said he was in charge of office decorations came into my office and asked: "Is there anything I can do for you?"

"Yes. I want to have this paneling sanded and restained (I love the soft atmosphere of natural wood), and I'd like to get some new carpeting and more useful modern furniture in here."

"Oh, Jeez. You can't do that. I'm sorry," he quickly responded.

"Why not?"

"We only decorate the offices every few years. And they are all done the same. It's the same way with the furniture. Maybe I can get you an extra table or a lamp or something like that." He was apologetic as hell. But rules were rules.

I told him to forget it. So I put a couple of pictures of my family around and decided I'd better get used to this funeral parlor office.

One rule on The Fourteenth Floor was that we should frequently use the executive dining room, especially at lunch. GM wants its managers to eat together whenever possible. It was a facet of team play. If you were in town you were expected to eat in the executive dining room unless there was pressing business elsewhere. The practice is encouraged in many American companies. The rationale is that in the relaxed atmosphere of a lunch or dinner managers get to know each other and communicate better. This leads to a closer-knit executive team and better management. That purpose is worthwhile. But most of the time management meals end up in small talk about the same things. And too often those things are office gossip and bitching.

Nevertheless, eating in the executive dining room was

standard operating procedure at General Motors. Some guys ate there morning, noon and night. To eat there you had to attain a certain management status within the corporation. I think the level was a department director or above. Otherwise, you couldn't eat there unless someone who could invited you.

As in the offices outside, there was a pecking order even in the executive dining room. To the left of the main dining area was the "executive committee dining room" where the top corporate officers met every day for lunch. If the daily lunch in the main dining room was akin to the team meal, I guess this was the coaches' meeting. I don't know what went on in those "executive committee" lunches. I never got that far.

For all of its aura of power and mystery, The Fourteenth Floor abounded in rumors, gossip, pettiness and role playing which contradicted the implied atmosphere of precise and calculated management at work. The bickering exposed the great image of GM management as something quite different from the giant, perfectly coordinated machine we all were led to believe it was. This image was a facade covering a network of bickering and backbiting that worked as a gremlin in the management machine.

Rumors were a way of life "upstairs." Sooner or later the rumor mill ground out gossip, true and untrue, about every executive. However, there always seemed to be rumors circulating about President Edward N. Cole. A tireless worker, Cole was a dedicated engineer who would become totally consumed in a project almost to the exclusion of everything else around him, a trait common among engineers. The drive with which he attacked various projects, whether they were new engines, like the Wankel, or a carburetion process, made it hard for his peers and superiors to turn Ed Cole down. He became a super corporate salesman in the process.

Stocky, but by no means fat, Cole had a winning smile and an almost shy manner when the topic strayed too far from engineering, which belied a very strong will and hard-nosed attitude. He was a master corporate politician who could deal harshly with those opposed to his ideas or his positions on major corporate issues. He started at General Motors when he was only 21, rose through the engineering ranks, became general manager of Chevrolet from 1956-61 and capped his 44-year career with General Motors as its president from 1967-74. (He died tragically in a May 1977 plane crash.)

For much of his seven-year tenure as President, Ed Cole was the first and final word in the corporation on product decisions. Such corporate strength made him a visible target for rumors.

One rumor spread by the financial staff concerned a trip he made to the Kennedy Space Center for one of the moon shots. He took a company plane for the junket and brought along a party of friends, including GM dealers, business associates and their wives. He put the whole affair on his expense account.

As the story, gleefully told to me by one finance staff member, went, Chairman Gerstenberg bounced the expense account and said Cole would have to pay for the trip himself. The tab was in the thousands of dollars. Only a few people at the top besides Cole knew what had happened, and the matter should have been quietly settled there. I found out within hours after Cole's expense account was bounced back to him. Talk of the incident ran rampant through the corporation. It should never have left The Fourteenth Floor, but people were scurrying around the divisions talking about it. I thought the whole thing was demeaning and embarrassing to Cole and derogatory to the office of the president.

Cole was also at the center of another long-standing rumor told to me by several members of the finance staff. The word was that not once after he was elected president of GM in 1967 did the Chairman, James M. Roche, set foot in Cole's office. Roche's growing dissatisfaction with Cole's presidency was widely discussed in GM. But whether he refused to step inside of Cole's office or not, I don't know. I do know that if the rumor was false it was malicious and destructive to corporate morale.

The Cole-Roche conflict spilled into the public domain in February, 1969. The whole affair started in Laredo, Texas, at a press tour of Uniroyal's new tire-test facilities. At lunch, the head of Uniroyal's tire division, Harold Barrett, told Tom Kleene, automotive writer for the Detroit *Free Press,* that GM was soon to begin taking delivery of the new bias-belted tires to offer on their cars that spring. He also indicated that GM was paying a premium price for the tires and probably would pass the extra cost on to the customers.

The story upset The Fourteenth Floor, as the blabbering of any supplier does. A short time later in a Detroit press conference, Roche told reporters the company had "no plans" for the tire. Cole was at his side when Roche answered the tire question. But the very next day, in Houston, at the annual National Automobile Dealers Association convention, Cole confirmed Barrett's remarks to a somewhat amazed Kleene, adding that GM would be asking a premium price for the tires.

Kleene wrote a second story from Houston repeating what Cole had told him, which contradicted Roche's statement the day earlier. When the story ran, Roche was in an uproar and so was The Fourteenth Floor. The public relations people denied that GM had any plans for bias-belted tires and repeated verbatim to inquiring reporters the chairman's statement at the Detroit press conference two days earlier. *The Wall Street Journal* then ran a story following the general theme of "Who's Running General Motors?" Some people inside the company were beginning to wonder themselves. The issue eventually died, but the wounds never healed. The company's troubled credibility took a decided turn for the worse that spring when General Motors offered Uniroyal's bias-belted tires on some of its car lines at premium prices, just as Cole had said.

When I moved to The Fourteenth Floor, festering hostilities among members of upper management became open wounds which marred the picture of camaraderie and professional respect that GM executives pushed so hard in public. The same guys who were slapping each other on the back and shaking hands in public were going after each other's jugular in private.

Within one 10-day span in late 1972 Cole openly criticized then Chairman Gerstenberg and the financial staff in front of a group of divisional engineers for "meddling in product decisions about which they knew nothing"; while Terrell, my boss, who reported to Cole, was telling underlings and just about anybody who would listen at cocktail parties in suburban Bloomfield Hills that "no one is president of General Motors. Ed Cole is just the chief engineer." While Terrell's apparent quarrel with Cole and Cole's beef with the financial people should have been carried on in the privacy of the executive suite, they instead were putting their stories out for all those around and below in the corporation to see.

The result of all this bickering was crippling to corporate and divisional morale. The general managers of the car divisions were complaining almost daily that these skirmishes on The Fourteenth Floor were getting in the way of the company's business because no one in the divisional operations of GM could get timely decisions from corporate management on problems that affected day-to-day business. My worst fears were rapidly being confirmed: That GM's success at the time was far more due to its tremendous economic power and total dominance of the market than to management competence. It took much better management to run Ford, Chrysler or American Motors.

The bickering and politics of The Fourteenth Floor made unpleasant what I quickly perceived to be a dull job as vice-president for Car and Truck Group. Practically everyone who went upstairs from a division said life up there was a drastically different kind of existence, completely lacking in the satisfactions that were experienced in the divisions. Bud Goodman, who was executive vice-president for Automotive Operations in the early 1960s, said that on The Fourteenth Floor you felt like you'd lost your effectiveness because you couldn't get things done.

At the time, this reaction seemed to me to be consistent with the difference in the two jobs: In the divisions you were a doer, and in the corporate management you were an overseer. If, as a member of the divisional management, you were attuned to the day-to-day pressure of running the business, then you surely would find the pace different on The Fourteenth Floor where the emphasis presumably was on planning, administering and formulating policy.

As I moved up in the company management during the 1960s, I began to realize that a corporate executive felt that he'd lost his "effectiveness" because he wasn't really doing that much. When I finally moved upstairs, Goodman's words took on even greater significance because I saw that the job not only wasn't fulfilling, but often consisted only of what my boss wanted me to do. Soon after I got into top corporate management, Terrell started giving me what I considered to be little, stupid, make-work kinds of assignments, things which I thought should have been decided further down the line.

Some of these things, which had little or no impact on the business, were an insult to a person's intelligence, especially if that person was a GM manager with 17 years in the company and a good track record. They were things which my secretary could have done. As I recall, he asked me to catalogue service parts numbers and to prepare reports on the size of parts inventories.

Whether he thought these assignments were well conceived or not, I sure as hell knew they weren't. It seemed so damn ridiculous to be spending my time reporting on inventories, when General Motors and the automobile industry were enveloped in a myriad of problems from soaring production costs to increasing federal control to the mounting energy crisis. What a waste of a $600,000-a-year executive's time on these assignments. But nevertheless, there often was a list on my desk of these assignments from Terrell. Finally, I passed them on down the line or just quit doing them.

About the same time, I was suddenly inundated with tons of paperwork, the likes of which I had never seen as an executive before or since. There were literally 600 to 700 pages a day to be read and processed. Some of it was important material, such as performance reports from the divisions. Most of it, however, was unimportant to this level of management—like a lease agreement to be signed for a new Buick zone office in St. Louis. As with Terrell's assignments, most of these matters should have stopped somewhere far down the line. But somehow these matters were ending up on The Fourteenth Floor.

Part of this mountain of daily reading material was generated by a practice of "preinformation" for almost every meeting held on The Fourteenth Floor. Each executive attending a meeting was to see in advance the text of any presentation to be given. There were never to be any surprises. Each executive was to read the text before the meeting and then sit through the formal presentation. If we were to get a program proposal from the marketing department on Tuesday, we were to have the text of that program in hand by Friday or Monday.

The practice seemed wasteful to me because we'd get the same material at least three times: when we read the text, heard the presentation of it in the meeting and then read the minutes of the meeting. If there were subsequent meetings on the program, we might get the same presentation six times or more. The only results of this practice were bad. It tied up valuable executive time which could better have been spent elsewhere and often led to ineffective and boring meetings.

In the presentations I attended on The Fourteenth Floor often up to a third of the audience of executives was asleep. Not loud, snoring sleep, mind you. Just quiet repose. They would sit in their chairs, arms folded, heads on their chests, quietly dozing. If it was a film presentation and the lights were turned off, half the meeting could be asleep. The effect on the executive giving the presentation, especially if he was from the lower levels of management, was devastating. I can still see various members of management quietly dozing off in their chairs while a young executive from somewhere like the GM Parts Division, exuding enthusiasm, tried to run through a presentation he had spent a month preparing. His ego probably never recovered.

Once, when I was making a presentation to the Marketing Policy Group, I looked up from the prepared text to make eye contact with my audience only to discover five or six executives were asleep. "Am I this goddamn dull that I'm putting all these guys to sleep?" I thought. "Maybe it's the subject matter? Or that they don't give a damn?"

I decided it was one or the other. If they didn't care, in many cases it was because they already knew what was going to be said. They had read it all, the whole damn presentation, the night before. Why shouldn't they sleep? I must confess that I practically slept through some of the meetings up there. Not only because I already knew what was going to be discussed, but because of the trivia which formed the basis of some of these meetings.

These weren't just chance meetings of several executives in the hallway, or impromptu gatherings in one of the

Fourteenth Floor offices. These were full-blown, scheduled-in-advance meetings with anywhere from seven to twelve members of top management present. And any one of them could have decided the matter himself or delegated it to an assistant.

In 1972, for instance, we had seven or eight meetings over how to dispose of 4,000 Chevrolets which were built in violation of the EPA pollution standards. Through an engineering mistake, these cars weighed more than they were allowed to under the EPA emission certification procedure. The problem was that the engines in these cars were approved only for a lower weight level and these cars exceeded that level by 5 to 50 pounds or so. Some of these cars were already in dealers' hands. If we wanted to sell these cars, we had to put in engines which met the pollution standards for the weight classification. A secretary in an engineering department could have told us what should be done given the facts we had. The cars had to conform to the law.

But instead of letting some guy down the line in Chevrolet marketing or engineering handle the decision, the problem was brought to The Fourteenth Floor. A series of meetings were held on the illegal Chevrolets. Terrell called breakfast meetings at the Tech Center, lunch meetings in the executive dining rooms, afternoon meetings and even a dinner meeting. He kept assigning different aspects of the problem to me. Can we take some weight out and leave the engines in? Can we reweigh the cars? Is there a loophole in the law that will let us sell these cars? I kept telling him, "We have only one decision: Make the cars conform to the law, if we want to sell them." That is exactly what we eventually did but only after tying up hundreds of hours of executive time in worthless discussion over the problem.

We had a somewhat related problem a year earlier, in the fall of 1971. Our Norwood, Ohio, assembly plant went on a long strike during the summer which ran right through our new model changeover period. This was the time of year when we shut down to replace the tooling for the 1971 models with the equipment for the 1972 models. It was early September and the problem this time was that the strike left about 400 Chevy Camaros and Pontiac

Firebirds in process along the plant's two assembly lines. As 1971 models, they were in violation of the 1972 pollution and safety standards which had gone into effect September 1. There was simply no way we could build these cars and sell them. It was too costly, if at all possible, to make them conform.

The options to us were obvious: We could either scrap the cars and use the parts in our service operations, or we could build the cars and give them away to mechanics classes in schools around the country and take a tax deduction. The latter was the more attractive alternative because, as I recall, under the tax laws we could deduct the manufacturer's suggested retail price of the cars, which was well over the actual cost of production. We'd be deducting about $4,500 a car when our cost was only about $1,900 or $2,000. It was a quick solution to a $1-million problem. In terms of a then $35-billion-a-year corporation, it wasn't a life-and-death proposition.

But that problem, too, was brought to The Fourteenth Floor. Terrell scheduled what seemed like interminable meetings over the cars, 10 or 12 separate meetings, which were long and drawn out. This time the result of our stalling was more than wasted executive time. Piddling around actually got the company into hot water. At one of the meetings, somebody suggested that we sell the cars in Canada where the safety and pollution laws were less stringent.

So we set out to peddle these cars in Canada. The only trouble was that some public-spirited guy at the Norwood plant leaked the plan to the Canadian press which jumped all over "giant General Motors" for trying to sell in Canada cars which were too dirty and unsafe for the United States. At a time when Canadian nationalistic spirit was rising and "ugly American" ownership of Canadian industry was under attack, the decision to try to sell these Camaros and Firebirds in Canada was the worst thing we could have done.

We were embarrassed by the bad publicity and, of course, had to scratch the plan. We were not done, though. The meetings over the cars continued. It was decided we should try to sell them overseas. That plan was nixed when someone pointed out that 400 Camaros and Firebirds are just about a lifetime supply of those cars for any country overseas. So when it was all said and done, the corporate consensus was that the only thing we could do was donate the cars to mechanics classes and take a tax write-off of about $2 million.

The most embarrassing, and probably the most ridiculous, meeting I attended "upstairs" involved a presentation to the Industrial Relations Policy Group in the fall of 1972. A young guy from the labor relations staff was talking about an obscure personnel point which he proposed that we change. It was an insignificant matter by any corporate standard, having to do, as I remember, with adjusting a transferred employee's pay rate upward to correlate with the cost of living in his new locale. It simply meant that what may be a great salary in someplace like Selma, Alabama, isn't worth much in New York City. If a guy gets transferred from Selma to New York, he should get more money to maintain his standard of living. So what were we doing in a big meeting of top brass listening to this presentation? I couldn't answer that question.

Looking around I counted up about $10 million worth of executive talent listening to and watching this presentation of cost-of-living graphs, color slides, industry analysis charts and company-by-company comparisons. The presentation finally ended. A couple of guys who were dozing in their seats blinked awake, and the room of executives looked toward the chairman for an indication of what we were going to do, as usually happened. The chairman in this case was Richard C. Gerstenberg, a fairly trim, hard-working finance man, who was born in Mohawk, New York, and presented a friendly, folksy, almost farm boy manner common among other GM executives. Gerstenberg's speech was often salty, but not offensive, and his delivery staccato and forceful. He snapped, "Goddamnit! I don't like to be surprised."

We were all stunned because the point of the meeting was so insignificant anyway. "What is Gerstenberg so surprised about?" I thought.

"We can't make a decision on this now," he continued. "I think we ought to form a task force to look into this and come back with a report in 90 to 120 days. Then we can make a decision."

He then rattled off the names of the members of the task force he was appointing. There was an eerie silence after the chairman spoke. It lasted for what seemed like half a day. The whole room was bewildered but no one had the courage to say why.

Finally, Harold G. Warner, the snow-white-haired, kindly executive-vice-president, who was soon to retire, broke the silence. "Dick, this presentation is the result of the task force that you appointed some time ago. Most of the people you just appointed to the new task force are on the old one."

Everyone became a little nervous and somewhat embarrassed. Gerstenberg flushed in the face and then said something which I cannot remember. I guess we accepted the recommendation from the Industrial Relations Policy Group on the matter, but I remember saying to myself as the meeting ended:

"What the hell am I doing here? I can't spend the next 17 years of my life up here doing these kinds of things."

It was a realization for me that for the first time in my life the joys of work did not overbalance the drudgery. For the most part, until I got to The Fourteenth Floor, I enjoyed my work, even though I was questioning certain aspects of our business.

From the first day I worked as an engineer for Chrysler through the Chevrolet experience (except for a brief period when I offered to quit in 1971), my jobs were interesting and demanding. Now all of a sudden the pleasure was gone. I hated my work. I was depressed by the lack of stimulation from my assignments, bored with most of the meetings on The Fourteenth Floor, and inundated with paperwork to read, most of which was of little consequence. "This is supposed to be a planning job," I remember thinking, "but I feel like a file clerk. I've spent many years learning to be a good executive. Now I can't use that knowledge."

I was trying to bring a set of new eyes to the job of group executive, as one only can do in the first few months in a new position. But I had no time to perform the real function of my position. Instead, I was being tied down and totally consumed by this constant parade of paperwork and meetings.

I knew that adapting to the job meant that pretty soon I would just be a carbon copy of the guy I replaced, and I didn't want that. So I set up a meeting with Vice-Chairman Tom Murphy to whom I had reported when he held the job I now held. His full name is Thomas Aquinas Murphy, an Irish Catholic with a broad face and a winning smile. His receding hairline precedes a thicket of bushy hair brushed straight back. When I first got to know Murphy, his hair was mostly black. Today it's gray. He has aged visibly since he became chairman of the board on December 1, 1974.

To all who knew him, Murphy was an understanding man. And I sought his help now.

"Tom, I think I know what has to be done for the long-term health of GM. But I don't get any time to work on it. I just don't get any time to plan my days because of this array of meetings, inane assignments and tons of paperwork."

He responded, "Hell, John, when I had that job I never got to plan one minute. It was completely planned for me. The job just drags you from place to place. You don't have time to plan. It is not that kind of a job."

I was surprised at Murphy's response. I thought that perhaps he didn't understand the depth of my objections to what was being done on the Fourteenth Floor.

"Well, that's exactly what's happening to me, and I don't consider it satisfactory," I said. "The system is deciding what I should be working on and what is important; I'm not. I'm not doing any planning of the direction of the company, and this is a planning job. No one else seems to be planning either. We're in for trouble . . . the gap between GM and the rest of the country is widening."

Murphy didn't say much further. I suddenly realized that what I felt was a problem and weakness of life on The Fourteenth Floor, he and others thought was "business as usual." They were quite happy to let their jobs drag them from one place to the next, trying to solve problems as they came up, but not getting into the kind of long-range planning that Fourteenth Floor executives were supposed to be doing. The kinds of planning I am sure Mr. Sloan intended when the policymaking function of the company was entrusted to these top corporate officers.

I later mentioned my frustration to Cole and he told me: "You've got to go through the steps. This job is part of the process." That process didn't look very attractive and fulfilling to me.

So I quit doing the things I thought weren't worthwhile to the job, as I perceived it. I skipped meetings I felt I could contribute little to. Instead, I would just read the minutes of these meetings. The only ones I attended regularly were the meetings of the Engineering Policy Group, and the Administration Committee, which brought all of the division heads, staff vice-presidents, and Fourteenth Floor management together.

I generally passed up the executive dining room at lunchtime. Instead, I'd work through the lunch hour, work out at the Uptown Athletic Club across the street or take a walk outside just to clear my head.

It quickly evolved that I wasn't a "member of the team." Management interpreted my absence from meetings as defiance. And there was a growing feeling that I wasn't interested in the work or contributing to the job. I was being regarded with distance by more and more of the executives on The Fourteenth Floor, which impaired my ability to perform.

As if corporate troubles weren't enough, I was experiencing great difficulties in my personal life, going through a divorce from my wife, Kelly, and fearing that I was going to lose my son, Zachary, in the process. Kelly and I were married in April, 1969, shortly after I moved to the Chevrolet Division. Tall and blonde, she was young, 20, and never accepted by the tight social circle of GM wives who were much older. While we rarely socialized with GM people, we were frequently thrust together at corporate functions or in the suburban clubs of Detroit, and the reaction to her, while not hostile, was cool and diffident.

Kelly's California background and the cool reception she received in the automotive circles made her yearn for more time back home. The combination of this and my extended work schedule (six- and seven-day work weeks, 10-12 hours a day) by the late fall of 1972 produced an untenable relationship for both of us.

A year earlier, when things were better, we had begun

adoption procedures on my son, Zachary, who now was a close part of me. Even though my marriage was beginning to crumble, I wanted "ZT" more than anything else. We often played in the morning before I went to work and at night when I got home. A one-year trial period for the adoption was almost up, and I feared that the troubled state of my marriage would unfavorably influence the decision to let me finalize the adoption.

This combination of utter frustration with my job and a somewhat aberrant personal life had me more depressed than I had ever been in my life. I lost 20 pounds. Some days I would just sit in my office brooding about my troubles. I wondered how everything could have suddenly gone so wrong, so fast. I asked myself, "Why can't I cut it here on The Fourteenth Floor? Dozens of people who talked about how boring it was up here, survived. They made the necessary adjustments. What is wrong? Is it my fault that I can't communicate the frustration with this job to my superiors? Am I wrong, and is the system right?"

Groping for answers to the questions of my depression, I got support where I least expected it—Ed Cole. In a casual conversation, he said one day, "If I was your age, John, I'd get the hell out of here so fast, that you wouldn't believe it. The opportunities in this business are gone. Especially for a guy like you who can get things done. There are a lot of people around here who should stay up here because this is the best they can do. The system protects them. But the opportunities for you are too great."

I was surprised at Cole's candor. Here was a man who had given all his working life to General Motors, from engineer to president. He had battled through the system, become a part of it and then reached the summit—president of General Motors. And yet after all of this, he was admitting that he wouldn't do it over again.

This had to be a hard admission for a man to make. Cole said essentially the same thing in an interview in *Newsweek* shortly before retiring in September, 1974. He enveloped his true feelings in a recital of his frustration with the job because of government intervention and the restrictions that this placed on the fun of the business. But I'd seen Ed Cole in the corporate committee battles, heard the snipings behind his back and watched his power base

35

erode as the financial side of the business took control of
the corporation. I knew the real reasons behind the comment that, "I wouldn't do it again." And I thought: "If
Ed Cole, who had been to the summit, wouldn't do it
again, there is no reason for John De Lorean to stay and
try to reach for the summit."

I again went to corporate management and told them
I wanted to resign. I talked with Murphy, who now was
vice-chairman, on a friendly basis, about my wishes. Earlier, when I had told Murphy I wanted to resign, he responded, "Jeez, I don't see why you want to leave. Nine
chances out of ten, when Cole leaves, you'll be the next
president."

Those were powerful words, because it was becoming
obvious internally that Murphy was one day going to be
GM's Chairman. But this time he was more receptive to
my proposal, although he tried to dissuade me.

In January, I wrote a stinging and critical analysis of
GM's management and system. The criticisms were aimed
directly at a lot of corporate people and their actions. I
felt many of the people around and above me would be
shocked by this report, which I sent to Terrell. I figured
he would get the report to the right places in management
in a hurry. He did.

I had two objectives in sending the memo. If it was at
all possible, in a last-ditch effort, I wanted to jar management into a realization of the deep-rooted problems upstairs. Since I was pretty sure this would not be effective—
because my previous efforts at reform were not well received—I figured this memo would demonstrate to management that we could no longer exist together and that it
was in their best interests to let me resign on my terms,
which were to leave and receive my accrued bonus. I
needed the money for the transition period between this
job and what I was going to do next. I figured I had to
leave quickly, because if I stayed on the job much longer
the attempts to discredit my business reputation would hurt
me.

Nobody said anything to me about the January memo
to Terrell. But it wasn't long thereafter that I talked with
Murphy and his attitude had changed markedly.

"John, I may have done you a disservice in the past

when I said you should stay with the corporation. It is pretty obvious you are unhappy and perhaps you should leave."

Either he or Terrell then told me that the Cadillac Division was going to locate a new dealership in Lighthouse Point, Florida, that I could have it if I wanted it, and that my bonus would be paid to me. I accepted, and the process was set in motion for me to leave The Fourteenth Floor.

CHAPTER THREE

Loyalty—Team Play—The System

Goddamnit! I served my time picking up my bosses at the airport. Now you guys are going to do this for me.
— PETE ESTES TO JOHN DE LOREAN.

Choosing among executives for promotion is a difficult task at best, but one which is vital to the success of a business. If two people vying for the same job are equal in talent and performance, and one is a friend, I will most likely choose the friend. That's human nature. If the other, however, is obviously more accomplished than my friend, the job would go to him or her. The point is that merit always surpasses friendship in matters that pertain to business promotion. This was not always the case in General Motors. But it is a practice I tried to follow closely because ultimately it is the best practice for the good of the corporation.

A classic test of this precept occurred when I was running the Pontiac Division. There was a guy in our marketing organization who was personally offensive to me. Whenever he got near me he just bugged the hell out of me. He was a blowhard and a name dropper, two traits which I find especially unlikeable.

At the same time, however, he was doing a helluva

39

job for the Pontiac Division. Every job we gave him, he did to perfection. And every time he did, I'd ask, "How the hell can a guy I can't stand be doing such a good job?" But he continued to perform, and the reports I got from his superiors corroborated my observations about his work. So I promoted him several times in the four years I ran Pontiac. It was hard to do, but his performance demanded it. After promoting him I would just stay the hell away from him.

I cite this extreme example because as I grew in General Motors it became apparent that objective criteria were not always used to evaluate an executive's performance. Many times the work record of a man who was promoted was far inferior to the records of others around him who were not promoted. It was quite obvious that something different than job performance was being used to rate these men.

That something different was a very subjective criterion which encompassed style, appearance, personality and, most importantly, personal loyalty to the man (or men) who was the promoter, and to the system which brought this all about. There were rules of this fraternity of management at GM. Those pledges willing to obey the rules were promoted. In the vernacular, they were the company's "team players." Those who didn't fit into the mold of a manager, who didn't adhere to the rules because they thought they were silly, generally weren't promoted. "He's not a team player," was the frequent, and many times only, objection to an executive in line for promotion. It didn't mean he was doing a poor job. It meant he didn't fit neatly into a stereotype of style, appearance and manner. He didn't display blind loyalty to the system of management, to the man or men doing the promoting. He rocked the boat. He took unpopular stands on products or policy which contradicted the prevailing attitude of top management.

At General Motors, good appearance meant conservative dress. In my very first meeting as a GM employee in 1956 at Pontiac, half the session was taken up in discussion about some vice-president downtown at headquarters who was sent home that morning for wearing a brown suit. Only blue or black suits were tolerated then.

I remember thinking that was silly. But in those days I followed the rules closely.

Style and personality in the corporate mold means simply that a GM executive is a low-profile executive. What is to me most memorable about the corporation today is the letters G and M, and not the people behind the letters. A General Motors man rarely says anything in public that adds the least bit of color or personality to those letters G and M. He identifies his success with the corporate success. And that success is measured in dollars earned per share. This system is best documented in its results.

The GM chairman annually is one of the least recognized businessmen in America. General Motors in the U.S. is almost twice the size of Ford Motor Company and yet the spokesman for the industry is Henry Ford II, chairman of Ford Motor Co. Former Ford President Lee A. Iacocca, who now is president of Chrysler Corporation, is better recognized than either of GM's top officers, Chairman Murphy or President Estes. Among GM's upper management today there is not a memorable one in the bunch. They want it that way. Even though GM in the past has produced some of the most memorable men in American business history—Billy Durant, Pierre S. du Pont and Alfred P. Sloan, Jr., William S. (Big Bill) Knudsen (Bunkie's father), and C.F. (Boss) Kettering—no one individual is permitted to stand out in the corporation today. When one does, he is rebuked, ordered to disappear into the wallpaper.

Management guards that prerogative jealously. Terrell told me to stay the hell out of the newspapers when I went to the Fourteenth Floor. One year while I was running Chevrolet, Bob Lund, then sales manager and now the head of that division, appeared every Saturday afternoon during the fall on ABC-TV's college football game of the week to award Chevrolet scholarships to schools of the game's outstanding players. He about killed himself doing it because he worked hard all week and then spent weekends flying around the country to these games. I got a call from Terrell one day. "Get Lund off of the TV." He was getting too much publicity for the GM team to tolerate. At season's end, Lund disappeared. Chevrolet still sponsored the games, but the scholarships were awarded by the network announcers.

On another occasion, one of the industry trade magazines was running "house ads" each week in which one of the titans of the automotive world would endorse the publication. It was a campaign to increase circulation and advertising revenue. The ads featured the likes of Henry Ford II; Robert Anderson, then president of Rockwell International; and others saying, in effect, "I must read this publication each week to keep up on the business." They asked GM if our President, Ed Cole, would do one of the ads. An executive familiar with the incident told me that Tony De Lorenzo, vice-president of Public Relations, told the publication: "We can get Cole for you if you promise that you won't use De Lorean."

If your appearance, style and personality were consistent with the corporate stereotype, you were well on your way to being a "loyal" employee. But loyalty demanded more. It often demanded personal fealty, actual subservience to the boss. You learned loyalty as you learned the business. Loyalty was talked about openly. It was part of team play. Pete Estes often talked about the need for "loyalty to your boss." He demanded it. He got it.

My introduction to "loyalty" was as assistant chief engineer at Pontiac. The division was staging a "ride and drive" program in San Francisco. "Ride and drive" programs were common to the engineering departments of GM. They were test sessions set up around the country for top engineers and divisional brass to drive and grade a fleet of cars for performance, durability, handling, gasoline mileage. We'd test competitors' cars, too. In this case, we were testing Pontiacs with a newly designed carburetor. There were about ten engineers in San Francisco for the four-day test.

I was showering in a motel near San Francisco International Airport the morning of the first day out there when the bathroom door flew open practically taking the hinges off in one jerk. I was shocked by the noise and I threw open the shower curtain and saw Estes who was chief engineer at Pontiac and my boss. The spitting image of Tennessee Ernie Ford, Estes was usually happy and pleasant. This time, however, he was red-faced and mad. "Why the hell wasn't someone out to meet me at the airport this morning? You knew I was coming, but nobody was there. Goddamnit, I served my time picking up my bosses at the airport. Now you guys are going to do this for me," he barked.

The thought had never even crossed my mind until then. I figured we were just supposed to get out to the West Coast on our own and be on time for the ride and drive session. I quickly became aware, however, that the pecking order at GM, as at many major U.S. companies, demanded that inferiors on the corporate ladder cater to their superiors. It was called "brown-nosing" a professor in college, KMAing (kiss-my-assing) when it was done by a supplier to a customer, and "loyalty" when it was done inside GM. As a rule, bosses were to be met at the airports by their charges. The bigger the boss at General Motors, the bigger the retinue waiting at the airport terminal. A chief engineer required a show of at least one assistant engineer and maybe a local plant official. A divisional general manager commanded more. If he traveled to St. Louis to give a speech, waiting for him at the airport would be the local plant manager, the head of the regional and zone sales offices and the local public relations guy. Traveling with him would be at least one executive from home, usually his public relations director. These men would pick him up, carry his bags, pay his hotel and meal bills and chauffeur him around night and day.

The greatest shows of force were reserved for the chairman of the board. On a trip he would often take several top executives with him, even if they had no worthwhile purpose in accompanying him. When he got to his destination, it would seem as if half of the area's GM employees were there to greet him—local sales managers of the car divisions, top plant people, chauffeurs. It was expected and demanded.

I discouraged the practice at Chevrolet. I often told our regional and zone office people that unless we had specific business to discuss, I would rather have them working on the job than meeting me at the airport. They would just have some kid meet me at the airport and give me a ride into town. One time in particular, I spoke to a luncheon of McGraw-Hill editors and executives in their midtown Manhattan headquarters. It was an off-the-record lunch that publications and publishing houses often have with business and political figures. I got a ride from the airport to their offices, walked into the lobby and got into an elevator where I ran into one of the company's vice-presidents. "You're John De Lorean. You are going to speak to us today, aren't you?" he asked.

"Yes."

"Well, where are your public relations people or your assistants?"

"Back in Detroit working, I hope." The man was a bit shocked at the answer because the GM executives he had known, and there were many, all traveled with retinues befitting only the potentates of great nations. The incident made quite an impression on him because I have heard the story several times since that meeting.

My personal feelings are that time spent traipsing after the boss is unproductive and wasteful of executive talent and ability. I didn't quarrel with the show of importance but rather with the system that made such fawning an essential part of the underling's job. It created an obvious servant-master relationship between the bossed and the boss. When the tally sheets were reviewed for promotions, as much credit was given to an executive's "form" as to his actual performance. It was like picking a suit of clothes because of its style without examining the quality of the cloth. In the end, the real corporation—the shareholders —suffered.

On occasion, key sales and management people in the field had to leave their jobs and pressing business in Kansas City, or Butte, Montana, to fly to St. Louis or Minneapolis in a show of force to greet the boss from Detroit who was touring a plant there or giving a speech before the Rotary Club. A dealer 500 miles away, back home, may have been going down the tube while these field people were meeting the boss at the airport, buying him dinner, picking up his hotel bill, and wasting a couple of important days in the process. But they were doing their jobs. They were team players and loyal employees. And when it came promotion time, they were promoted even though that dealer may have gone down the tube. Often, although not always, a sycophant with a mediocre or even poor work record was promoted over a performer who wasn't a fawner.

The practice of fawning over the boss gave birth to all kinds of ridiculous practices. One was the use of a secret network in the corporation to find out the likes, dislikes and idiosyncrasies of the boss. The information was usually passed on from one secretary to another. It was used by underlings to please their superiors. Display their loyalty. If the chairman liked Chivas Regal served in a hub-cap, there would be a bar full of it and a dozen wheel-covers waiting in his hotel room wherever he traveled. His favorite scotch would be the only scotch served at a dealer reception. If the boss liked to read murder mysteries before retiring, there'd be a veritable library of murder mysteries when he walked through the doors to his suite.

This network of intelligence served up information which provided the most outlandish example of "loyalty" that I have ever heard of inside General Motors or out. And I heard it several times. It involved a Chevrolet sales official at a rather low level of management for this feat extraordinaire. It showed how deep in GM management the loyalty system ran.

In preparing for the sales official's trip to this particular city, the Chevrolet zone sales people learned from Detroit that the boss liked to have a refrigerator full of cold beer, sandwiches, and fruit in his room to snack on at night before going to bed. They lined up a suite in one of the city's better hotels, rented a refrigerator and ordered the food and beer. However, the door to the suite was too small to accommodate the icebox. The hotel apparently nixed a plan to rip out the door and part of the adjoining wall. So the quick-thinking zone sales people hired a crane and operator, put them on the roof of the hotel, knocked out a set of windows in the suite, and lowered and shoved the refrigerator into the room through this gaping hole.

That night the Chevrolet executive wolfed down cold cut sandwiches, beer and fresh fruit, no doubt thinking, "What a great bunch of people we have in this zone." The next day he was off to another city and most likely another refrigerator, while back in the city of his departure the zone people were once again dismantling hotel windows and removing the refrigerator by crane. It was the most expensive midnight snack ever eaten by a GM executive.

While loyal employees attended the boss's personal needs with care and dispatch, they attended his corporate decisions with unwavering support, even if they thought the decisions were wrong. This was business loyalty. It not only capitalized on a natural inclination to support the man at the top. It made it mandatory.

This practice as I knew it flourished under Frederic G. Donner, who was chairman of the board of General Motors from 1958 to 1967. Short, stocky, with a stern face, Donner had all the emotion of a pancake.

He was cold and calculating in his approach to business. To Donner business came ahead of anything else. And business to him meant business his way. He would rarely tolerate views opposed to his. He refused to rediscuss previous decisions, even in the light of new information. "We already decided that!" he would snap. And that was the end of any attempt to reopen old business.

With such closed-mindedness at the top, a guiding precept of management soon developed. "Thou shalt not contradict the boss." Ideas in this kind of a system flowed from the top down, and not in the reverse direction. The man on top, whether he was a plant manager, department head or divisional general manager, was the final word. Each executive in turn supported the decisions of his boss right up the ladder. The chairman, of course, in this system had the final say on everything unless he parcelled out power to those around him. In Donner's case he was the unquestioned authority on financial matters. He would tolerate opposing views on product matters and usually gave authority for such matters to the president. But even in this area if he felt very keenly about a product decision, his way was the way the corporation went. The sovereignty of the president in product matters was generally as unchallenged as was Donner's overall authority, because the president got his power from Donner. What Donner and his men thought and supported became what the company thought and supported. Their attitudes were the prevailing attitudes. The system stayed on even though Donner retired in 1967. When I pushed for a program for drastically reducing the weight and size of all General Motors cars in 1969-70, I sporadically had President Ed Cole's support. When I did, the program was red hot. When I didn't, it died.

This system quickly shut top management off from the real world because it surrounded itself in many cases with "yes" men. There soon became no real vehicle for adequate outside input. Lower executives, eager to please the boss and rise up the corporate ladder, worked hard to learn what he wanted or how he thought on a particular subject. They then either fed the boss exactly what he wanted to know, or they modified their own proposals to suit his preferences.

Original ideas were often sacrificed in deference to what the boss wanted. Committee meetings no longer were forums for open discourse, but rather either soliloquies by the top man, or conversations between a few top men with the rest of the meeting looking on. In Fourteenth Floor meetings, often only three people, Cole, Gerstenberg, and Murphy would have anything substantial to say, even though there were 14 or 15 executives present. The rest of the team would remain silent, speaking only when spoken to. When they did offer a comment, in many cases it was just to paraphrase what had already been said by one of the top guys.

Terrell was the master of the paraphrase, although he was by no means the only practitioner. He often parrotted the views of Chairman Gerstenberg with unabashed rapidity. So often did he do this that the practice became a joke. Divisional general managers and their staffs entertained each other over lunch with various impressions of Terrell paraphrasing Gerstenberg in an Administrative Committee meeting. The dialogue would go something like this:

> Gerstenberg: Goddamnit. We can not afford any new models next year because of the cost of this federally mandated equipment. There is no goddamn money left for styling changes. That's the biggest problem we face.
>
> Terrell, after waiting about 10 minutes: Dick, goddamnit. We've just got to face up to the fact that our number one problem is the cost of this federally mandated equipment. This stuff costs so

47

much that we just don't have any money left for styling our new cars. That's our biggest problem.

Gerstenberg: You're goddamn right, Dick. That's a good point.

It was humorous to witness and replay at lunch, but it was sad to realize that executives could build credibility in this way. Top managers were sitting back in their chairs saying: "What a helluva hard-charging, decisive guy this is."

Terrell was by no means alone. Many Fourteenth Floor executives operated in similar ways. What they did to the Donners, Roches, Gerstenbergs, and Coles of the corporation, the divisional general managers often did to them. Simply regurgitated to the boss his own ideas. These lower managers were identified as the young turks of the corporation. They were loyal employees. They knew exactly where the power resided at the top. They were more than willing to play up to that power and rise in the company in the process. When the boss said "jump," they never asked "why," only "how high."

A system which puts emphasis on form, style and unwavering support for the decisions of the boss, almost always loses its perspective about an executive's business competence. Even if the man in power is a competent businessman, but adheres to the system, the chances of his successors' being equally competent are reduced because they are graded not on how they perform as businessmen but on how they perform as system-men. Once they get into power, they don't tamper with the system that promoted them. So a built-in method of perpetuating an imperfect management system is established. This is what I feel has happened at General Motors. Not that every executive in an important position is incompetent. There are very many fine and talented men in GM management today. Nevertheless, top management has some less than competent executives who may be good system-men but poor managers of people and trustees of the corporation. And the system which promoted them is so firmly entrenched that it most likely will continue to promote mediocrity to The Fourteenth Floor, often stifling the progress of more talented executives.

Not only is the system perpetuating itself, but in the act of perpetuating itself the system has fostered several destructive practices which are harmful to executive morale. They developed from the psychological need, as I see it, of less competent managers to affirm in their own minds a logical right to their positions, even though the basis for their promotions was illogical by any business-performance standard. Once in a position of power, a manager who was promoted by the system is insecure because, consciously or not, he knows that it was something other than his ability to manage and his knowledge of the business that put him in his position. He knows that he is one step or more past his Peter Principle equivalent. He thus looks for methods and defense mechanisms to ward off threats to his power base.

Donner, as far as I know, had unassailable credentials as a sound financial mind. He was a product of the Alfred P. Sloan–Donaldson Brown (a financial expert in the early days of GM) school of thought on financial control, which not only guides General Motors but also a whole host of American businesses. He was not a knowledgeable product man. Finance men aren't and usually can't expect to be. But Donner, as chairman, wanted to affirm for all that he was the boss. He went about this through a system of calculated promotions of "loyal" employees and management by intimidation.

From him developed what I call "promotion of the unobvious choice." This means promoting someone who was not regarded as a contender for the post. Doing so not only puts "your man" in position, but it earns for you his undying loyalty because he owes his corporate life to you. The "unobvious choice" is a devoted follower of the system who has nothing noteworthy in his background to mark him as a promotable executive. He often is surrounded by team players who are more qualified for the promotion.

A study of the past 10 years of General Motors top executives and an examination of their business biographies makes it obvious that some men with undistinguished business careers moved to the top and in many cases occupy positions of power within the corporation today. An understanding of their benefactors makes their ascension more explicable. In many cases, they were "unobvious choices." If the question were asked, "Would a man of these qualifications be chosen from outside the company for this post?" the answer would always be a resounding, "No!"

Donner himself was not an "unobvious choice," but as far as I know, he was the first major GM executive to promote an "unobvious choice." It happened in 1958. Harlow Curtice was then president and chief executive officer and about to retire. Red Curtice was warm, flamboyant, exciting, and as strong a product man as GM has ever known. Though he occasionally acted with a heavy hand, he had the compensating balance of being right most of the time. As chief executive officer he was the top corporate official. It was widely assumed in the corporation that his successor would be either Cliff Goad or Bud Goodman, two competent and strong executive vice-presidents.

The board was meeting in New York on a hot August day in 1958 to announce the successor not only to Curtice but also to Chairman Albert P. Bradley. I had been at Pontiac only about two years. But I was in a suite in the Book-Cadillac Hotel in downtown Detroit with a bunch of Pontiac people: Bunkie Knudsen, the divisional general manager; Pete Estes, chief engineer; Bob Emerick, the Public Relations director; and one or two other people. We were anxiously awaiting a call from New York. The phone rang and Bunkie picked it up. Suddenly his face dropped like frosting melting off a cake. He put the phone down and said: "Jack Gordon is the new president."

No one expected that. Even though John F. Gordon was group executive for the Body and Assembly Operations, he wasn't considered a corporate heavyweight. Not alongside Goad and Goodman.

We also learned that Donner not only was named chairman, as expected, but also chief executive officer. It was obvious that this hard-nosed finance man was going to run General Motors in the post-Curtice era. And it was just as obvious that Gordon was his "unobvious choice" for president. From then on, promoting the "unobvious choice" became a method of management. It was practiced more on the operations side of the business than the financial

50

side, because the operational side is vast, offering a greater field for promoting the "unobvious choice."

James M. Roche's selection as president to succeed Gordon was an "unobvious choice." He also succeeded Donner as chairman in 1967. A kindly, grandfatherly man, and a hard worker, Roche nevertheless, did not have a particularly distinguished career in General Motors, although before his rise to power he served a stint as general manager of Cadillac and several top corporate posts. Unlike many around him, however, I think Roche had a great sense of the corporate responsibility. He was not able to get this theme pushed through the corporation, however, perhaps because he was not forceful enough. It was obvious that he, like everyone else, was dominated by Donner.

Under the Donner-Roche regime a combination of Donner's arrogance and Roche's willingness to go along with the boss led to two of the most embarrassing public relations blunders in the corporation's history. First, in 1965, Donner abominably performed before Senator Abraham Ribicoff's Subcommittee on Executive Reorganization. He refused to, or could not, answer the simplest of questions about GM's operations and financial performance. Second was the whole sordid episode in which the company tailed Ralph Nader. Roche apologized to Nader, the Congress, and the country for the incident, and GM paid $425,000 in damages in an out-of-court settlement with the consumer advocate.

Donner also promoted to The Fourteenth Floor an "unobvious choice" in Roger M. Kyes, whose accomplishments at Frigidaire and then GM Truck & Coach Division were lackluster. Kyes in turn brought along his "unobvious choice," Dick Terrell, whose whole GM career was spent in non-automotive operations, first, Electro-Motive Division and then Frigidaire Division. From Terrell came his "unobvious choice," Reuben R. Jensen from the Allison Division.

Not one of these three was a distinguished businessman or had a reputation in the corporation for exceptional management ability. For Terrell, running Electro-Motive was an undemanding task since the division has a hammerlock on the nation's locomotive business. Its profits are good but small in their contribution to the total GM profit picture. His tenure at Frigidaire was marked by one distinguishable note. When he left the division, a corporate study recommended that GM all but fold the division by selling off its appliance business. Were it not that General Motors' car divisions at one time were required to buy Frigidaire air-conditioning equipment, for often more than similar systems could be purchased on the outside, the division would have been immersed in red ink. (GM recently sold the entire division.) Yet Terrell clung to the coattail of Kyes and moved from the appliance division to The Fourteenth Floor as vice-president for Non-Automotive and Defense Group; then in 1970 to executive vice-president for Car and Truck, Body and Assembly Operations, succeeding Kyes, even though he'd never worked a day in an auto division. He eventually became vice-chairman and one of the top three corporate officers of General Motors, before retiring in January 1979, at age 60.

Behind Terrell tagged Jensen, a virtual unknown who spent all his GM life in the Hydra-matic Division making transmissions, until October of 1967, when he was made head of the Allison Division. The Allison Division, which made gas turbine engines, military vehicles and locomotive parts, during this tenure was modestly successful. Eventually, at his urging. it was merged with the Detroit Diesel Division in 1970. The merger came about only a few months after Jensen was moved to The Fourteenth Floor to head the Non-Automotive and Defense Group, succeeding Terrell. Two years later, he was moved over to care for the car and truck operations although the only part of the car he had ever manufactured was the transmission. After a few months, heading up car and truck operations, Jensen was put in charge of GM's vast overseas operations. Today, Jensen is an executive vice-president for Worldwide Components and Power and Appliance operations.

Whether these "unobvious choices" were unrecognized as capable, astute businessmen was unimportant; they were well-recognized as hard team players, loyal to their bosses and the system which promoted them.

In watching the promotions of Kyes, Terrell, and Jensen while others who I felt were more competent were overlooked (I'd gladly name them were it not that such mention might ensure them anonymity in the corporation), the words of Mr. Sloan take on new significance: "I happen to be one of the old school who thinks that a knowledge of the business is essential to a successful organization." That is simply not the case today at GM.

There were and are men in positions of power at GM who do not know the business they are running. Many were not good businessmen in the areas with which they are familiar. "Promotion of the unobvious choice" has put some of them into their positions. Others simply played the loyalty system game so well they just moved up the corporate ladder every few years. What developed in some cases is "management by crony" which Sloan denounced as detrimental to a corporation. Among upper management of GM's operations there are not many proven, successful executives. There are some with potential who have not served sufficient time in the divisions to bring to The Fourteenth Floor the type of broad experience and confidence that only time and achievement can produce.

Insecure, an executive often resorts to defense mechanisms to affirm psychologically his position. Intimidation is a favorite tool, and once again the art of management by intimidation as I know it at GM began with Frederic Donner. He was the master intimidator and often reverted to gimmicks to show his power.

One time in an Administrative Committee meeting he asked the head of GM Truck & Coach Division:

"How many buses did you build last month?"

The executive replied: "Approximately three thousand" or a rounded figure like that. It was an approximation.

Donner scowled and snapped back something like: "Last month you built three thousand, one hundred and eighty-seven vehicles." Whatever the figure was, it was precise.

It was obvious to most of us in the meeting that Donner had just looked it up since the precise figure wasn't all that important. But the fact that he would rattle off the exact production figure in such an authoritarian, arrogant manner told us just one thing, that Donner was trying to make the point, "Look how I know this goddamn business, people! Look what a mind I have!"

The Donner memory game is not new to GM or American business. But it is a management cheap shot. It was used often inside GM's hallowed corporate walls but never with the devastating effect that it was used by Donner.

Very few men are gifted with a photographic memory. Pete Estes is one who is, and in this respect he is brilliant. He is one of the very few people I have ever met with such an amazing memory. He can remember what he had for lunch on this day a year ago. But in dealing with top GM executives, you could get the notion that The Fourteenth Floor had a corner on the memory market. This is because GM executives take copious notes of almost every conversation they have and often use them to give the impression that they know everything that was ever said or done in the company. In meetings I would see them taking notes. Other times, after casual conversations, they would hustle back to their offices to jot down what was said by whom and to whom.

Note-taking of itself is a good practice because it can provide an executive with instant references to refresh his memory about business matters and keep him on top of his job. I often take notes. But it becomes a bad practice when it is used to intimidate.

In a conversation I had one time with Jim Roche, when he was chairman, we were discussing something less than significant like the development of a new tooling process. I offered a thought on the matter and he replied something like: "Well now, wait a minute. We talked about that two years ago, and you said just the opposite of what you are saying now. Why has your position changed?"

He didn't have a note in front of him. "Holy Moses!" I thought. "I'm talking with a goddamn genius here." I couldn't remember what I had said two years previously and I was somewhat embarrassed. Later, I learned about Roche's habit of taking detailed notes on everything and referring to them later. He became mortal once again.

Everyone at GM takes notes, though. Tom Murphy, the current chairman, takes notes, although in his case they aren't used to intimidate, but rather to keep abreast of the business. Nevertheless, during the Federal anti-trust suit against Ford and GM for conspiring to fix the prices of the fleet car sales, it was learned that Murphy had taken detailed notes during an Administrative Committee meeting at which GM supposedly discussed pricing policy for fleet sales. The notes were subpoenaed which scared the hell out of The Fourteenth Floor until they were declared useless because no one could decipher them. Murphy writes in letters about two printer's points high and no one could read them.

Donner had his corporate imitators. Roger Kyes learned the art of intimidation at the master's knee. He didn't play the memory game, but he tried to intimidate executives by talking unceasingly about what a business brain he was. He often took up two-hour meetings in his office with nothing more than a lecture to captive divisional people about how he saved one division after another. He told me on several occasions that he knew more about the car business and my operations than I ever would.

On one occasion shortly after I took over Chevrolet, he pulled me into his office and said, "I have made a private study, and the whole problem with Chevrolet's inventory mess is centered on 50 parts classifications. Clear them up and you've solved Chevy's problems."

He said it with such authority that I figured we'd better get onto that problem first. I went to Chevy's manufacturing and purchasing people. "Kyes told me about his private study and that it revealed that the whole problem centers on 50 parts classifications. Let's identify them right away, and get it solved."

They answered, "If there was a study made, we sure as hell don't know of it." And neither did any of the managers on down the line right into the manufacturing plants. If Kyes made a study he didn't bother to talk to a single soul in Chevrolet.

My own analysis soon showed me that Chevrolet's inventory problems were a helluva lot more complicated and fundamental than the misclassification of 50 parts. Kyes just made up the solution to the problem and picked the number 50 right out of the air. He was trying to dazzle me; it didn't work, but it intimidated a lot of other GM executives.

Kyes, to my way of thinking, was the consummate corporate bully. A man unfortunately given frighteningly bad looks, he used his features to his advantage. He once referred to himself as "one mean, ugly sonofabitch." At six-feet four, he was an imposing figure of a man with a harsh and foggy voice and penetrating look that made executives wilt.

He was a hatchet man in the corporation and relished the job just as he relished a similar duty while he was assistant secretary of Defense in the Eisenhower Administration. His proudest moment, he would tell anyone, was when a *Look* magazine article called him "The hatchet man in the Defense Department." He cherished the role and played it to bravura performances. One of his duties was to tell has-been executives that they were going to take early retirement. He bullied more than a couple of men into taking early retirement. If one rebelled, he'd gather a case against the executive, break the results to him and then give him the option of being fired or taking early retirement. On one occasion, he built up a case against an executive charging that "he did not travel enough to keep in touch with his operations." Then Kyes turned around and charged another executive whose "time was at hand" with traveling too much. "You're never home minding the store," he told him. In some of these cases, it was publicly announced that this or that executive was taking early retirement for health reasons. The word around the corporation was, "When Kyes tells you that you're sick, you're sick."

He threatened me with firing often when I ran Pontiac and Chevrolet. The threats were made in private when he objected to something I did which wasn't the way he wanted it done. One time, though, he threatened me in public, and I fought back.

All of the divisions were ordered to cut back on personnel. We were given specific areas in which to cut back. Included in my order was the dismissal of a handful of test drivers for Chevrolet Engineering at the GM Tech Center. It seemed like a ridiculous directive because we would still have to have the testing done. But we would have to go outside of the company to get it done and end up spending a helluva lot more money. So I practiced that old corporate trick of foot dragging. I didn't fire the drivers. A review of the cutback program was being conducted at an Administrative Committee meeting. I was asked about the dismissal of the test drivers and answered something innocuous like: "I'm working on it."

Suddenly Kyes boomed back: "If you can't fire those goddamn guys, then we will get somebody who can. If you can't do it, you don't know how the hell to do your job."

The words stung like arrowheads. I was thoroughly embarrassed at the dressing down in front of my superiors and peers. I was livid and started to yell back at him but stopped short and held my peace. After the meeting I went straight to Ed Cole's presidential office and said: "If you don't get that ugly sonofabitch off my back, I'm going right into his office and pinch his head off."

"Jeez, John," Cole said leaping up from his desk. It was the most violent outbreak he'd seen amidst the almost churchlike quiet of The Fourteenth Floor. "Cool it. Relax. I'll speak to him."

But I couldn't cool it. So I stormed down the hall into Kyes office.

"You sonofabitch! If you embarrass me with a tirade like that again, I'll knock you on your ass. Right in front of everybody."

He turned white and rattled off something about wanting to impress me with the importance of his orders. That was the end of it. He never confronted me in such a manner again in public. But his craggy visage haunted me until he retired from GM in 1971. Sadly for Kyes, his usefulness to the company waned in his last couple of years. He was taken out of active management at the age of 63 and made an assistant to the president until age 64 when he ironically took an early retirement. It may have been a case of Roger Kyes telling Roger Kyes he was sick. He died a year later.

I use Roger Kyes as an example not to desecrate his memory but rather to point out the adverse influence he had on my career at General Motors. He embodied many facets of a man made by the GM system. He was a team player. Loyal to his superiors and the system—to a fault.

CHAPTER FOUR

How Moral Men Make Immoral Decisions

"We feel that 1972 can be one of Chevrolet's great years. . . . Most of the improvements this year are to engines and chassis components aimed at giving a customer a better car for the money. . . . I want to reiterate our pledge that the 1972 Chevrolets will be the best in Chevrolet history. . . . We recognize that providing good dealer service is the surest way to keep quality-built Chevrolets for 1972 in top quality condition. . . . This is the lineup of cars for every type of buyer that we offer for 1972. Cars that are the best built in Chevrolet history. . . ."

The words seemed to fall out of my mouth like stones from an open hand. Effortlessly. Almost meaninglessly. It was August 31, 1971. I was powergliding through the National Press Preview of 1972 Chevrolet cars and trucks at the Raleigh House, a mock-Tudor restaurant-banquet hall complex in suburban Detroit. The audience was filled with reporters from all over the country. In their midst was a plentiful sprinkling of Chevrolet managers. The new product presentation and question-answer session went smoothly, and I was stepping down from the podium and receiving the usual handshakes and compliments from some of the sales guys and a few of the members of the press when a strange feeling hit me:

"My God! I've been through all this before."

59

It was a strange feeling because somehow I was detached from it all. Looking down on myself in the banquet hall surrounded by executives, newsmen and glittering Chevrolets. And I was questioning why I was there and what I was doing. The answers were not satisfactory.

"This whole show is nothing but a replay of last year's show, and the year before that and the year before that. The speech I just gave was the same speech I gave last year, written by the same guy in public relations about the same superficial product improvements as previous years. And the same questions were being asked by the same newsmen I've seen for years. Almost nothing has changed."

I looked around the room for a brief moment searching for something, anything that could show me that there was real meaning in the exercises we were going through, that the national press conference and the tens of similar dealer product announcements I conducted across the country were something more than just new product sales hypes. But I found nothing.

Instead, I got the empty feeling that "what I am doing here may be nothing more than perpetuating a gigantic fraud," a fraud on the American consumer by promising him something new but giving him only surface alterations —"tortured sheet metal" as former chairman Frederic G. Donner used to say—or a couple of extra horsepower and an annual price increase. A fraud on the American economy, because I always had a vague suspicion that the annual model change may be good for the auto business in the short term but that it wasn't good for the economy and the country. Couldn't the money we spent on annual, superficial styling changes be better spent in reducing prices or in improving service and reliability? Or seeking solutions to the sociological problems which our products were creating in areas of pollution, energy consumption, safety and congestion?

And a fraud on our own company because, when General Motors began to grow on the principle of annual model changes and the promotion of something new and different, cars were almost all alike with the same basic color—black. There was room for cosmetic changes as well as substantial advancement in technology with new and better engines, more sophisticated transmissions, improved performance and comfort characteristics.

But now there was nothing new and revolutionary in car development and there hadn't been for years. As a company, we were kidding ourselves that these slight alterations were innovative. They were not. We were living off the gullibility of the consumer combined with the fantastic growth of the American economy in the 1960s. Salting away billions of dollars of profits in the process and telling ourselves we were great managers because of these profits. This bubble was surely going to break, I thought. The consumer is going to get wise to us, and when he does we will have to fight for a long time to get back into his favor.

Those feelings during the preview led me to tell newsmen during lunch that I would probably leave the auto industry when I was age 55 or so, to get involved in helping find answers to America's problems. There was skepticism and disbelief in their voices as we talked about this subject. They didn't know that I had petitioned management to let me resign from the corporation to take a dealership in San Jose, California. Nevertheless, the newsmen wrote about my lunchtime revelation.

The Fourteenth Floor went through the ceiling when the stories appeared the next day saying I was going to forsake General Motors in eight or nine years. It looked to them as if I was trying to force their hand by saying: "Make me President by then or I will quit."

To anyone in the corporation who asked about them, I explained that my luncheon comments, though not irrevocable, were sincerely motivated and that I was having some internal conflicts about my job. My doubts about the worth of the annual model change were just a part of a growing concern I had about the general level of morality practiced in General Motors, in particular, and parts of American business in general.

It seemed to me, and still does, that the system of American business often produces wrong, immoral and irresponsible decisions, even though the personal morality of the people running the businesses is often above reproach. The system has a different morality as a group than the people do as individuals, which permits it to willfully produce ineffective or dangerous products, deal dictatorially and often unfairly with suppliers, pay bribes for business, abrogate the rights of employees by demanding blind loyalty to management or tamper with the democratic process of government through illegal political contributions.

I am not a psychologist, so I can't offer a professional opinion on what happens to the freedom of individual minds when they are blended into the group management thought process of business. But my private analysis is this: Morality has to do with people. If an action is viewed primarily from the perspective of its effect on people, it is put into the moral realm.

Business in America, however, is impersonal. This is particularly true of large American multi-national corporations. They are viewed by their employees and publics as faceless. They have no personality. The ultimate measure of success and failure of these businesses is not their effect on people but rather their earnings per share of stock. If earnings are high, the business is considered good. If they are low or in the red ink, it is considered a failure. The first question to greet any business proposal is how will it affect profits? *People* do not enter the equation of a business decision except to the extent that the effect on them will hurt or enhance earnings per share. In such a completely impersonal context, business decisions of questionable personal morality are easily justified. The unwavering devotion to the bottom line brings this about, and the American public until now has been more than willing to accept this. When someone is forced into early retirement in a management power-play or a supplier is cheated out of a sale by under-the-table dealings, the public reaction is generally, "Oh, well. That's business." And management's reaction is often, "It's what's on the bottom line that counts." A person who shoots and kills another is sentenced to life in prison. A businessman who makes a defective product which kills people may get a nominal fine or a verbal slap on the hands, if he is ever brought to trial at all.

The impersonal process of business decision-making is reinforced by a sort of mob psychology that results from group management and the support of a specific system of management. *Watergate* certainly proved what can happen when blind devotion to a system or a process of thought moves unchecked. Members of the Nixon Administration never raised any real questions about the morality of the break-in and the coverup. The only concern was for the expedient method to save the system. So too in business. Too often the only questions asked are: What is the expedient thing to do to save the system? How can we increase profits per share?

Never once while I was in General Motors management did I hear substantial social concern raised about the impact of our business on America, its consumers or the economy. When we should have been planning switches to smaller, more fuel-efficient, lighter cars in the late 1960s in response to a growing demand in the marketplace, GM management refused because "we make more money on big cars." It mattered not that customers wanted the smaller cars or that a national balance-of-payments deficit was being built in large part because of the burgeoning sales of foreign cars in the American market.

Refusal to enter the small car market when the profits were better on bigger cars, despite the needs of the public and the national economy, was not an isolated case of corporate insensitivity. It was typical. And what disturbed me is that it was indicative of fundamental problems with the system.

General Motors certainly was no more irresponsible than many American businesses. But the fact that the "prototype" of the well-run American business engaged in questionable business practices and delivered decisions which I felt were sometimes illegal, immoral or irresponsible is an indictment of the American business system.

Earlier in my career, I accepted these decisions at GM without question. But as I was exposed to more facets of the business, I came to a realization of the responsibilities we had in managing a giant corporation and making a product which substantially affected people and national commerce. It bothered me how cavalierly these responsibilities were often regarded.

The whole Corvair case is a first-class example of a basically irresponsible and immoral business decision which was made by men of generally high personal moral standards. When Nader's book threatened the Corvair's sales and profits, he became an enemy of the system. Instead of trying to attack his credentials or the factual basis of his arguments, the company sought to attack him personally. This move failed, but, in the process, GM's blundering "made" Ralph Nader.

When the fact that GM hired detectives to follow and discredit Nader was exposed, the system was once again threatened. Top management, instead of questioning the system which would permit such an horrendous mistake as tailing Nader, simply sought to preserve the system by sacrificing the heads of several executives who were blamed for the incident. Were the atmosphere at GM not one emphasizing profits and preservation of the system above all else, I am sure the acts against Nader would never have been perpetrated.

Those who were fired no doubt thought they were loyal employees. And, ironically, had they succeeded in devastating the image of Ralph Nader, they would have been corporate heroes and rewarded substantially. I find it difficult to believe that knowledge of these activities did not reach into the upper reaches of GM's management. But, assuming that it didn't, top management should have been held responsible for permitting the conditions to exist which would spawn such actions. If top management takes credit for a company's successes, it must also bear the brunt of the responsibility for its failures.

Furthermore, the Corvair was unsafe as it was originally designed. It was conceived along the lines of the foreign-built Porsche. These cars were powered by engines placed in the rear and supported by an independent, swing-axle suspension system. In the Corvair's case, the engine was all-aluminum and air-cooled (compared to the standard water-cooled iron engines). This, plus the rear placement of the engine, made the car new and somewhat different to the American market.

However, there are several bad engineering characteristics inherent in rear-engine cars which use a swing-axle suspension. In turns at high speeds they tend to become directionally unstable and, therefore, difficult to control. The rear of the car lifts or "jacks" and the rear wheels tend to tuck under the car, which encourages the car to flip over. In the high-performance Corvair, the car conveyed a false sense of control to the driver, when in fact he may have been very close to losing control of the vehicle. The result of these characteristics can be fatal.

These problems with the Corvair were well documented inside GM's Engineering Staff long before the Corvair ever was offered for sale. Frank Winchell, now vice-president of Engineering, but then an engineer at Chevy, flipped over one of the first prototypes on the GM test track in Milford, Michigan. Others followed.

The questionable safety of the car caused a massive internal fight among GM's engineers over whether the car should be built with another form of suspension. On one side of the argument was Chevrolet's then General Manager, Ed Cole, an engineer and product innovator. He and some of his engineering colleagues were enthralled with the idea of building the first modern, rear-engine, American car. And I am convinced they felt the safety risks of the swing-axle suspension were minimal. On the other side was a wide assortment of top-flight engineers, including Charles Chayne, then vice-president of Engineering; Von D. Polhemus, engineer in charge of Chassis Development on GM's Engineering Staff, and others.

These men collectively and individually made vigorous attempts inside GM to keep the Corvair, as designed, out of production or to change the suspension system to make the car safer. One top corporate engineer told me that he showed his test results to Cole but by then, he said, "Cole's mind was made up."

Albert Roller, who worked for me in Pontiac's Advanced Engineering section, tested the car and pleaded with me not to use it at Pontiac. Roller had been an engineer with Mercedes-Benz before joining GM, and he said that Mercedes had tested similarly designed rear-engine, swing-axle cars and had found them far too unsafe to build.

At the very least, then, within General Motors in the late 1950s, serious questions were raised about the Corvair's safety. At the very most, there was a mountain of documented evidence that the car should not be built as it was then designed.

However, Cole was a strong product voice and a top

salesman in company affairs. In addition, the car, as he proposed it, would cost less to build than the same car with a conventional rear suspension. Management not only went along with Cole, it also told the dissenters in effect to "stop these objections. Get on the team, or you can find someplace else to work." The ill-fated Corvair was launched in the fall of 1959.

The results were disastrous. I don't think any one car before or since produced as gruesome a record on the highway as the Corvair. It was designed and promoted to appeal to the spirit and flair of young people. It was sold in part as a sports car. Young Corvair owners, therefore, were trying to bend their car around curves at high speeds and were killing themselves in alarming numbers.

It was only a couple of years or so before GM's legal department was inundated with lawsuits over the car. And the fatal swath that this car cut through the automobile industry touched the lives of many General Motors executives, employees and dealers in an ironic and tragic twist of fate.

The son of Cal Werner, general manager of the Cadillac Division, was killed in a Corvair. Werner was absolutely convinced that the design defect in the car was responsible. He said so many times. The son of Cy Osborne, an executive vice-president in the 1960s, was critically injured in a Corvair and suffered irreparable brain damage. Bunkie Knudsen's niece was brutally injured in a Corvair. And the son of an Indianapolis Chevrolet dealer also was killed in the car. Ernie Kovacs, my favorite comedian, was killed in a Corvair.

While the car was being developed at Chevrolet, we at Pontiac were spending $1.3 million on a project to adapt the Corvair to our division. The corporation had given us the go-ahead to work with the car to give it a Pontiac flavor. Our target for introduction was the fall of 1960, a year after Chevy introduced the car.

As we worked on the project, I became absolutely convinced by Chayne, Polhemus and Roller that the car was unsafe. So I conducted a three-month campaign, with Knudsen's support, to keep the car out of the Pontiac lineup. Fortunately, Buick and Oldsmobile at the time were tooling up their own compact cars, the Special and

F-85, respectively, which featured conventional front-engine designs.

We talked the corporation into letting Pontiac switch from a Corvair derivative to a version of the Buick-Oldsmobile car. We called it the Tempest and introduced it in the fall of 1960 with a four-cylinder engine as standard equipment and a V-8 engine as an option.

When Knudsen took over the reins of Chevrolet in 1961, he insisted that he be given corporate authorization to install a stabilizing bar in the rear to counteract the natural tendencies of the Corvair to flip off the road. The cost of the change would be about $15 a car. But his request was refused by The Fourteenth Floor as "too expensive."

Bunkie was livid. As I understand it, he went to the Executive Committee and told the top officers of the corporation that, if they didn't reappraise his request and give him permission to make the Corvair safe, he was going to resign from General Motors. This threat and the fear of the bad publicity that surely would result from Knudsen's resignation forced management's hand. They relented. Bunkie put a stabilizing bar on the Corvair in the 1964 models. The next year a completely new and safer independent suspension designed by Frank Winchell was put on the Corvair. And it became one of the safest cars on the road. But the damage done to the car's reputation by then was irreparable. Corvair sales began to decline precipitously after the waves of unfavorable publicity following Nader's book and the many lawsuits being filed across the country. Production of the Corvair was halted in 1969, four years after it was made a safe and viable car.

To date, millions of dollars have been spent in legal expenses and out-of-court settlements in compensation for those killed or maimed in the Corvair. The corporation steadfastly defends the car's safety, despite the internal engineering records which indicated it was not safe, and the ghastly toll in deaths and injury it recorded.

There wasn't a man in top GM management who had anything to do with the Corvair who would purposely build a car that he knew would hurt or kill people. But, as part of a management team pushing for increased sales and profits, each gave his individual approval in a group to decisions which produced the car in the face of the serious doubts that were raised about its safety, and then later sought to squelch information which might prove the car's deficiencies.

The corporation became almost paranoid about the leaking of inside information we had on the car. In April of 1971, 19 boxes of microfilmed Corvair owner complaints, which had been ordered destroyed by upper management, turned up in the possession of two suburban Detroit junk dealers. When The Fourteenth Floor found this out, it went into panic and we at Chevrolet were ordered to buy the microfilm back and have it destroyed.

I refused, saying that a public company had no right to destroy documents of its business and that GM's furtive purchase would surely surface. Besides, the $20,000 asking price was outright blackmail.

When some consumer groups showed an interest in getting the films, the customer relations department was ordered to buy the film, which it did. To prevent similar slip-ups in the future, the corporation tightened its scrapping procedures.

Chevrolet products were involved in the largest product recall in automotive history when, in 1971, the corporation called back 6.7 million 1965-69 Chevrolet cars to repair defective motor mounts. The rubber mounts, which anchor the engine to the car, were breaking apart and causing the engine to lunge out of place. This action often locked the accelerator into an open position at the speed of about 25 miles per hour. Cars were smashing up all across the country when panicky drivers couldn't stop them or jumped out of them in fright. The defect need never have been.

At Pontiac, when I was chief engineer, we developed a safety-interlock motor mount which we put on our 1965 car line. It was developed because we discovered that the mounts we were using were defective. We made our findings and the design of the new motor mount available to the rest of the car divisions. None of them opted for it.

However, reports started drifting in from the field in 1966 that the Chevrolet mounts were breaking apart after extensive use. The division did nothing. Dealers replaced the mounts and charged the customers for the parts and labor.

When I got to Chevrolet in 1969, the reports about motor mount failures were reaching crisis proportions. When a motor mount failure was blamed for a fatal accident involving an elderly woman in Florida, I asked Kyes, my boss, to let me quietly recall all the cars with these problem mounts and repair them, at GM's expense. He refused on the ground that it would cost too much money. By 1971, however, the motor mount trouble was becoming widely known outside of the corporation because unsatisfied owners were complaining to local newspapers, the National Highway Traffic Safety Administration and several consumer groups.

The pressure began to build on GM to recall the cars with these mounts. Soon GM began to repair these cars at company expense, but it refused to recall all the cars, preferring to wait until the mounts broke in use before doing anything. Bob Irvin, of the Detroit *News*, who was receiving huge numbers of complaints, began to write almost daily stories about the mount trouble and GM's steadfast refusal to recall all the cars.

The fires of discontent were further fanned when Ed Cole, who was opposing the recall internally, was asked by a reporter why GM continued to refuse to recall the cars. He replied that the mounts were not a problem and that anyone who "can't manage a car at 25 miles per hour shouldn't be driving." It was an unfortunately callous remark, for which I am sure Cole was later sorry. But he became more rigid in his stance against a recall campaign. So I wrote a memo to my immediate boss in 1971, Tom Murphy, and it said in part:

> *At this point in time, it seems to me that we have no alternative (but to recall the Chevrolets). Certainly if GM can spend over $200,000,000 a year on advertising, the $30 or $40,000,000 this campaign would cost is not a valid reason for delaying. Certainly, it would be worth the cost to stop the negative publicity, even if management cannot agree to campaign these cars on moral grounds.*

Murphy received the memo and returned it to me, refusing to accept it.

Finally, about a month or so later, under the weight of government, consumer group and newspaper pressure, GM recalled the 6.7 million cars with defective engine mounts. The price was about $40 million to recall the cars and wire the engines to the car so they wouldn't slip out of place when the mounts broke.

But the cost was much greater in the incredibly bad publicity GM received because of its unwillingness to admit its responsibility for the defect and to repair the cars on its own. It was really a case of the corporation taking an attitude of "the owners be damned" when it came to spending the money it needed to fix the engine mount problem.

The motor mount affair reflected a general corporate attitude toward the consumer movement, an attitude shared by some American businesses in a wide variety of industries. The reason that consumer advocates, such as Ralph Nader, have emerged as public champions, and that city, state and national governments have set up offices to look after consumer affairs, is that people have legitimate beefs about the quality and safety of the products they are buying. If almost everybody who bought products was happy with them, there would be no Naders at the local, state or national level. And even if there were, their cries would fall on deaf ears.

Car service is an example of an area of wide consumer displeasure today. At best, automotive service is poor. Car owners are suspicious of their dealers' service. More and more people are turning to the corner gasoline station mechanic for service, even though the nearby dealer is supposedly the specialist at fixing their car. The reason is that the auto companies, especially GM, have never committed themselves to improving the serviceability of the dealership.

A car dealer is judged by how many new cars he pushes out of the showroom doors in the front and not how he services them in the back. Dealers are graded primarily on their sales results, because this puts money into the corporate bank account and profit on the financial sheet. A big-volume dealer with a poor service operation is handled very gingerly by the manufacturer. Unfortunately, he often gets better treatment from the company than the dedicated, conscientious dealer with lower volume who invests heavily in a proper service facility.

The relationship between the company and its retail dealer body is a study in paradox. The corporation depends on its dealers to market its cars and trucks. Without the dealer body, GM or its competitors could not stay in business. Dealers and their businesses represent about half the total investment in General Motors.

The local Chevrolet or Buick dealer often is the only personal contact a customer has with General Motors. His perceptions of GM and its car divisions come from the way he is treated at the retail sales level. Such interlocking needs between the dealers and the company would seem to dictate a close and friendly relationship between the two.

In some cases, most often with high-volume dealers, this is the case. More often, behind the smiles, handshakes and backslapping of dealer-company sales meetings, there is an adversary relationship which is contrary to the practical dictates of business. Dealers often don't trust the company and vice-versa.

I found the majority of car dealers I worked with to be hard-working, sound and honest businessmen. In their struggles with the corporation, the dealers received the short straw more times than not.

There were some bad and dishonest dealers as well as good ones. Some, for instance, were notorious for cheating on warranty claims.

Chevrolet division in late 1974 purged practically two entire zone sales offices when it uncovered a dealer warranty fraud scheme which was working with the help of the zone officials. This scandal was more than a routine case of fraud, however. The Chevrolet service manager for the Boston Zone was murdered in the scheme.

Conversely, in many instances, dealers performing legitimate warranty repairs to customers' cars had their claims for restitution disallowed on a purely capricious basis, a practice I fought against.

The tone for an adversary relationship between company and dealers has been set, I think, by shoddy treatment of the dealer body. While General Motors owes its very existence today to its dealers, the manner in which

71

GM has manipulated and browbeaten them falls into the area of questionable ethics.

When I got to Chevrolet, the dealer body as a whole was very distrustful of divisional and corporate management because it had been left with a string of broken promises about new product developments and the exclusivity of its markets. In one instance, Bob Lund, Chevy's general sales manager, and I were asked to attend a Fourteenth Floor meeting to report on how Chevrolet dealers would react if Pontiac dealers were given a version of the compact Nova. At the time, our dealers were selling every Nova they could get into their dealerships. They also had been promised by corporate management that they would have this compact car market all to themselves among GM's divisions.

Before the meeting "upstairs," I was called into a small top management conference by Kyes and told that if I opposed a decision to give a Nova derivative to Pontiac, the small-car program I was pushing (the K-car project) would be taken from Chevrolet. Nevertheless, in the meeting I opposed the move, along with Lund, on the ground that our dealers couldn't get enough Novas as it was and that we had to keep our promise of exclusivity to them.

Lund and I were wasting our breath; the corporation gave Pontiac a version of the Nova called the Ventura. As it turned out, Pontiac dealers had trouble selling their compact cars while Chevrolet dealers lost sales that they practically had in the bag. They were livid at the double-talk they had been given by The Fourteenth Floor. And my small-car program was never approved.

This was not an isolated case. The dealers are often bounced around at the whim of corporate management. And it is a wonder that car dealers have not formed an organization like the National Football League Players Association to represent their consolidated interests before the manufacturer. In the past, when GM effected a price cut to meet its competition or improve the sales of a particular car line, the cut often came out of the dealer's markup.

In other words, hypothetically assuming that GM announced a four percent price reduction on a $3,000 car, this would be a drop of $120 on the sticker price of the car. The public would praise the corporation's move, but what it wouldn't know was that the price of that car to the dealer from the company hadn't changed one bit. The company had lowered the manufacturer's suggested retail price by $120 by narrowing the profit spread between that price and the price of the car to the dealer. If the spread was 21 percent, it fell to 17 percent. The price reduction came out of the dealer's potential profit.

The company often leans on its dealers to maintain or increase its own profit levels, with little regard to the dealer's business climate. After the Arab oil embargo there was a sharp drop in big car sales. GM's big car divisions watched their business drop 50 percent or more. The plight was the same for the dealers, yet GM continued to force big cars on dealers with no relaxation in the payment schedules.

I thought that GM should give its dealers 90 days free interest, and I told people so, even though by now I was out of management. Instead, management maintained its standard billing program—payment in full 20 days after the cars are received. When the corporation provided General Motors Acceptance Corporation (GMAC), which finances dealer inventories and retail purchases, with a $500-million interest-free loan during the crunch, none of the interest break was passed on to the dealers. GM dealers didn't get a one-tenth of one percent reduction in their loan rates because of the free loan to GMAC. So GMAC made money at the dealers' expense, and that compounded the business troubles for the dealers during the auto recession.

A practice which I opposed in GM was the constant pressuring of dealers to buy their service and aftermarket parts from the General Motors Parts Division (GMPD), when they could get some of the same parts cheaper from the warehouse distributors of the AC Spark Plug and Delco Products Division.

The situation was complicated. GMPD was a business of $400 million a year or so, primarily set up to give GM car and truck dealers a single source for the parts they need to repair vehicles or sell over-the-counter. The parts they offered included spark plugs, condensers, oil filters and shock absorbers made by other GM divisions such as AC and Delco products.

These divisions, however, also had their own network of warehouse distributors, which sold primarily to non-GM dealers, repair shops and gasoline stations. Both the GM car dealers and the warehouse distributors bought their parts at similar discounts, in some cases 25 percent. The dealers got this discount from GMPD, and the warehouse got them from their home division.

There was some overlapping of business, however, a problem which no one ever sought to straighten out. The distributor could also sell to the GM dealers. When they did, they received an additional discount from the divisions to make the sale profitable. Otherwise, they could offer the dealer no better deal than he could get from GMPD. Whatever this additional discount was, the distributor often offered to split it with the dealer. When this happened, the dealer could get the part cheaper at the distributor level than he could from GMPD.

Nevertheless, to keep GMPD viable, pressure was constantly applied to the dealers to buy parts from GMPD at a higher price. When GMPD held a big sales push, a car division sales or service representative would be given a quota of say 25,000 spark plugs to sell.

He'd walk into a GM car dealer and say, "Your quota is 1,000 spark plugs." If the dealer balked, he was badgered and browbeaten by the sales representatives of his own car division to meet his quota. In the end, a balking dealer knew that the company held the upper hand because it could get even in many different ways, one of which was to slow up deliveries to him of hot-selling cars. Sometimes, large-volume dealers who were important to the corporation could fend off this pressure without fear of reprisal. But, more often than not, dealers had to knuckle under and buy the parts from GMPD at a higher price than they could get elsewhere.

During one dealer service meeting at Great Gorge, New Jersey, an east coast dealer complained about being badgered into buying GMPD parts. He said he had just weathered a couple of bad business years and added:

"I couldn't get anybody to come out and help me save my dealership, or help me with my business problems. But I had seven different people call on me, including the regional manager (of the division), about taking my quota of these goddamn spark plugs from GMPD that I could buy cheaper somewhere else. It cost me a lot of extra money (thousands of dollars) each year to buy parts from the GMPD." There were other such cases.

In a somewhat different situation, there was a Chevy dealer in Florida who was the low bidder on the sale of a large fleet of cars. To win the bid he had to price the cars very close to his own cost. So, to save about $35 a car, his bid included Motorola radios instead of the GM-built Delco units. This $35 represented most of the profit for him per car. When the dealer ordered the cars from Chevrolet, sans Delco radios, the company representative contacted him and made it clear that, unless he bought Delco radios for the cars, his order would be delayed three to four months. Such a delay would bring the cars to the dealer much later than the delivery date promised to the fleet consumer. The Florida dealer was forced to buy Delco radios, and he made very little profit on the sale of these cars, while GM made thousands of dollars on the Delco radios alone. Later, I ran into a divisional guy who was gleeful in his replay of this case, crowing about how he forced this dealer to take company radios.

In many respects, I felt that the dealers had carried the division and the corporation through rough sales periods. Chevy's dealers kept the division afloat during the mid-1960s. Our thanks for their help was to constantly put the squeeze on them for every last nickel of corporate profit. Our policies with dealers were shoddy. What we were doing was often a blatant violation of our own precepts of free enterprise.

When we were called down before Congressional hearings to explain our side of the growing problem of governmental control of the industry, a frequent defense of our business was that we needed to preserve the free enterprise system. "In a free market, the customer is the winner. And the true principles of business prevail because the customer decides which businesses are successful and which are not," the corporation would tell any willing ear.

Yet, within our corporate walls, we engaged in business practices which were not only monopolistic, but sometimes were downright violations of the free-enterprise system. We stifled competition. Our dealers weren't always free to

75

run their businesses as they saw fit. We were forcing them at times to buy our parts and products at inflated prices.

We certainly could not tolerate the use of inferior parts by our dealers in repairing General Motors vehicles. But we sure as hell shouldn't have forced them to pay higher prices for our own parts than they could get elsewhere in the company. And, in situations where they had the choice of choosing our product, such as Delco radios or a competitor's product of similar quality, we should have had to sell the dealers on the merits of the GM product over the competition. That is what free enterprise is all about. We shouldn't have forced our dealers to take the GM product. If General Motors was buying a product from one company, it would buy it the cheapest way. That is just good business. Therefore, I felt what we were doing with our dealers was immoral and probably illegal.

So I told the Chevrolet sales executives, who were our dealer contact people, that we were never again going to force our dealers to pay more for a product they could get cheaper elsewhere. That was an order. There would be no more intimidation of Chevrolet dealers by the field sales force about buying spark plugs from GMPD. Our dealers could get GM parts where they got the best price.

Word quickly got to The Fourteenth Floor about this directive (I think it took less than an hour). I got a call that Mr. Kyes wanted to see me in his office immediately. When I got there, he was red-faced and mad. He launched a 15-minute, blistering attack on me as a person, citizen, employee and businessman. I was verbally raked up one end of executive row and down the other. I thought he was going to fire me on the spot. His diatribe ended on a typically low note:

"You don't know how business is done. You're a goddamn amateur, De Lorean."

"That's just the way I feel. You don't solve the problem of an unequal discount structure on our parts by intimidating the dealers into paying a higher price. What you should do is look for a way to fix the problem," I responded.

I left his office. My order stuck. Chevrolet people stopped pressuring our dealers to take parts from GMPD.

Not all GM dealers fared poorly in their association

with the company. Some profited quite well by their friendships with top executives. Hanley Dawson, a big company dealer in the Midwest was one who profited exceptionally well from his corporate friendships, especially with Ed Cole.

On one occasion, Cadillac decided to sell all its "company stores," which is an inside term for retail dealerships which are owned by a division of the corporation. One of these was the Rush Street "store" in downtown Chicago, which is a prime location for a Cadillac dealership. The property and building were leased on a long-term agreement with Prudential Life Insurance, as I recall.

So valuable was the land that Prudential wanted to buy the lease back from Cadillac for a price that was in the millions. But the division wanted the valuable location. Harry Hollywood, an assistant sales manager at Cadillac, said he wanted to buy the Rush Street Store. He had been a general manager of this dealership prior to coming into Cadillac management in 1967. And it was well known in the corporation that he was brought into GM then by Chairman Roche with the promise that when he wanted to go back into the retail business, he would get a Cadillac dealership. So Hollywood was exercising this option when he bid for the Chicago dealership.

The company told him the selling price would require Hollywood to come up with something like $500,000 to $800,000 of his own money. This was a staggering sum for Hollywood. He couldn't afford it and had to turn the deal down.

Shortly thereafter Cole set up an arrangement which permitted Hanley Dawson to buy the same dealership with only about $350,000 or less of his own money. It was blatantly unfair to Hollywood, who might have been able to raise $350,000 or less but had no chance of coming up with $150,000 to $450,000 more. For him the selling price was as much as half-a-million more than it was for Cole's friend Dawson. I don't think it was anything personal against Hollywood. It was a "business decision," not a personal decision.

There are scores of Harry Hollywoods (he has a Cadillac dealership in Florida now, fortunately) in every American industry, who are run over by the system. General Motors, I think, probably treats its employees as well as any American company. But the treatment of its employees is financially oriented, not personally oriented.

When a hard-working executive slips up along the way, or finds himself on the wrong side of a corporate argument, or grows too old in his job, having given his best years to the company, he is eased into early retirement. The corporate rationale is very simple. The executive is given severance pay and a retirement pension that should keep him comfortable for the rest of his life. With that, the corporation management feels that it has discharged its obligations to the executive.

The corporate obligation is considered purely in financial terms. No one considers the effect on the executive's life and pride. After years of service, he is suddenly jobless, no longer a part of the corporate fraternity to which he has given his life's blood.

Suppliers often feel the brunt of corporate power, pressure and influence. A GM decision to stop buying one part from a particular company can send that firm into bankruptcy. GM and its auto company cohorts hold the power of life and death over many of their suppliers. In most cases that power is exercised responsibly. In some cases it is not.

During the development and introduction of the subcompact Vega, a problem arose in controlling emissions on the engines with two-barrel carburetors. We asked GM's Rochester Products Division to help us work on this problem. Its executives refused. We had to add a $25 air pump to these engines to burn exhaust gases more effectively. It was a costly and unsatisfactory remedy to the problem.

Holly Carburetor Co., an independent supplier, however, gladly worked with us on the problem. It developed a different type of two-barrel carburetor which promoted better combustion of the fuel in the engine. We were able to meet the pollution standards with this new carburetor. We could get rid of the expensive air pump and improve engine performance. This saved Chevrolet about $3 million per year.

Now, development of such a new product by an outside supplier carries with it an implicit gentleman's promise by the company that the supplier will get some of the business. Suppliers sometimes do not take out patents on such work, or if they do, they give their client free access to the design. In this case, when Rochester Products Division found out about the Holly breakthrough, it got panicky that it was going to lose the Vega business. The corporate management came to Rochester's aid and threw out Holly as a possible supplier on the carburetor it designed, and it gave the job to Rochester. Chevrolet's Director of Purchasing, George Ford, a tremendous man of sound integrity, brought the problem to my attention. We fought our way to the top of the corporation. Holly was finally allowed to keep a little piece of the business.

GM management did a similar "number" on the Kelsey-Hayes Company, which developed a single-piston disc brake only to have General Motors appropriate the design and build most of the parts internally.

The morality of such arbitrary action compelled me to write a memo to my superior, Tom Murphy, after the Holly incident in August of 1971, and send a copy to Ed Cole. It said in part:

> *Obviously, Holly will never help us again—and Rochester will never again heed one of our threats to go outside—so that the next time the $3,000,000 a year (cost savings) will go down the drain. Needless to say, the impact on our technical and purchasing people has been great—because we have made them a party to a questionable, shabby business practice against their will.*
>
> *I have instructed our people to stop getting outside quotations in competition with Allied Division, since it is unfair to ask a firm to spend time and money preparing a quote when they have no chance at the business. I should point out that outside quotes have enabled Chevrolet and GM to reduce our product costs by over $30,000,000 per year, over the past two years.*
>
> *In my opinion, this decision was shortsighted— and is one of the main reasons that General Motors has not led in a significant technical innovation since the automatic transmission. Power steering, reheat air conditioning, power brakes, power win-*

*dows, disc brakes, the alternator and the two-way
tail gate all originated with our competitors.*

The memo concluded:

*To my mind, a supplier who makes a significant
contribution earns some business—to use our suppliers otherwise is immoral. To use the size and
might of General Motors in this way borders on
illegality and invites antitrust action.*

I never got a reply to this memo, but my dwindling
stock as a team player fell a few extra points.

GM's dearth of product innovations, which I felt would
be prolonged by its shoddy dealings with suppliers, produced an unquenchable thirst for information on what the
competition was doing in product areas. This thirst led the
company into areas which I felt were of questionable legal-
ity. So concerned was management with the plans of the
competition, especially Ford, that the final okay on product
programs was often delayed until we received the latest
up-to-date intelligence on Ford's product programs.

I was told by Lou Bauer, once Chevrolet Division's
comptroller, that, when Bunkie Knudsen took over Chevrolet in 1961, he was shocked to find on Chevy's payroll
two men who worked for and spied on Ford. They worked
in Ford's product planning area and passed on new product
information to Chevrolet for a price. Knudsen, I was told,
fired the spies the day he confirmed their existence.

Later, when I was at Chevy, an executive walked into
my office one day with a copy of Ford's complete marketing program for the coming model year. He said that
copies were being distributed all over the corporation. I
was surprised but later I learned that it was corporate
practice to maneuver such information out of the competition. When Ross Malone, corporate counsel at the time,
learned of this, he severely admonished the entire Administration Committee for this action. I was proud of him.

This practice reached a height of sorts when several of
us walked into a meeting of the Administration Committee,
sometime after 1971, and found the top corporate officers
poring over a very confidential "spread sheet," that listed
all of Ford's product costs. This report gave the definitive

breakdown, product-by-product, of what it cost Ford to build and sell its cars. It was the kind of information which, for our products, never got off The Fourteenth Floor. GM top management wouldn't even let the divisional management in on all the corporate costs, let alone the competition. But somehow, top management had gotten this information about Ford and they were studying it with deep concentration when again General Counsel Malone was incensed. He snapped, "Goddamnit! You guys shouldn't be doing this."

His voice was at once angry and pleading. It was obvious to me that Malone thought that what was taking place had serious legal overtones.

After he spoke, someone scooped up the Ford cost reports and hustled them off to one of the front offices. None of us at the divisional level ever heard about the report again. Now, I am sure that the men studying these confidential cost sheets and giving their approval to a system which procured them would be outraged at the suggestion of similar conduct in their personal lives. Like most Americans, they were probably angered by the disclosures in the wake of *Watergate* that the CIA, U.S. Army, FBI and other government agencies spied and gathered intelligence on unsuspecting citizens. And yet, in business, they were justifying the very same sort of conduct on the grounds that "this is business."

General Motors took its place in the line with scores of other American businesses in promoting what I think are, at the very least, improper political campaign contributions from its top executives. The system was complicated and far more secretive than the outright corporate political gifts for which a number of major corporations have paid fines and their top executives have been fined or sentenced to jail.

Nevertheless, General Motors solicited from its executives substantial political contributions which most likely totalled in the hundreds of thousands of dollars during a national presidential campaign. Off-year campaigns, state and local contests, produced proportionately lower amounts.

The contributions program was operated, as I understood it, by the financial side of the business with assistance from some people on the public relations staff. The finance staff apparently collected the money and a few PR people distributed it with guidance from The Fourteenth Floor.

There were two tiers to the system. Middle and upper middle management were generally allowed to contribute a sum of money to the party of their choice. However, once an executive reached upper management levels (divisional or corporate), it was decided for him how much he would contribute and to whom it would go. As a general manager, I can remember the divisional controller walking into my office with a sheet of paper that apparently had been given to him by the corporate finance staff. On the sheet was written my name and the amount I was to donate to that year's election campaigns—national, state or local. I was told to make a check out to "cash" for the amount assigned to me and give it to the controller who returned it to the corporation. Once the check was made out, an executive did not know to whom or for whom the political contribution was made, or in the manner it was made: whether it was an anonymous cash contribution, one that was made in his name or a corporate gift. All the executive knew was that he wrote out a check to "cash" for the predetermined amount.

The sums were big. For a GM vice president, it was maybe as much as $3,000 in a presidential campaign, less for an off-year congressional election and so on down to a few hundred dollars for a city election.

I participated in the system several times at Pontiac. I cannot recall whether I made the donations myself or wrote a check to "cash." But finally, I just couldn't accept the practice, and I refused to participate. The whole thing seemed wholly improper. Whether the money was donated in my name or not, it was still a corporate gift over which I had no control. What's more, my franchise to vote and donate as I saw fit was too important to me as a citizen to delegate it to management or some guy on one of the corporate staffs. The corporation has no right to tell any executive how to vote, or to know how he votes.

After I refused to participate in the contribution program at GM on several different occasions, top management hit the roof. As in the past, the chore of trying to bring me in line fell to Kyes. When I entered his office at his request, he was ready for battle.

"John, you'd better damn well play this game," he said. "If you don't, you are telling us you aren't on the team. We don't think highly of guys who aren't on the team at GM."

Then he sought to reduce the questions and doubts in my mind to merely a matter of money, the common rationalization in business.

"We take care of you at bonus time. When you make this contribution you get that back as part of your bonus. And if you don't make it, then you aren't going to get that much bonus."

The meeting ended angrily, as usual, with neither of us giving an inch. I continued to boycott the political contribution system at GM, and instead made personal donations to candidates I thought were worthy. And I must admit I never noticed an inexplicable drop in the bonus I received for my work at GM thereafter.

While these business practices, to which I and a number of other GM executives at varying levels objected, involved questionable ethics exercised for the good of the business, there were disturbing activities in upper management in which executives used their positions of power and knowledge to profit *personally* in corporate business. These were by no means widespread and perhaps confined to only a few individuals. My contact with them came often in a tangential or strange way. In one instance, when I was directing Pontiac, several GM dealers were purchasing the troubled National Car Rental Co. for almost nothing— less than $4 million. The price, as I remember, was 2 or 3 dollars per share.

While they were doing this, they also worked a deal with upper corporate management for GM to provide $22 million in advertising assistance, because National was going to emphasize GM cars in its business and promotion. The confirmation of this arrangement was known only to a few people. But once it became public the stock of the company would surely jump in value. One day one of the participants in the purchase of National came to me and said, "You've got to get some of this stock. We're buying it at

$2 to $3 a share." I said, "That's an obvious conflict of interest. I can't do it."

He said, "Hell, I'll buy it for you and keep it in my name. Tell me how much you want." I refused his second offer because it was wrong and what's more, once you let a guy do something like that, he owns you forever. You're his puppet. He was irritated by my refusal and said, "Hell, we're doing it for—" and he named a high-ranking GM official. It was quite a surprise. I never personally verified whether the guy this dealer named was in on the deal or not, which is why I am not disclosing the names involved. But I do know that word was rife through the corporation that officers were making bundles from insider information on National Car Rental Company stock. So well-known was this rumor in the company, that management conducted an investigation and demanded to examine National's stockholder list to see if any GM executives were on it. There were none. But then there wouldn't be if the stock was held in someone else's name.

On yet another occasion when I was at Chevrolet, word got around that company and divisional executives were speculating on land around the Lordstown assembly plant in Ohio. Since these people would be privy to our plans for the Lordstown area, they could buy the land and sell when its value rose as GM increased its activity in the plant area. I wasn't aware which executives were supposedly involved.

Again the corporation conducted an investigation and apparently fingered several people, including one of our Chevy managers. Word was that the culprits were going to be fired. One day, the Chevy executive in question walked into my office obviously nervous and excited, and snapped: "If you guys make something out of this, I'm going to blow the lid off this goddamn thing."

"What the hell do you mean?" I asked.

He replied by telling me the name of a real estate man in the Lordstown area who he said was acting as the agent in these land transactions and who was willing to implicate top corporate managers in the speculating venture. Some of the executives the Chevy man mentioned to me were the same ones who were trying to have him fired in the brewing scandal. I told the guy I knew nothing about the

84

matter and was not a part of the firing action. But he must have put the same threat to his prosecutors in the corporation because it wasn't too long before this executive who was on the verge of being fired was plucked from Chevy management, promoted to a corporate job and given a $5,000 raise.

CHAPTER FIVE

My Life in Autos and Pontiac

At 31 years of age, in the summer of 1956, I was facing the most important decision of my life. One of the happiest periods of my life was ending. My employer, the Packard Motor Co., was merging with the Studebaker Corporation. As head of Research Development for Packard, I was being asked to move to South Bend, Indiana, the headquarters of the merged company. Both Packard and Studebaker were in trouble. The merged company did not appear any stronger than its two components. So I decided to leave.

I had two job offers to choose from. It was a choice between David and Goliath. One offer was from Thompson Products, a small, Cleveland-based auto parts supplier which wanted a Research & Development director who could become vice-president of Engineering in a few years. The Thompson people said their informal management setup would permit me to get into all facets of the business including marketing, manufacturing and finance. It was similar to the job I was holding at Packard, one which I enjoyed immensely.

The second job offer was from the Pontiac Division of General Motors, which wanted a director of Advanced Engineering. This was a new job and a new department for any GM division. While the job appeared more confining than the Thompson position, this was an opportunity to work for the world's largest industrial corporation, the king automaker. The starting salaries were the same, about $14,000.

I was leaning toward Thompson because I felt I simply was not cut out to be a big-company man. Big companies and their bureaucratic superstructures put me off. I always liked to work in a place where you knew everybody and everybody knew you. I studied the two job offers in every detail and in the process also examined the aspirations of my life as formed in my background.

Automobiles were the central focus of my life from its start on January 6, 1925. I was the oldest of four sons born into a tough, lower-middle-class neighborhood near Six Mile Road (McNichols) and Dequindre, on Detroit's near east side. My parents were immigrants to the United States where they met and married, although I don't know when or where.

Zachary R. De Lorean, my father, came to this country from Alsace-Lorraine in his late teens. The thirteenth of fourteen children, he was a big man at 6'1" and 220 pounds and enjoyed a certain amount of physical violence. Not that he was mean, but he got into his share of fights, sometimes after having a few beers with the boys after work. Throughout his life he held jobs that were physically demanding. He was a sheepherder in Montana, a steel-worker and then a policeman in Gary, Indiana, and finally a millwright in a Ford foundry in Detroit.

Part of my dad's inclination toward fisticuffs came from a deep frustration caused by his inability to communicate effectively and thereby capitalize on his mechanical genius. He was uneducated when he came to the U.S. and he couldn't speak English. Though he eventually mastered the language, he always spoke with a trace of an accent.

I remember when he hand-carved out of wood a complete machine tool for contouring pistons. It was his own design, about the size of a large desk, and had about 100 moving parts including gears, levers and shafts, each piece precisely carved by hand. The toothwork in the gears alone was amazing. If I had it today, it would be an incredible work of art. He showed the machine to his bosses at Ford, and I think parts of it were incorporated into working

88

machines at the plant. I do know that the frustration with his inability to verbally get out the things that were inside of him eventually led to a serious drinking problem which resulted in the breakup of our home.

My mother, Kathryn, was an Austro-Hungarian born in Salzburg. She came to this country as a child and, therefore, had some formal English-language education. She was an incredible woman both in her ability to relate to people, and, to generally manage our family. Very religious, she had an affinity for the neighborhood churches more than the big denominational variety because she chose her churches more on the basis of her friendships than on a specific abiding creed. Much of her life she worked as a tool assembler for the Carboloy Products Division of General Electric, which is on east Eight Mile Road at the northern boundary of Detroit.

We lived in a small frame house. My parents had a bedroom in the back of the house next to the kitchen, while my brothers, Chuck, George and Jack, and I shared two bedrooms in the middle of the house. From my father we acquired a mechanical sense, and I can remember putting cylinder heads on Model A's with my brothers before I was ten.

Kids are inherently happy if you give them half a chance, and I thought we had a pretty happy childhood. Part of the reason is that while we had the humble surrounding that come with lower-middle-class existence, we didn't know we were being deprived of some of the great fruits of American life because we didn't have the means of instant communication then as we do today. So while we didn't have a lot, we also weren't aware of what other people had. That comfortable picture was shattered one day when I was about 13, and two classmates, a brother and sister, at Nolan Intermediate School asked me to their house for dinner. They lived in a very plush area known as Palmer Woods, at Woodward and Seven Mile Road. And while their house wasn't the biggest in the area, it was the largest I'd ever been in. I remember feeling awkward at dinner, not sure of how to act or eat. The conversation covered some things I'd never heard of, like going to summer camp and traveling on vacations. Vacations, for the most part, when I was young, meant getting out of school and playing around the house for three months. The experience opened a new vista for me. I began to realize what things were possible and available in America.

There was tension in our home. Some of it came from unemployment. Each summer the auto industry shut down for two or three months to change over from one model to another. There were no supplemental unemployment benefits then. A shutdown meant the family had no steady income from my dad, even though he did what he could working as a carpenter. When he was working steadily at Ford, there were occasional tensions which centered on the job itself. One incident in particular stands out. I was probably six or seven and was awakened in the early morning by loud banging on the front door. My dad answered the door and was pushed aside by a couple of the legendary Harry Bennett's goons who proceeded to ransack the home in search of tools or auto parts they thought were stolen from the Ford foundry. My dad never took as much as a wrench from the plant, but this didn't preclude him from a random search. I can remember peering down the hallway and seeing these big men in dark clothing throwing things around our house. My mother rushed all of us into a bedroom and shut the door. We sat there in silence listening to the crashing of furniture and banging of doors as they went through the house. Later we were too afraid to ask any questions. I guess we just accepted it as part of my father's working life.

To these occasional problems was added a growing rift between my parents. As I got older my father's drinking problem increased. Quarrels became frequent and unbearable. Since divorce was not socially acceptable then, there were prolonged separations, three as I can remember. With each separation my brothers and I would move with my mother to Los Angeles, where she had family, and then back to Detroit and a reconciliation a year or two later. Eventually, it was obvious that the marriage wouldn't work, and my parents were divorced in 1942. I was 17 at the time, and we stayed permanently with my mother in Detroit. We saw very little of my dad after the divorce. He died at age 61 of throat cancer.

Before my mother died I was able to set up an independent trust for her with General Motors stock and other securities. She was able to enjoy some of the fruits of America that had been denied her most of her life. Her funeral was an incredible testimonial to her life. I was amazed at the wide collection of people who came to the Vasu-Lynch Funeral Home. There were old neighborhood friends, businessmen, people from work, churchmen and the guy who owned the corner gas station whom she hadn't seen in 15 years. The crowd was a cross-section of Americana, topped by a bearded drag racer in a leather jacket, who had just broken his back when his "sling shot" dragster flipped. He was in a body cast from the buttocks to the neck. Friends helped him into the funeral home. I can't remember his name, and I never did find out how he knew my mother.

It was in returning to Detroit after one of our sojourns to California that my somewhat carefree life took a decided turn toward a vocation. We'd been in California for over a year, and I was 13 when we came back to Detroit to be reunited with my dad. I started school in the fall at Nolan and didn't know what the teachers were talking about. The California schools at that time apparently were so bad that a year out there put me completely out of touch with my classmates in Detroit. I had to work harder than I ever had trying to catch up. When high school came, I chose Cass Tech instead of nearby Pershing High School because my best friend at the time was going to Cass. My grades were marginal, and I was accepted on probation. Cass Tech was the equivalent of a school for honor students. It was two long bus rides from my house, and it generally enrolled only the cream of Detroit's students, especially those with technical or artistic leanings. The faculty and administration tolerated no time wasting. If you weren't serious about your studies, you were out. I was still quite behind the rest of the students and had to develop tremendous work habits to catch up and then stay even. I eventually caught up and in the process acquired a competitive spirit and zest for work that is with me today. This experience proved to me how important it is to develop to your potential. I often wonder if I hadn't gone to Cass whether I would have ended up a malcontented factory worker like my father.

After Cass Tech, I won a scholarship in engineering to

Lawrence Institute of Technology in Detroit. After two years at Lawrence Tech, I was drafted and spent the better part of three years in the Army. The most significant fact of my military career is that I never got out of the United States, getting a variety of stateside assignments instead. I was discharged and went to work as a draftsman for the city of Detroit's Public Lighting Commission until I had enough money to enroll again at Lawrence Tech. I not only had to pay my own way now, but I had to provide some of the support for my brothers and mother. So I worked in the non-school hours, helping direct a dance band. The job began at 8 p.m. and ended at 2 a.m. Classes started at 8 a.m., so I learned to get by on four to five hours sleep at night, a habit I still have today.

During the summers, I worked at Chrysler's Jefferson Avenue assembly plant and the Murray Body plant. I decided to specialize in industrial engineering, which was a particularly hot field at the time. On one class assignment, I was sent into the Murray Body plant, where I had worked as a laborer, to do "time-and-motion" studies. There are few things which make union workers madder than "time-and-motion" studies where a guy stands at a work station timing how fast a worker does his job. They see it as added management pressure to extract more than a reasonable share of work from the worker.

Oblivious to this, I went into the plant with a new clipboard and stopwatch in hand to begin the study when suddenly these guys started hooting and yelling at me in red-faced anger. They were doing everything to intimidate me but throw tools. I thought, "Hell, I don't really want to do this for a living." That ended my thoughts about becoming an industrial engineer.

When I graduated from Lawrence Tech, I looked for a non-engineering job. I was an introvert up to that point—down deep I guess I still am—and I decided that if I was going to make it in life, I'd better overcome this shyness. So I got a job selling life insurance. At first it was an excruciating experience, because I would set an appointment with a prospect at his house, then I would drive around in my car for an hour trying to get enough courage to go and ring his doorbell. I would pray that he wouldn't be home. But he usually was, and before long I became familiar with the job and more at ease with people than I had ever been. Most of my clients were engineers, and I avoided the usual sales baloney that insurance people have to go through. Instead, I developed a very analytical program which appealed to an engineer's logical mind. It was a matter of "here is what you are making, these are your dependents, here is how much insurance you should have and what it will cost in dollars and cents." There was no glad-handing and I didn't use scare tactics. The technique worked well, and in about ten months I sold about $850,000 worth of life insurance and won a trip to Bermuda in a sales contest. But once I accomplished what I wanted from this job, building up my confidence, the work became dull and boring. I found selling itself interesting, though, so I took a job as a sales representative for the Factory Equipment Co., a now defunct distributor of mechanical power transmission supplies. For the most part I sold conveyor systems to the auto industry.

Eventually, this job palled on me and I realized that my real interest was engineering and the automobile industry. I applied and was accepted at Chrysler Institute with the help of my uncle who was a foreman in the Institute's experimental group. There I went to school on the co-op plan, working and studying at the same time. When I wasn't studying engineering I was working in various departments for three-month periods to learn the business.

I graduated with a master's degree in automotive engineering in 1952 and continued to work at Chrysler. In my impatience, I found this work too narrow and confining. In addition, I felt Chrysler was too big a company for me. At age 27, I quit Chrysler Corporation and went to work for Forest McFarland, the head of Research and Development for the Packard Motor Car Company. He put me to work on central hydraulic systems and the development of the new Ultramatic Transmission. For me, this was the perfect setup. The experience was invaluable. Packard was small enough that an engineer had to do many things— design a part, work with the machinist as he built the first part (I even machined a few myself), help put the part together with the car and then test it. If everything worked out, then I'd go to the guys in production and work with them to make sure the part was built and assembled prop-

93

erly. I was excited by the work, so I put in long hours and learned more in four years with Packard than I would in any similar time since. Forest McFarland was a patient and understanding man who taught me much.

It was while spending time in the backshop with skilled craftsmen that I learned from them a philosophy of life which I adopted for myself. These fine old tool makers worked hard and were very proud of their craft. They kept their big tool boxes right underneath their work benches. If you looked at them the wrong way or dealt with them in any manner other than a man-to-man, professional fashion, they would simply reach under their work benches without saying a word, throw their tools into the big box, lock it up and leave. That was it. Each guy figured, "What the hell, I don't have to take this from anybody. I'm a pro. I know this business and I am not depending on you or anyone else." From the time I first witnessed how these craftsmen worked, on a basis of respect and professionalism alone, I thought, "What a great way to be. To be so good at your job that you never have to kiss anyone's fanny to keep your job." From that experience, in part, I developed my own philosophy: That I would work extra hard at whatever I was doing to become so good at it and that I would never have to kiss anyone's fanny to keep my job. And I never have and I never will. At times later, my GM associates and superiors called this attitude arrogance and aloofness. It wasn't. I was practicing what I thought was the soundest basis for a business relationship—mutual, professional trust and respect. And I have tried to treat people who've worked with and for me in this same way, like a craftsman at Packard.

This philosophy combined with my scientific-technical training served me well in managing people and business later in life. A scientific background taught me to approach problems logically by breaking each problem into its components and then determining the solution. Clearly identified, most problems are easily solved. And my philosophy of learning each job thoroughly has given me confidence in my own ability. I have been able to delegate responsibility more easily than most managers. The combination of my training and philosophy, I think, has produced creative atmospheres in the businesses I've managed in which employees know their responsibilities and are unafraid to make decisions.

Less than four years after joining Packard, I was named to succeed McFarland, who went to Buick as assistant chief engineer. It was a big jump for me. And it was from this position that I was now contemplating a new business life apart from Packard. It was also the enjoyable Packard experience that was pushing me toward Thompson Products.

My contact at GM was Oliver K. Kelley, an assistant to GM's vice president of Engineering. He was a talented engineer and a headhunter for the engineering staff. In this case he was given the assignment of bringing some key Packard people to GM. He sent me to four GM divisions: Buick, GMC Truck & Coach, Hydra-matic and finally Pontiac, where I met Bunkie Knudsen.

I was impressed by Knudsen, the general manager, but unimpressed by the chief engineer he sent me to see. He was a nice old guy wearing high-top shoes and a suitcoat stuffed with cigars. A few words with him and I thought, "What an old lady's division this is. I don't want to work here."

I told Kelley and Knudsen. "No thank you." But Kelley persisted, saying that I should give GM a try for a few years. If things didn't work out I would still be young enough to start a career somewhere else. He asked me to go back and talk with Bunkie. I did and Knudsen continued to impress me with his candor, knowledge and low-key attitude.

He told me that he was going to change Pontiac around completely and that an essential part of this change was the creation of the Advanced Engineering Department. He also told me that "High Tops" was retiring and he introduced me to Elliott M. (Pete) Estes, who was to be the new chief engineer. I liked Pete immediately. I believed what Bunkie told me and decided to go to work for Pontiac instead of Thompson Products. Pete began at Pontiac on the same day, September 1, 1956.

I was really a square guy when I came into Pontiac Division, completely unsophisticated in the methods and machinations of corporate life. I couldn't tell you the name of the chairman or the president of GM. I had never heard of Bunkie Knudsen or his father William S. (Big Bill) Knudsen, who was a big name in the pioneering days of the industry and the formation of the modern General Motors Corporation. In fact, the only GM people I knew were the transmission engineers because that was the part of the business I had been working on at Packard. However, under Bunkie I grew in knowledge of the automobile business and General Motors. I owe him a lot. For some reason, he singled me out and decided to expose me to all of the facets of running a car business. He made a deliberate program out of the education of John De Lorean. I remember going with Bunkie to meetings with the corporate brass at the GM Tech Center and watching corporate management in action. He introduced me to legendary GM executives who were also some of the most prominent and powerful names in the world automobile industry— Harlow Curtice, Albert P. Bradley, Frederic G. Donner and Alfred P. Sloan, Jr.

It wasn't long before I realized that to survive and move ahead in a corporation I had to become much more sophisticated in my approach to business because, as an executive rose in management, he had to rely less on his technical training and more on his ability to sell his ideas and programs to the next level of management. When I was just an engineer somewhere down the line working on a technical problem, everything affecting me was within my grasp. All I had to do was solve this particular problem and I was doing my job. But now, as head of Advanced Engineering, I had to anticipate and predict product trends and then sell my programs for capitalizing on those trends.

Bunkie was a good teacher. He shunned office politics. But he also understood them. He knew how to sell programs and still operate outside of the personal-political arena. He knew what facets of his proposals would electrify his superiors and how to present those proposals to the different factions of the corporation—finance, sales, styling, engineering and manufacturing. I was amazed by the skill and ease with which he operated. And I was most impressed at how he worked with people. As a young kid, he learned the auto business from his father. He worked summers in the plants at Pontiac, and when he became general manager he still remembered those with whom he worked, calling them by name. When we walked through the plant, he'd stop to talk with a press operator he'd known 25 years earlier. The guy might make a suggestion, and Bunkie would listen earnestly. I saw his compassion for people, perhaps best exemplified when he kept a top department head on the job despite his all-consuming alcoholism. When people were urging Bunkie to fire this man, who'd been given countless warnings and reprimands, he refused. On occasions, he not only covered for the guy but personally handled some of his duties when he was too incapacitated to work.

It was obvious that Bunkie was confident and assured in his position. He tried to fool no one because he didn't have to. And no one tried to fool him. He was results-oriented, never rejecting an idea out of hand, and willing to discuss old matters if new information surfaced. He was a master at managing people and business, and I tried to incorporate his ideas and techniques in my style.

My education in big business started and thrived under Bunkie but by no means ended when he moved to Chevrolet in 1961. I learned from Pete Estes, his successor, and then I was my own mentor, succeeding Estes as head of Pontiac.

Pete Estes and Bunkie Knudsen were entirely different people and managers. Where Bunkie was quiet and reserved, Pete was outgoing. Unlike Bunkie, who learned the business from his father and had a certain respect in the corporation because of that, Pete was a product and devotee of the system that was emerging in the late '50s and '60s. A man responsive to the political winds of the corporation, Pete Estes covered his political flanks well. While Pete was hard-working and a competent engineer, he typified a type of politically alert executive who grew in popularity and rose through management ranks when I worked for General Motors. Such executives increased in number, and from them I observed techniques which could be employed to handle political problems with savvy and dispatch. One technique involved the sticky matter of expense accounts.

There seemed to be constant hassles over expense accounts at General Motors, mostly because of the dual responsibilities of each division's financial people who reported to the general manager and also to the corporate financial staff. As head of a division's financial staff, the comptroller was responsible for approving divisional bills. So he was in a position to undermine a general manager simply by refusing to okay expenses or by reporting what he felt were excess expenditures to the corporate people.

The general managers had a rough go of it whenever they wanted to pass through questionable expenditures, such as the bills for a midwinter sales meeting of divisional executives and a few top dealers held in the south. These were questionable expenditures because the meetings had little business value and could easily have been held in Detroit. But instead they were held in warm, expensive climates. The Eldorado Country Club in Palm Springs, California, was a particularly popular spot for meetings like these. The three- or four-day routine was fun-oriented and simple: a business session each morning followed by swimming, golf, lavish cocktail parties, delectable meals and after-dinner entertainment. The bills ran into the tens of thousands of dollars, and the comptroller was expected to pay the tab. If he objected, the general manager had the choice of proceeding with the party under the implied threat that the corporation would be on his back for the expenditures, or cancelling the outing. But there was a political way out of this dilemma—invite the comptroller and his wife on the outing, even though they had less reason to be at a sales meeting than anyone else there. This handled the problem nicely and neatly. Once the comptroller accepted the invitation, he sure as hell couldn't turn down the bill, or blow the whistle on the divisional management.

I don't think we had many, if any, boondoggles of this sort when I ran Pontiac or Chevrolet, so I didn't get locked into any squabbles with the divisional comptroller or the corporation over our divisional expenses. But I did run afoul of the corporation over my personal expense account and in the process learned a great deal about corporate life. The battle point came over my refusal to play a silly expense account game in which the object was for top managers to try to keep their personal business expenses to the bare minimum through ruses and gimmicks which wound up costing the corporation money instead of saving it.

As the general manager of a division, I approved all the expense accounts of those who worked for me, with, of course, the approval of the comptroller. However, I had to submit my own expense account to the divisional comptroller for the approval of the financial staff "upstairs." The financial staff felt that top management should have small expense accounts. I guess a small figure gave the semblance of a lean, well-controlled corporation, and provided a shockingly low figure for the chairman to give shareholders if the question of executive expense was raised at the annual meeting.

It was obvious that in running a $35-billion-a-year corporation, or a division like Chevrolet, which was then about one-third that size, management was going to incur substantial expenses for travel, lodging and entertainment in the general operations of the business. So in exercising their management responsibilities while keeping their personal expense accounts at the poverty level, executives went through all sorts of financial gymnastics to avoid expenses. They always let underlings pay their bills and then approved the underlings' expenses; used company planes when a commercial flight would have done the job; or let suppliers pick up the tab.

The results were ridiculous. The chairman in any given year might have had an expense account of only $5,000 when his actual expenses, including the use of corporate aircraft, were many times that. A divisional general manager could have a similar total while his director of Public Relations produced an expense account quantum jumps from that because he was running around picking up all of the bosses' tabs. A couple of executives might take a company plane to New York at a substantial cost to the corporation (GM has a fleet of corporate planes), when the same two could have flown commercially then for less than $300.

I thought the system was ridiculous, so I took commercial flights when I could, and picked up my own meal and hotel bills instead of letting the public relations or sales department do it. If we sponsored a legitimate dealer sales meeting, I paid whatever my share of it was. After a business trip, I just handed all the receipts I accumulated to my secretary and let her fill out my expense account.

One year, my total expenses were about $25,000, everything included. I was called by my boss who said that all of the executives' expense reports were being accumulated for the shareholders' meeting and that mine was being bounced back to me because it was too large. He said that everyone else turned in reports which were much less, so I would have to reimburse the corporation for one-third of my expenses—about $8,000—from my own personal funds. I refused on the ground that my expenses were legitimate and the system of accounting was screwed up.

I said, "This is pure baloney. The whole thing is a big facade."

My boss responded, "Your principle may be right, but you are going to kill yourself trying to establish it."

I argued with the financial staff over the whole matter, but they would not budge. In the end I settled just to get rid of the hassle by paying a portion of what they said I owed, even though the expenses were bona fide costs incurred while managing Pontiac. I was not bothered again at Pontiac even though I didn't much alter my system of expense reporting.

However, a similar occurrence cropped up at Chevrolet. So I gave all my receipts to the divisional auditor and said, "You go over every expense I have and make damn sure they are legitimate. If they aren't, throw them out." He did and then I submitted my expense account. It was kicked back by the financial staff. I asked the auditor what was up and he said: "I went through everything, and as far as I am concerned everything is legitimate. But they are just out to hassle you. You know you are on Oscar Lundin's list and that's just the way it is." I had to settle out of my own pocket again. The damn thing is that if I'd have wasted money on company planes and played the silly game of letting the sales and PR people pick up the bills, no one would have complained. Eventually, on some occasions, I did just that because fighting the system was costing me too much money. It was actually costing me personally to save money for the corporation.

These were infuriating battles to lose because they were so ridiculous. I learned from each conflict.

Perhaps the rudest awakening to what playing corporate politics was all about occurred when I was running Pontiac. We were concerned about the quality of Pontiac cars as they reached the customer. Our dealers complained that our cars were not top quality when they received them from the factory, and Pontiac customers were becoming quite upset. I decided a good way to take care of this was to check each car before we shipped it. So the manufacturing and distribution people devised a program called "recheck and repair" (R & R) for examining each car as it was produced and repairing any defects on the spot. We ran a pilot program and the cars shipped from this small pilot drew raves from the dealers. They said these were the finest quality cars they had ever gotten. I showed the program to Edward D. Rollert, vice-president for Car and Truck Operations. He liked it. I told him we wanted to install the whole program in a vacant plant in the Pontiac complex, that it would involve about a $400,000 expenditure, and that we needed corporate approval immediately to be into operation for the new model start-up. He said, "Go ahead. Get this thing started and follow up with the paper work for corporate approval."

We commenced and got the R & R operation in smooth working order when Rollert called me to say that his boss James E. (Bud) Goodman, executive vice-president and head of the whole domestic automotive operation, wanted to come out to see the Pontiac Division operations. "Great," I said, "but he has to see our car preparation center too." Rollert said that would be fine. We set a date, and then went to work to get the division in order and prepare the R & R operation for its first corporate visitor.

When Goodman arrived, I was proud as hell as I ushered him into the new-car preparation center. It was beautiful and in full swing when he turned around suddenly, looked sternly at Wright Cotton, our divisional comptroller, and snapped, "Who approved this expenditure?"

Cotton coughed, sputtered and looked longingly at me. I was a bit surprised at Goodman's question but quite confident that all was right since I had Rollert's word to "go ahead." So I turned to Rollert for the answer to Goodman's question. But Rollert without batting an eye snapped, "John, who approved the expenditure for this?" I didn't know what to say. I wasn't sure what was happening.

Before I could collect my thoughts, Goodman snapped

again at a shaken Cotton, "You know you could be fired for this. We have a dual control system at GM for approving this kind of an expenditure."

Rollert was right behind Goodman and by now was saying to me, "John, you could get fired for letting something like this happen. What made you guys think you could spend this kind of money without corporate approval?" I was flabbergasted. I didn't say anything in front of Goodman because all I had from Rollert was an oral commitment which he could deny. And besides, if I embarrassed him now, there was no telling what would happen to me because I still had to work with the guy. But right after the incident I grabbed him in private. I was livid and demanded:"What the hell happened there?"

"Well, John," he chuckled, "You just learned something about corporate life."

I did indeed. And there were numerous times in the future in similar situations and in corporate meetings when I watched a top executive who had given his commitment to support a proposal or project quickly switch sides when he sensed that his boss or the prevailing corporate attitude was decidedly against the proposal. If in the process he left a friend and associate stripped of support and standing naked in the conference room, he ran up to him afterward and said something like, "I'm awful sorry about that. You know how those things go."

CHAPTER SIX

The Pontiac Revival

In 1956, when Semon E. Knudsen took the reins of the Pontiac Division, the auto industry and the city of Pontiac, Michigan, were full of rumors that GM was going to shut down this troubled car division. Annual sales were a paltry 233,000 units. Management morale was low and dropping lower each day. The once proud "Oakland" Division (renamed Pontiac in 1931) was losing money, and the word around the division was that GM would assign the Pontiac name to another car division to let the Pontiac dealers down slowly. There was precedent for such a move. In the depression of the 1930's, GM combined the manufacturing operations of Buick and Oldsmobile divisions, and Pontiac and Chevrolet divisions while the company rode out the economic storm. This seemed to give validity to the stories that Pontiac's days were numbered. Thus Bunkie's assignment to Pontiac meant he had to revive the division quickly or preside over its funeral. It was a classic business challenge and one that he would be equal to.

Pontiac was too small an operation to have any complicated problems. The problems were basic and twofold: Its management was old and entrenched, and its products were dull and therefore not accepted by the public. Pontiac's sales penetration had fallen from 7.4 percent to 6.0 percent in just one year, from 1955 to 1956. Further drops lay ahead before he could get the product programs turned around.

In his first moves, Knudsen brought in new management. In engineering he hired Pete Estes and me. He also conducted market research surveys to find out how the car was viewed by Pontiac owners, and the car-buying public at large. Such surveys were almost unheard of in GM at the time, but they served Pontiac well. The results showed that the Pontiac had no distinctive image at all among its owners and potential customers. It was a solid, reliable and sturdy car which evoked no discernible emotion one way or the other. Knudsen told us that this was a good situation because we would not have to first combat a negative image before building a new one.

Reviving Pontiac would be a difficult, but certainly not impossible, task. With only a small share of the market, we did not have to seek growth through a broad-based appeal to the American consumer as did Ford or Chevrolet with their 20 to 30 percent shares of the market. Instead, we could find a niche in the market and exploit it. We could choose where we wanted to be in the market by being daring, innovative and by taking chances. We could ignore over half of the whole auto market in our marketing effort and still grow. And that is precisely what Knudsen did. The image he would build for Pontiac was that of a youthful, exciting, fast-moving car. An innovative design leader, Knudsen was the first in the industry to recognize the emerging importance of the youth market, not just in automobiles but in everything from fashion to food. Capricious, energetic, and impressionable, America's young people have always been excited by cars. But their influence in car buying increased as the post-World War II economy grew, producing two-, three- and even four-car families. As the post-war baby boom generation matured, it became a trend-setting market unto itself.

The best opportunity for growth in the automobile market is still in the youth market, where buying preferences are not rigid. Once you get into markets for people 35 and older, customer preferences become firmly established and difficult to change.

The new Pontiac people recognized that the youth market was Pontiac's road to growth, as Knudsen sought to turn an old lady's car division into a freewheeling, forward-thinking operation. He scrapped the traditional Pontiac Indian head hood ornament and silver-colored side streaks. In fact, for over several years, Pontiac led the industry in completely de-chroming cars, giving automobiles clean features uncluttered by wide, gaudy chrome side-stripping. Andy Court, an economic analyst with the corporation, deserves credit for noticing this trend. He once said to me: "You know, people's tastes are much better than you guys give them credit for. They don't want all that junk on the side of their cars." Eventually, we cut weight wherever we could. We tried aluminum bumpers and grilles. And later we lowered the car, by the use of a torque box frame I'd invented. This frame lowered cost by $25 per car, reduced weight and provided much better side impact collision protection than the cruciform frame Pontiac had previously used. Bigger engines were added to the car lines, and performance and handling were improved by varying axle ratios and adding new suspension systems. Soon we had very fast, exciting cars, and a distinctive Pontiac ride and feel. Our products were more powerful and smoother riding than those of Chevrolet, our internal competitor. But we had to prove this to the people who bought new cars.

To do so, Bunkie promoted a massive Pontiac effort in the burgeoning world of automobile racing. It was the first extensive effort of any automobile division. Later, Ford surpassed this effort when it spent millions in the mid-to-late 1960s on its GT endurance racing program overseas, and its Indianapolis, stock car and drag racing efforts at home. With a Pontiac we knew would perform outstandingly, our cars were entered into the Grand National stock car and drag racing circuits. Soon Bonnevilles and Catalinas were cleaning up the stock car racing schedule from coast to coast. They were driven by the likes of Marvin Panch, Joe Weatherly and Cotton Owens. Fireball Roberts took the field at Daytona, on the beach, before the current asphalt speedway was built. On Utah's Bonneville Salt Flats, Mickey Thompson blasted the Challenger I to 400 miles per hour, a land speed record, behind the power of four Pontiac V-8's. Jim Wangers, who worked on the Pontiac account at our advertising agency, MacManus, John and Adams (now D'arcy, MacManus & Masius, Inc.),

105

piloted his own Catalina to top stock eliminator honors in the big league of drag racing. For every race he was winning, young kids with their Pontiacs were taking home armfuls of top drag strip prizes from L. A. to Detroit to Miami. It was exciting to watch the image of this once dowdy division change almost overnight. In our best year, Pontiacs won 43 of 52 top stock car races. The car with an exciting image was now the talk of America's youth, the hottest product in the business. Pontiac's new image was firmly implanted in the minds of the car buyers.

Our product program was supplemented by a revitalization of Pontiac advertising which previously was at best nondescript. One particular campaign, the "Wide Track" promotion, stands out. It was born in the most unusual way. As head of Advanced Engineering in 1957, I was working with Chuck Jordan of GM Styling on developing a new independent rear suspension system for an advanced model car. We ran into a problem mounting the suspension system on convertible models, which were the rage of that era. To do the job, we had to spread out the rear wheels. And to make the car look right, we had to do the same thing to the front wheels. This gave our big cars a 64-inch tread (the distance between the center of the wheels on the same axle).

We put the car into clay mock-up form and the two of us were amazed at how the car looked so much better planted on the ground with the wider tread. It looked more stable and sleeker than the standard Pontiac. The reason was that in the 1950s, car bodies became wider and wider while the chassis underneath did not. So most of the industry's cars looked very high above the road. Widening the tread gave the illusion of lowering the car. The instant Bunkie saw the car he said, "Let's put that on a production car." So we went into a crash program widening the tread on our standard car line for the 1959 model. The name "Wide Track" somehow became affixed to the new look. And it was instantly recognizable that this was a desirable feature, not only from a styling standpoint but also from a safety standpoint because the wide tread gave the car more stability in turning corners and maneuvering on the road.

When it came time to devise an advertising campaign

for our new cars, the agency was not too excited by the name "Wide Track." But Pontiac people told me that in the meetings with the agency Bunkie insisted that they call the new look the "Wide Track Look" and make that the central theme of the campaign. The agency did and the campaign turned out to be far and away the best advertising campaign that ever came out of General Motors when I was there.

Within five years under Bunkie, Pontiac was thriving. Our sales increased dramatically to hit 373,000 units. Penetration went from a low of 4.9 percent in 1958 to 6.4 percent in 1961. Pontiac jumped from the sixth largest division to the third behind Chevrolet and Ford. We were pumping millions of dollars of profit into the corporate treasury, and the dealer body was gleeful with its successes. The city of Pontiac which at one time thought it was going to go down the tube with the Pontiac Division, was grateful for the turnaround. When the city remodeled its downtown in 1964, it built a large circular street surrounding the downtown—and named it Wide Track Drive.

In 1961, for his resuscitation of Pontiac, Knudsen was made general manager of Chevrolet, the division once headed by his father. His recommendations that Estes succeed him as head of Pontiac and that I be named chief engineer were approved by the corporation.

The momentum built into Pontiac was now fantastic. The division's morale was high, and the freewheeling atmosphere established by Knudsen was conducive to creative thinking and innovation. The rest of the corporation was somewhat in awe of Pontiac. We heard little from The Fourteenth Floor, apparently because no one up there wanted to interfere with a good thing. We used this atmosphere to advantage under Estes's direction and later my stewardship. From 1962 to 1969, three-fourths of the corporation's innovations originated in Pontiac. Some were big successes like concealed windshield wipers, endura bumpers, high-performance engines and improved suspension systems. Others were not. The radio antenna embedded in the windshield is an innovation which I promoted. It looked good and solved the problem of antennas breaking off in car washes, but in its first few years it left something to be desired in performance. Another less than successful development was the 1961-63 "rope drive" Tempest. The car featured a four-cylinder engine made simply by cutting a V-8 in half, with a torsion-bar (the rope) in place of a standard three-point prop shaft for taking the engine power and carrying it to the rear wheels. The invention worked but never went well with the rear end transmission and axle combination on the car. There was no mechanical problem, but the car rattled so loudly that it sounded like it was carrying half-a-trunkful of rolling rocks. When the compact Tempest became an intermediate-sized car in 1964, the "rope drive" and the four-cylinder engine were dropped.

Nevertheless, our successes outweighed our failures. A goodly number of the 200 patents and pending patent applications I have amassed over my lifetime came out of my work at Pontiac. We were looking everywhere for innovations. In car crazy Southern California in the late 1950s, we spotted a styling trend. The kids and the custom shops there were filling in the front ends of their car grilles or extending the fenders with plastic to eliminate the bulging-eyes look of the headlights. The trend was called "Frenching-in" the front end, and it became the focal point for our 1963 Grand Prix, which led GM into the personal, luxury car market.

The Grand Prix got started as the first "clean-look" car. We designed a special edition of the standard car line with a new and different roof and a practically chromeless body. The car looked sheer and elegant. We figured that this kind of a car with Pontiac's now distinctive handling and performance would give us a good entry in the luxury end of the market. When we showed the car to the corporation in 1961, management flatly refused to give us money we needed to tool up for it. Estes was mad as hell and so was I, so we decided to bring it out anyway. Without the money for the tooling, we had to keep the same essential roof line of the standard Pontiac. But we spruced this car up inside, while taking off the chrome outside. We called it the Grand Prix. It sold 40,000 units as a 1962 model. That shocked everyone. The next year, we brought it out as a new model, complete with a new roof. It was an instant and even bigger success as a 1963 model. The car became a mainstay of the Pontiac line. For the 1969 model, when I was heading the division, we added a bold-nose front end and took several hundred pounds of weight out of the car by reducing its size from a standard to an intermediate body. The car soared to even greater sales heights, returning as much as $1,500 a unit profit to the company in its first couple of years.

The most memorable product coup while I was at Pontiac, however, was the birth of the muscle car craze. Despite the racing success, we were searching for a way to keep the Pontiac image vibrant and youthful. At the time, the corporation was introducing a larger body and chassis for the erstwhile compact car lines in Pontiac (Tempest), Buick (Special) and Oldsmobile (F-85). Sales of these cars as compacts had not set the world on fire, so the company decided to make them bigger, sell them for more money and explore a new market which became the intermediate-sized car market. The cars were attractive and lightweight, carrying small six-cylinder engines.

I love to drive a good performing car, and so we put a 326 cubic-inch, V-8 engine in this lightweight Tempest, tested it and discovered that the car was surprisingly quick and exciting to drive. When we put a big 400 cubic-inch V-8 into the car, it was even more exciting. It was an electrifying car. It gave you the feeling and performance of an expensive foreign sports car. But it was basically a low-cost car to build. A car that most people could afford. We took the Tempest with the two big optional engines, stripped the car down to bare essentials, added heavy-duty brakes and suspension system for safety, threw in three two-barrel carburetors for performance and readied the car for production. Only this time Estes didn't tell the corporation about it. I agreed with this approach. The Engineering Policy Group technically should have been consulted about putting these bigger engines into the intermediate car, but we were afraid they would turn us down or take so long to give their approval that we wouldn't get the car into production on time.

Because the car reminded me of a fast, foreign sports car, I suggested we call it the GTO (after a Ferrari coupe being raced in Europe called the Gran Turismo Omologate). The GTO was introduced as a 1964 model in the fall of 1963.

Pontiac's General Sales Manager, Frank Bridges, didn't think the car would sell at all, and he refused to schedule more than 5,000 GTO's for production. But when the car went on sale, it was an instant hit. Within four weeks of its introduction, we were vastly revising GTO's production schedules upward. We sold about 31,000 the first year, 60,000 the second year and 84,000 the third year. The GTO gave birth to the muscle car craze of the mid-1960s. We caught the rest of GM's car divisions flat-footed. They followed suit later, as did our outside competitors—Ford with the Torino Cobra and Mach I Mustang, Plymouth with the Road Runner and a host of others. But our car became the center attraction in a GTO craze. Ad man Wangers personally launched a national GTO promotional campaign centered around a rock group, Ronnie and the Daytonas, whose hit record "Little GTO" sold well over a million singles, capitalizing on the excitement of the car and the "surfing sound" of the Beach Boys. The market was full of GTO shirts, shoes, emblems, and the car and its appeal knocked the youth market over. For $3,200, the GTO was within reach of most pocketbooks. And if America's teenagers couldn't afford a GTO that day, the success of the car meant they were going to think Pontiac first when they could.

When the corporation management got wind of the car shortly before it was introduced, it was mad. But the GTO was too late in its development to be stopped. And when the car took the market by storm, The Fourteenth Floor certainly wasn't going to order us to stop selling it. Nevertheless, in retrospect, I think that our circumventing of the Engineering Policy Group was the single most important occurrence that later led that Group to become far more involved in the day-to-day engineering decisions of the automotive divisions, a move which eventually hurt the company's ability to respond quickly to new emerging markets.

The momentum that Knudsen established in Pontiac remained long after he left for Chevrolet. By 1964, Pontiac, under Estes, climbed to 690,000 sales. In 1965, he was promoted to Chevrolet, following Knudsen who moved to a group vice-presidency. Then I moved into the driver's seat at Pontiac.

In many respects the division was easy to run. But there were two areas which I felt needed attention. For one thing, with our concern for reviving and rebuilding Pontiac, we ignored the condition of our plants which were getting old and run-down. They needed immediate attention. In addition, it seemed to me that with our new image and success we now needed emphasis on marketing and a harder sales push to achieve handsome payoffs in increased market penetration and improved sales volume.

Our plants were dingy operations, unbefitting our new, youthful product image. It was not a hard problem to cure. But to cover the costs I tried to increase sales volume as we modernized our plants one by one. The project culminated in the construction of a modern Pontiac headquarters building, which I helped design. Unfortunately, 12 months before the ribbon cutting took place for the new headquarters, in 1970, I was moved to Chevrolet.

With the concept of Pontiac firmly planted in the public's mind, I sought ways to improve and embellish that concept. It was obvious from the cars our dealers took in trade that we were eating out of Chevrolet's trough. So I tried to push harder into that area. We devised a neat, two-seat sports car, not totally unlike the Corvette, which I begged The Fourteenth Floor to let us build. But it wouldn't. So we had to do what we were doing best, and that was taking the cars which the corporation permitted us to build and adding the distinctive Pontiac performance and handling characteristics. The 1968 Firebird was an example of this practice. The Firebird was an offshoot of the Chevrolet Camaro. When GM moves into a smaller-car market, it always gives the first entry in that market to Chevrolet Division, which is GM's small, less expensive car division. Later, Pontiac may be given a version of the car, and sometimes Buick and Oldsmobile.

It was widely known in the mid-1960s that General Motors was rushing through the Camaro project to give Chevrolet an answer to the popular Ford Mustang. As the only head-to-head competitor of the Ford Division, Chevy was to have first crack at that market. But I pushed long and hard to get a version for Pontiac. And I guess because of my persistence, management agreed to let us have a version of the sporty compact car only six months after the introduction of the first Camaro in the fall of 1966. We took the Camaro, studied it and gave it a lower look by adding a different, tighter suspension system. When we brought out the Firebird in early '67, it was a measurably better performing and handling car than its sister, the Camaro. And it sold well, adding large profits to the division and enhancing Pontiac's brighter image.

On another occasion, I was after the United States Rubber Company (now Uniroyal) to give us something different in a tire. Their staff came up with a sharp-looking tire with a thin red line between the tread and the rim. They called it the "Tiger Paw" and began a big advertising campaign with this theme. We offered the new tires as options on Pontiac cars and adopted a similar "Tiger" theme in our advertising, which featured Barbara Feldon, later of TV's "Get Smart," growling like a tigress as she extolled the virtues of Pontiac from a tigerskin rug. The dealers liked the campaign, and speciality shops were selling tiger tails to Pontiac owners who were hanging them from their trunk lids. Unknown to me, however, Chairman Jim Roche was doing a slow burn over the advertising, apparently because he felt the tiger image was too vicious and unfavorable for the corporation. He called Ed Rollert, my boss at the time, who called me at home one night and said: "John, get that goddamn tiger out of your ads." That was the last Pontiac Division saw of the tiger.

While looking for a marketing-advertising edge, I had our staff conduct intensive research studies on our cars and on the features which most appeal to car buyers. From these we learned that the noise level of a car is a primary criterion by which owners judge the quality of a car, but one rarely showing up in market tests. Noise levels may not be mentioned often in a survey which asks, "What do you look for in a car?" But they are big factors in an owner's dislike of a car. So we went out to GM's Milford (Michigan) proving grounds, where the corporation has one of the most complete and sophisticated acoustical departments in the business, and we asked the sound engineers to make our car as quiet as they could. The results were terrific. The noise level of the cars which they developed were lower than in the Rolls Royce. So we prepared a series of ads with a Pontiac prominently displayed in front of a softened image of a Rolls. We didn't mention the Rolls Royce by name, but instead simply said that the Pontiac was quieter than the "world's most luxurious car." The ad ran in one magazine as I remember, and Cadillac Division went through the roof. "Rolls is our competitor, not Pontiac's," the Cadillac management roared to The Fourteenth Floor. After a quick meeting upstairs in the GM Building, we were told to pull the ads. We did, but Cadillac did not pick up the theme. No one did, until Rolls ran its "the loudest thing at 60 miles an hour is the clock," advertising campaign. Ford Motor Co. introduced a similar "quiet car" campaign later. Both were very successful in selling cars for Rolls and Ford.

The biggest barrier to vastly increasing Pontiac sales, it became apparent, was the lethargy of our own sales department. It had a pretty soft job because our youthful products were selling themselves. And while the sales management was composed of a great bunch of guys, these executives were older men with dated selling techniques. They often just sat in their offices, smoked cigars, talked on the phone, and allocated cars when there were shortages. I knew that with a more aggressive effort we could increase sales. I figured we could improve the sales effort without any wholesale purge of our sales staff by simply increasing the pressures on the staff to push more aggressively.

My first move was to get Ed Cole, the president, to let me increase Pontiac's inventories. When the division was in trouble in the era before Knudsen's general managership, the inventory levels were kept low by the corporation so that the company and the Pontiac dealers wouldn't have too much money tied up in the poorly selling cars. The Pontiac inventories, therefore, were consistently lower than the inventories of any major-selling car line in the industry. We were losing business because of inventory shortages. Increasing these inventories would force the sales staff to work harder to sell them, and it would give Pontiac dealers a wider assortment of new cars to sell right off their lots.

The sales people didn't like my move one bit. They rebelled against it. To show them that I was absolutely intent on increasing the division's sales volume, over any and all protests, I called a sales meeting for 7:45 a.m. every day of the week. In the meeting with me were the general sales manager, the head of car distribution and one or two of the assistant general sales managers. We would go over the very latest sales statistics from the field, dealer-by-dealer, zone-by-zone and region-by-region. We would discuss any problems that were cropping up in our markets and then plot the strategy to solve them.

This pressure worked. Pontiac set all-time sales records in 1967 and 1968. We further solidified our position as the third best-selling division in the industry by increasing our lead over fourth-place Plymouth. Pontiac dealers suddenly became the top-volume leaders in several of the major U.S. markets, including Chicago and the Auto Capital—Detroit. Our growth was coming primarily out of the hide of Chevrolet, and this had Chevy dealers in a dither. The first quarter of the 1969 model year (October to December, 1968) set an all-time sales record for Pontiac of 252,000 units. My prediction of September, 1968, that Pontiac sales would top one million units for the 1969 models, seemed to be a cinch, for one thing because the 1969 Grand Prix was the hottest selling car in the industry. When I left Pontiac for Chevrolet in early 1969, I urged the division to keep the sales pressure on and capitalize on the momentum we had working. But it wasn't long before I noticed that Pontiac was lowering its production schedules, taking tens of thousands of cars out of the production plans which I had made. By the end of the 1969 model year, Pontiac management eliminated about 100,000 units from our original production plans. Instead of setting a new sales record with the 1969 models, the sales of these cars fell far short of the record units sold in 1968. I was blamed by some of the press and some GM people for hanging Pontiac with a poor-selling product lineup. The truth is, if the pressure I applied to the sales department had been maintained, Pontiac would have sold every car we planned to sell and possibly more. Since then, Pontiac has declined. It has dropped from the third-best-selling nameplate to a distant fourth place. And strangely, the

114

division lost sight of the image and market it built in the 1960s. Some of its cars became bigger, slower and less stylish. The excitement of the 1960s vaporized in the 1970s, and with it the innovative leadership and electrifying youth image of the Pontiac cars. It is hard to believe, but Pontiac slowly took on some of the characteristics of an old lady division again.

CHAPTER SEVEN

Big Problems at Chevy

*You weren't my choice for general manager. I
am stuck with you. But you are goddamn well
going to do this thing the way I want it done, or
you're going to be gone.*
— ROGER M. KYES TO JOHN DE LOREAN

It was Saturday morning, February 1, 1969. I was taking
a long weekend vacation in Palm Springs, California, to
golf with friends at the Thunderbird Country Club. I felt
great. Pontiac was coming off its third record sales year in
a row. We had sold almost 900,000 cars in the 1968 model
run. The over one-million 1969 Pontiacs I was confidently
predicting we would sell, would make us only the third
division in automotive history to sell that many. Ford and
Chevrolet were the only other million sellers. We were
solidly entrenched behind them as the industry's third leading nameplate.

After a few days of golf and relaxation here in Palm
Springs, it would be back to Detroit to put the finishing
touches on the 1970 lineup of cars and to get cranked up
for the spring selling season.

In my foursome were three friends, Bill Holt, Jim Ford
and Fred Kammer, and I was shooting a few strokes over
par. I lined up my tee shot on the twelfth hole, when the

caddie master hurried up in a golf cart and said that I had a phone call in the halfway house at the ninth green. I hopped into the golf cart, rode to the halfway house and picked up the phone. On the other end was my boss, Roger Kyes.

"John," he said. "You've been named general manager of Chevrolet."

"Great," I said. "I'll be back as soon as I finish the round."

"No," Kyes replied sternly. "You'll come back right now." With those instructions, I sent word back to the twelfth tee that I wouldn't be finishing the round. Instead, I packed my bags and caught the first plane back to Detroit.

At 8 a.m. the next morning, Sunday, I met with Kyes and President Ed Cole at Cole's home in Bloomfield Hills, where they informally told me that I would be replacing Pete Estes as Chevy's general manager. Pete would be moving up to group vice-president for the Car and Truck Operations. My place at Pontiac would be filled by F. James McDonald, who had been my general manufacturing manager at Pontiac before switching to a similar job at Chevy about a year previously. All of this information was formally confirmed Monday morning in New York when I met with Chairman Roche in his New York office.

I was honored and somewhat shocked by my appointment to the Chevrolet job. I had just turned 44, which made me the youngest general manager of GM's car divisions. I wondered why I had been chosen for the Chevy job. Roche said it was because of the fine job I had done at Pontiac and that he wanted me to do the same thing at Chevy. This really worried me because there was very little similarity between Pontiac and Chevrolet.

Chevrolet is the flagship of General Motors' five car divisions. It is the heart of GM's automotive business, accounting for almost half of all GM's North American sales and in a good year up to half of the profits. Since World War II, it has been the largest-selling American nameplate for all but two years, 1957 and 1959, when Ford took over that spot briefly. In its 68-year-history, Chevy has sold over 100 million cars and trucks. With annual sales of over $11 billion in 1973, for instance, Chevy sits bigger than all but a handful of the world's largest companies. If tomorrow it was broken away from GM, Chevy would be close to the size of the entire Ford Motor Company in America, and much larger than Chrysler or American Motors combined. Alone, it would be one of the largest auto companies in the world.

The contrast between Chevrolet and Pontiac was like day and night. Pontiac was small, with one assembly plant. It had only a small number of employees compared to Chevrolet which at that time operated 11 assembly plants, numerous manufacturing plants and employed 140,000 people. Because it was relatively small, Pontiac was located in one spot, the city of Pontiac, Michigan, about 35 miles north of the GM building. It had only about 130 people in middle and upper management. They were a tight, cohesive team. It was a very simple business to run because you could talk with just about everyone every day or at least several times a week to discuss their problems. Nothing ever got too far out of hand.

Chevrolet was unwieldy, with facilities scattered around the country. It had hundreds of upper-management executives all over the place and that made communication difficult. Estes once told me: "Chevrolet is such a big monster that you twist its tail and nothing happens at the other end for months and months. It is so gigantic that there isn't any way to really run it. You just sort of try to keep track of it."

That assessment shook me up. When I followed Pete as head of Pontiac in 1965, that division seemed to be in control of itself. I knew the business immediately, and it wasn't too hard to keep Pontiac going and to make dramatic improvements. But Chevrolet was many times the size of Pontiac. I didn't know any of the Chevy people, and I really didn't know much about the division except that it was our number one internal competitor at Pontiac and we had been able to make some of our biggest sales gains by taking customers away from Chevrolet.

So shortly after I stepped into my office at Chevrolet on the first floor of the General Motors Building my reaction was, "God, I'm completely lost." It soon was very obvious that my first reaction was quite proper because I learned that Chevrolet was running completely out of control.

119

Kyes had said as much when he pulled me aside shortly after our meeting in Cole's home and said, "Chevy is in a mess, John. Estes can't get the job done." He gave me a number of charts, graphs and statistical analyses which showed that Chevrolet was declining in every part of the business.

Profit

Even though total dollar sales of Chevrolet increased almost every year, gross profit declined precipitously. Return on investment, which is a measure of how well you use assets, was to decline from 55.4 percent in 1964 to 10.3 percent in the 1969 model year. It was obvious from the trend established that Chevrolet was headed for a big loss in the 1970 model year, which Kyes said worried him and The Fourteenth Floor management.

Market penetration

Although Chevrolet was participating in the general boom in car sales which marked the 1960s, it wasn't booming as big as the rest of the industry. Thus, from 1962 to 1968 its share of the total market for domestic cars dropped from 31.6 percent to 24.2 percent. Much of that loss was to its number one competitor, Ford Division, which had managed in that time to cut the Chevy sales lead from 600,000 units to just about 200,000 units. Each percentage point drop in market penetration for Chevrolet meant roughly $100 million less gross profit for the corporation.

Product

Chevrolet was being beaten into new markets by its competitors, especially Ford, which was first into the compact car market with its Falcon, first into the sporty compact market with the Mustang, first into the modern truck-van market with the Econoline van, and first with the

120

two-way station wagon tailgate. Chevrolet was up to three years late in responding to these markets. What's more, Chevrolet's product quality was slipping in relation to Ford and its other competitors. This was most evident in the used-car market where a one-year-old Chevrolet at one time held a $250 advantage over a comparable Ford. By 1969, the two were selling for virtually the same price. This was threatening Chevrolet's strong position in the huge fleet leasing market where the resale value of the used car means the difference between making a profit or taking a loss to leasing companies such as Hertz, Avis or Peterson, Howell & Heather.

Dealer profit

The Chevrolet dealer body is the finest, the largest and the strongest in the automobile business. But when I got to the division literally hundreds of dealerships were up for sale primarily because as the division's profit and product quality slipped so did the dealers' profit and credibility. The net profit before taxes for the Chevrolet dealer body was dropping drastically from $308 million in 1963 to $202 million in 1969. And in that time the return on investment for the average Chevrolet dealer dropped almost in half from 27.8 percent to 14.7 percent.

Behind these statistical representations of Chevrolet's problems were mammoth organizational and business control problems in each one of the division's staffs and departments. A quick study of staff reports made it obvious that the business was undisciplined. This was evident in several major areas.

Finance

Strict adherence to financial controls was almost non-existent. Every department was outspending its budget every year. The Engineering Department hadn't met a budget in something like 15 to 20 years. Typically, in 1966 it was $13 million over its budget, $11 million over in 1968 and $15 million over in 1969. When problems developed in Chevy departments, the simple solution seemed to be to pour more money in. And generally, budget excesses were identified only after a project was completed—the money spent was totalled and compared to the amount budgeted.

Capital expenditures for expansion and improvement of plants and facilities were authorized in a helter-skelter manner. Each year the total expenses for capital improvement exceeded the division's depreciation by as much as 300 percent. However, these investments did not generate the improved productivity and profits necessary to justify them.

Perhaps the most widely confused aspect of the finance operation was the division's system of computer controls. Chevrolet's use of computers throughout the business was unsophisticated in relation to most of the automobile world. When computer controls were put into the division, no master plan was developed. Instead, the division was computerized on a department-by-department basis. Only the internal clerical work in each department was automated. There was little provision for department-to-department computer communication. There was no central control at headquarters. Interdepartment work, therefore, had to be done manually. For instance, the conversion of sales forecasts and orders to production schedules was done by hand.

This rather simplistic approach to the electronic computer age at Chevrolet produced two disastrous results. One was the totally inefficient use of Chevrolet's manufacturing plants, because there was no way to coordinate material control with sales orders. When a new-car order was placed by a dealer, it sat for ten days to two weeks until there was time available in a production plant: It was then read to see if the car ordered by the dealer could actually be built. (As many as 30 percent of all new-car orders have errors, such as a dealer mistakenly ordering a Nova with an engine which is not available for that car line.) If the order was correct, it was put into the production schedule. If it wasn't, it was kicked back to the dealer for correction and then sent back to the corporation where it sat for another ten days to two weeks before it was read a second time. If it was wrong again, it went through the whole process a third or fourth time, if necessary. The wait alone here could be two months or more.

Also, production schedules were given to assembly plant managers only a week in advance at best. The assembly plant managers did all of their own material ordering. Once it got a production schedule, plant management scrambled around to see if it had enough inventory to build the cars that were being ordered. If it didn't, an urgent SOS was sent to other assembly plants or to the internal parts manufacturing plants. It was "Panicville." Since the plants ordered their parts autonomously, headquarters never had an on-time record of plant inventories. Sometimes both the plant management and staffers at headquarters in Detroit were calling all around the country trying to locate material to keep the assembly lines running. And when they located a surplus of, say, brown steering wheels, the plant with the excess wouldn't release its surplus for fear that the following week its schedule would call for brown steering wheels. Sometimes the troubled plant, to be sure it could keep the lines running, would order brown steering wheels from more than one plant as a backup measure. If all the plants delivered, the once troubled plant would suddenly find itself awash in a sea of brown steering wheels.

This reckless system often had the poor guy at a machine in a parts plant working 60 hours one week trying to keep up with demands only to be given a short work week the next because there was now a surplus of the part he built.

As a result of poor coordination of materials, Chevrolet every year led the company in costs for interplant shipments, premium (mostly air carrier) freight shipments and inventories of obsolete parts at the end of each model run. Also, Chevrolet took up to twice as long to deliver a new car to the customer as did Ford. And the division could never give dealers an accurate date for new-car deliveries.

The second disastrous result of the Chevy financial staff's unsophisticated approach to computer control came at the start of the 1969 model run when it tried to alleviate some of the manufacturing foul-ups with a new electronic system designed to order the production of new cars, assign schedules to specific assembly plants and then bill the dealer for the cars. The old, mostly manual system was scrapped at the start of the model run in favor of the new system. But the bugs hadn't been entirely worked out of the new system. It simply did not work. The division was unable to invoice dealers for thousands of new cars which were shipped. At first, the dealers had no way to sell the cars because they didn't know the price of the cars. Some of the more enterprising dealers found ways to peddle the cars, but they weren't billed for them. Their sales were 100 percent pure profit. As much as two years later, dealers were laughing and quietly telling me that they had never been billed for certain cars. The division took the loss and I understood that was the single most important reason that Chevrolet management was changed and I was brought into the division.

What's more, as Chevrolet's sales penetration had started to decline, management panicked and tried to be all things to all people. The business as a whole was expanding, first with the addition of new markets such as compact cars like the Ford Falcon, intermediates like the Chevrolet Chevelle, sporty compacts like the Mustang, and sporty luxury cars like the Pontiac Grand Prix. There also were developing sub-markets within these new markets. The muscle car, with its stripped-down intermediate body around a powerful engine, was one highly successful sub-market. Divisional studies of Chevrolet's falling penetration indicated that Chevy wasn't offering the customer enough choice, so product lines were added ad infinitum. Chevrolet cars soon had 15,000 parts, with a combination of body types, engine sizes, colors, axle ratios and interior arrangements which was almost incalculable. We could build one million Chevrolets and not have two cars exactly alike. Truck lines were experiencing similar expansion. From 1963 to 1967, alone, the number of basic Chevrolet car models grew from 29 to 50 while truck models in that time grew from 124 models to 292. By 1969, Chevrolet was offering 179 different engine combinations for cars and 299 for trucks. There were 142 different axle combinations for cars and an astounding 440 possibilities for trucks. The totals were similar for suspension systems, optional equipment and color combinations. There were 165,000 different material order specifications for cars and trucks. The Chevrolet parts manual was over a foot-and-a-half thick.

Therein lay at least part of the problem in material control, product quality and general confusion throughout the division. The management system had grown up to handle one product line. It was never changed to cope with a now widely diverse business. Just inventorying this wide a variety of parts tied up millions of dollars that might have been better used elsewhere.

Organization

Chevrolet management was proud, hard-working and burdened by an almost impossible business system. It was without control or direction. The organization had grown without rationale as the division's sales increased, and furthermore it was totally uncommunicative with itself. The system of management in 1969 was essentially the same organizational structure of the immediate post-World War II days. This was inefficient. The system which ran Chevrolet when it was a one-car and one-truck line operation was incapable of running the Chevrolet Division which could produce two million or more dissimilar cars and trucks.

The division's answer to the growing proliferation of product and automotive markets was simply to add more management lines to the old management structure. As this developed, Chevrolet's always strong internal staffs grew distant. If they didn't communicate through the computer system, they also didn't communicate in person. I don't think it was a conscious decision by each department head that he would not keep in touch with his counterparts. I just think that the business grew so broad and distant that there was no viable means of keeping each facet of the business informed of the progress and developments in the other facets.

This lack of communication reached a zenith in 1968 when the sales staff decided to promote four-cylinder Novas. A massive advertising campaign was devised and a big promotion was set into motion. Ads in the media were accompanied by dealer promotions with the traditional bright-colored banners, loud commercials and assorted hoopla. Just about the time this campaign was being launched, the manufacturing people were completing a program of de-emphasizing four-cylinder engine production because sales had fallen off to such a point that there was practically no demand for them any longer. The manufacturing people had taken most of the four-cylinder equipment out of the plants or put it to another use. No one in management had bothered to check with manufacturing to see if the four-cylinder Novas that were being promoted could in fact be built. They couldn't. The campaign was launched, and suddenly the manufacturing people were inundated with engine orders six times their capacity to build. The results were disastrous. Everyone got burned. The manufacturing people because they couldn't meet dealer orders. The dealers because they couldn't supply the cars that the customers were ordering. And the customers because they could not get the cars that Chevrolet's advertising campaign convinced them they wanted.

A confused, over-managed, under-controlled division awaited me on my first day at Chevrolet, February 15, 1969. The staffs were not only depressed because their operations were on the decline, but they were skeptical of me, a young, upstart newcomer. They were cautious in their conversation with me. I was overwhelmed and befuddled by this vast cobweb of problems. And I didn't have any place to look for help. While Kyes often offered suggestions on how to get Chevrolet back into shape, it was obvious from the conversations I had with him and other top management that no one knew what was wrong with Chevrolet. But everybody was worried because the division was headed for red ink. Internally, I was offered four detailed analyses of the division's problems prepared by the financial staff, and these, too, turned out to be of little help because they simplistically analyzed only the effects of Chevrolet's problems—the drop in return on investment, the loss in market penetration and so on. They did not deal with the causes. I decided one thing, and that was whatever had been done in the past hadn't worked, and so it was probably wrong. So I wasn't going to do these kinds of things. I was going to try something different.

My most immediate problem was trying to get enough time to think over the division's problems. In my first week at Chevy, I couldn't get five minutes by myself. There was an endless parade of executives and staffers into my office to discuss all kinds of problems. They weren't significant things for the most part. They were minutiae. They wanted me to make every little damn decision that was to be made. The practice, I quickly learned, developed under my predecessor, Pete Estes, who because of his incredible memory could keep track of almost every small factor of the business.

In fact, he wanted to be involved in every aspect of the business. I couldn't. And I thought that to be effective here I had to work within my own limitations and concentrate on the broad overall concepts of the business and not get all tangled up in detail. So by the end of the first week I started telling people in the division that I didn't want to be involved in the smaller details of the business; that they were the experts in those fields anyway; and they should make the decisions.

On the bigger problems, I let it be known that no one could come into my office to discuss these problems without first having given them thorough study and then prepared a recommended solution. "Let's talk about the solutions to these problems, not just the problems themselves." This rule shook up some people who had grown accustomed to having the ear of the general manager several times a day. But it also, in a small way, started to boost executive morale because it put people on their own feet and gave them decision-making power which they didn't have before. Before long, the only problems coming into my office were accompanied by proposed solutions. And because of this it was easy for me to identify the real managers and the talented people through their ability to analyze problems and develop solutions.

In trying to get hold of the Chevrolet tiger, I concluded that the best way was to examine the division personally. So I set out on a three-month study to ascertain the seriousness of Chevrolet's sickness. First I met with Chevrolet managers and their staffs in the problem areas—finance, product, manufacturing, sales and marketing. I wanted their personal assessment of their problems. And I hoped that, by seeking their counsel, I would show them that I was truly interested in getting at the source of Chevy's problems and in the process combat the natural hostility toward me as an outsider who was coming in to tell the people how to run their business.

If the meetings were with home office personnel, as often as I could, I tried to meet in the employees' office rather than mine. This generally created a more relaxed atmosphere. Somehow, the boss's office has a stiff, formal air to it.

If the meetings were in Chevrolet's far-flung plants, I tried to keep the visits low-key and businesslike. Too often in General Motors, plant tours turned into Fourth-of-July-like celebrations, with great pomp and circumstance, for which the machines have been carefully polished and the plant manager and his staff are all smiles and handshakes. To keep this display to a minimum, I usually gave only a few days notice to the plant before I arrived. When management was reticent to discuss business, I asked direct questions like, "Why haven't you met your budget for three years in a row? What's the problem?" Often the guy would get a little defensive. His back would straighten and he might get a flushed look, but then he'd say something like, "Well, goddamnit, how the hell can I make budget? Here are my schedules, and you've changed them every three days for so long that I can't remember. In the old days when this plant was making a lot of money, we made only one engine. Hell, now we're making all of these different varieties, and it is impossible to schedule them."

Another plant manager might say, "Here, Chevy's got 40 different oil pans that we have to put on these cars. It's just impossible to schedule that many. When are we going to get that number down to something more reasonable?"

They soon were talking about their problems—which is what I wanted to hear. And I told them so.

They had been either lost in the maze between lower management and the top, or they didn't get attention because people were too busy trying just to meet production requirements. Nobody seemed to have the time to look over suggestions of how to improve the business. One plant manager had half-a-dozen or so plans for improving the efficiency of his operation which had never been approved. "I can't get anybody to listen to me," he lamented.

Where my inquiries into the business might make department heads or their staffs unduly apprehensive, I would contrive a reason for seeing these people. If the guy was a computer systems engineer I would dig out an article on a new IBM model and tell him I wanted to talk about it. Pretty soon the conversation would drift off of the new computer model and into an analysis of Chevy's systems problems.

I also talked to disgruntled employees, those who had left the division, and those who were still there but were not masking their hard feelings. They were unhappy. I wanted their analyses of the division's problems. Often you can learn more from an unhappy employee than you can from a happy one.

In almost every area I researched I was amazed how my first impressions were changed after talking with the people at work. From their performance results I felt that most of the Chevy people must be goofing off. After talking with them I saw that by and large Chevrolet's people, especially the middle and upper managers, were competent, and working harder and longer than most of their peers throughout the corporation. Yet they couldn't stay on top of their jobs. They were being hassled to death by a cumbersome management structure and management techniques. They were trying to cut grass with hand clippers instead of a power mower. Because of this there was an inherent inability in the system to crystallize clear-cut programs to improve the job the division was doing. Instead, when problems crept up, the solution was like putting another patch on an old inner tube instead of getting a whole new tube and throwing the old one out. No one in Chevrolet could take a meaningful step in a profitable direction.

While I was meeting with Chevy personnel, I also was meeting in the field with Chevrolet dealers. One of my early first encounters was with a meeting of the Chevrolet Dealers' Council. It was an openly hostile affair. Everyone was so mad that not a helluva lot was accomplished in the way of business. They were snapping at me:

"These cars you are sending us are lousy."

129

"Our advertising is poor, at best."

"Why does Ford always get better products than we do?"

"We don't believe anyone with the company anymore."

I had trouble keeping the meeting in order because everyone wanted to unload on me at once.

Afterward, I decided to go into the field and meet with the dealers in small groups to get at the heart of their problems. I scheduled two or three meetings a week with 10 or 12 key dealers in the country's biggest markets. As in the plant tours, I wanted to get away from the traditional GM dealer meetings. In those the executives would get together with 500 dealers and drink themselves into a midafternoon glow. Then the divisional general manager would get up and say something like, "We're going to go out and sell everybody in the world a Chevrolet loaded with optional equipment and make zillions of dollars for all of us." He would be followed by a seemingly well-rehearsed standing ovation and that was it.

So, instead, we had small luncheon meetings with key dealers. The lunch part was simple, down-played and quickly dispensed with so that we could get to the dealer problems. We only chose key dealers because about 80 percent of Chevy's business is done by 20 percent of the dealers and I figured if we could solve the problems of the key dealers, we would most likely be taking care of the smaller ones, too.

As with some of my meetings in Detroit, it was hard to get the dealers to open up. For one thing, they distrusted me, I guess, because when I ran Pontiac I was the enemy of Chevy dealers. We had managed to eat into Chevy's market and make our dealer body increasingly profitable. A story in *Business Week* magazine once quoted a Detroit Chevy dealer as saying that the city's two most profitable dealers were Pontiac dealers and that Pontiac division, not Ford, was his number one competitor. To get these dealers into serious discourse I prepared a list of simple but direct questions such as, "Why is Ford selling more Galaxie 500s than you are selling Impalas?" If I got one guy to open up, then I found the whole meeting would take off like a jet.

Several main problems surfaced from these meetings. As in the dealer council meeting, our dealers were angry over our lagging behind Ford in product innovation, the relatively poor quality of Chevy products (doors sometimes didn't fit properly, hoods were not in line with the fenders) and a general breakdown in relations between Chevrolet management and the dealers. The division had a very poor record of keeping its promises to dealers. We not only couldn't tell a dealer when he would receive his new-car orders, but we never attempted to fix that order response system after we told him we would. They didn't trust Detroit management. And what's more, they were still chafing from the bludgeon effect of an article in *Automotive News* fully two years before, in which Estes and General Sales Manager Lee Mays called Chevrolet dealers "fat cats" and blamed their intransigence for the division's declining sales. Ironically, that year the Chevy dealer body recorded its lowest gross profit of the decade—$187 million.

I promised them action and took copious notes at each meeting to make sure I had an accurate record of their complaints. It was obvious to me about this time that Chevy's ability to avoid a much more serious decline in market production during the 1960s was due to the strength, ability and perseverance of its dealer body.

Finally, I talked to people outside of Chevrolet and the corporation, competitors and non-competitors alike, about the division's problems. I talked with Bob Anderson, former Chrysler executive who is now chairman of Rockwell International, and Don Frey, former general manager of Ford Division and now president of Bell & Howell. I talked with guys at the other auto companies, with whom I have a long-time friendship established through my association with the Society of Automotive Engineers. And I also talked with advertising people in New York, and competitive dealers around the country. These people gave me frank analyses of Chevrolet's problems from the kind of objective perspective that only an outsider can give. I didn't tell my superiors that I was consulting with outside executives about the division's problems because the idea of going outside of GM was repugnant to them. The prevailing thought was that at GM we had the ultimate in management technique and ability. People should come to us or use our system to improve their businesses, but we surely could solve our own problems internally.

Within a few months I had visited perhaps 60 percent of Chevy's plants and talked with about half of our key dealers, as well as hundreds of Chevy managers and employees and competitors. I began to realize that Chevrolet's problems went to the roots of the division. There was not one facet of the business that didn't need overhauling. I thought to myself, I may not have my arms around the monster, but at least I am beginning to see its outline. That was an improvement.

A preliminary analysis of the division's trouble indicated that I needed to improve product quality and our overall system of marketing, institute a vast program to update and streamline the management organization, and introduce strict and fundamental controls throughout the division. With the problems identified, I began to work out a management strategy to solve them. What I didn't count on was the immediate surfacing of a more pressing problem with my bosses.

Up to then, I was doing what had not been done before. Sizing up Chevrolet for myself. Instead of sitting in my Detroit office ten hours a day listening to everybody's little problems, I was on the road meeting with managers in the field and getting a firsthand reading of their problems. Instead of plodding through mountains of paperwork every day, reading old analyses of the division's problems and ordering new ones, I was getting staff people to tell me exactly why they weren't getting the job done. However, because I wasn't doing the kinds of things that had been done before, and because I was out of town a large amount of the time, resentments were building up within fragments of the divisional management and on The Fourteenth Floor.

Pete Estes, who was now my immediate boss, for one thing was quite defensive at Administrative Committee meetings when I would talk about Chevrolet's problems. It was understandable. I supposed his nose was somewhat out of joint. For this I was sorry because nobody worked harder to cure Chevrolet's problems than he did. He gave it his best shot. But the division nevertheless got deeper into trouble. I suspect part of his problem at Chevrolet was that he was such a team player that he listened too much to what those above him said should be done to help Chevrolet. As a result, he didn't get to the heart of the problem. Still, his defensive attitude at committee meetings made my job all but impossible, especially when he opposed certain programs that I had to bring to him for approval. It was an untenable situation which I suspect the corporation brass recognized because within a year Pete was moved to head up GM's overseas operations and Tom Murphy was put in his slot as vice-president for Car and Truck Operations.

In addition to Estes' natural inclination to oppose and perhaps pooh-pooh my plans for reviving Chevrolet, I suspect that the Chevrolet financial staff, which was receiving much of my attention and had close ties with The Fourteenth Floor, was telling management there that I was goofing off on a bunch of junkets around the country to our various facilities. These complaints culminated in a call I got from Kyes' office. I was told he wanted to see me.

As executive vice-president for Car and Truck, Body and Assembly Operations, he had control of all GM's North American automotive operations. When I got into his office, it was obvious that he was irritated. First, he complained that I wasn't doing my job because I wasn't doing the things he suggested or the things that Estes had done before me. (I later learned that Estes was doing many of the things that Kyes had told him to do.) He said that I wasn't spending enough time in the office.

I told him, "I'm just trying to get a grasp of this thing. Doing more of what has been done already isn't going to save Chevrolet. That didn't work before and it won't work now."

It was obvious that he was in no mood to listen to what I was saying no matter how compelling my argument. After a few minutes of my talking, he bellowed, "You weren't my choice for general manager. I am stuck with you. But you are goddamn well going to do this thing the way I want it done, or you're going to be gone."

Sitting across from his mahogany desk I was shook. I said nothing to him but went downstairs to my office and thought the whole thing over. Then I decided, "If I'm going to get my fanny thrown out of GM, I'd just as soon get it thrown out for doing what I thought was right as sit here and let this thing go down the tube and not do anything."

After getting over the shock of Kyes' comments, I rejected them and their content in about the same amount of time it took him to deliver them. I mapped out a plan for Chevrolet's recovery, but at the same time I was worried that at any moment the axe could fall.

CHAPTER EIGHT

Turning Chevrolet Around

Not surprisingly, soon after Kyes gave me his "do-it-my-way-or-you-are-out" edict, rumors began flying throughout the corporation that I was going to switch places with Lee N. Mays, general manager of Buick. Only a few months earlier he had been my general sales manager at Chevrolet. Such a move would have been a demotion for me since Buick was about one-fifth the size of Chevrolet. It was even smaller than Pontiac. I never spoke to Kyes about the rumors. He never mentioned them to me. But it was consistent with his attitude toward me that Kyes would try to have me removed from Chevrolet. And if he did try, I suspect that management turned him down because they figured that I at least deserved a chance to take a shot at Chevrolet's problems.

The rumor ran through the corporation, and it was disconcerting and unsettling to Chevrolet personnel, whom I was trying to mollify and mold into a cohesive management unit. Nevertheless, we started to move on the division's problems. It was obvious that the organization had to be streamlined in order to cope better with the challenge of building and selling cars and trucks in the 1970s. And it was just as obvious that a streamlined management structure would be ineffective without modern and innovative

135

controls for the business. Getting this done would not be easy.

First there was the problem with Chevrolet management. It had tremendous pride, but it also was old—an average age in the 1950's—with a natural affinity for the status quo which comes with age. Many of them were not educated in the sophisticated use of computer controls and they found it hard to adjust from their established business methods to new techniques incorporating the speed of computers. In this light it is not hard to understand why Chevy's use of computer technology was undeveloped.

Second, there were strong feelings in the corporate and divisional management against tampering with the very basics of Chevrolet's organization. A fault that GM has had for a long time is its feeling that, since it sells more cars and trucks than anyone else in the world and makes far more money than any other automotive company, the GM way is the only way. At Chevrolet this corporate thinking translated into the theory that since Chevrolet is the number one nameplate in the American automobile industry it is unwise to tamper with its proven formula for success.

This malady is common in some businesses. It also is common in professional sports where management with a team that is old but still winning is often reluctant to bring in younger talent. The result is, of course, that one day the winning record stops because the players are too old to compete effectively. Management must take several years to rebuild the team and develop younger players to take the place of the old ones. Chevrolet, in many respects, was at this juncture. It was still number one in the industry and, by that count, a winner. But it was starting to fall. The rebuilding process would be slow, arduous and maybe impossible, if we did not act quickly.

The formula for change was basic. Overhauling the division's organization and bringing in a new and extensive system of controls would give us the form and tools we needed to manage the business. However, simultaneously we had to reverse quickly the plunging trend in Chevrolet's profits and market penetration through increasing our sales, bettering the quality of our cars and trucks, more effectively marketing these products and preparing innovative programs to cut costs and generate new income. To keep Chevrolet out of red ink in 1970 we had to move swiftly and in concert. We didn't have the luxury of installing new programs one at a time to see if they worked before going on to another. We had to do many things at once and be damn sure we did them right.

Organization

All of the division's eight major staffs and their many departments had severe organizational problems, some of them quite complicated and others relatively simple.

One of the biggest and yet simplest problems was in the manufacturing staff. It was overburdened with layers upon layers of management. Between a plant manager and my office there were no less than five levels of management. A plant manager reported to a city manager who reported to a regional manager who reported to a manager of plants who reported to the general manufacturing manager who reported to the works manager who reported to me, the general manager. Consequently, the manager of the Chevrolet Gear and Axle plant on Detroit's near east side who was only a few miles from my office, was almost light years away in terms of management reporting channels. There were five layers of decision making between a proposal for his plant and my approval.

Directing the revamping of the manufacturing organization was Jim McLernon, one of the brightest executives I know. He now is president of Volkswagen of America, Inc. I brought him into Chevrolet from the corporate manufacturing development activity which he directed. With McLernon coming in we moved several manufacturing staff executives to new jobs either in the staff or elsewhere in the corporation with The Fourteenth Floor's approval. The vacancies opened with these moves were filled with talented people I had known—like Bob McKee who became the division's director of Reliability (quality control) —or eliminated from the organizational chart.

In the manufacturing staff as well as in many of the division's activities, our reorganization was aided by the retirement of a number of executives who had reached the then mandatory retirement age of 65. Through this we were able to eliminate the whole level of city plant managers. Retirement vacancies in that level were unfilled, and the remaining spots were eliminated when their occupants were promoted to succeed retired regional plant managers.

Within two years we eliminated three levels of management in the manufacturing operations—city managers, managers of plants and works managers. This shortened lines of communication and when combined with my desire to drive decision making to the lowest level possible, it gave definite and clear responsibility to each level of management.

In the mammoth sales staff there didn't seem to be an organizational problem, at first. The sales operation was divided into 47 zone offices which had the day-to-day contact with Chevrolet's 6,000-plus dealer body. Zone managers reported to one of nine regional managers who in turn reported to assistant general sales managers who reported to the general sales manager. It appeared quite efficient for keeping close and direct contact with the huge dealer body. Nevertheless, the speed of communication between the zone office level and headquarters was almost tortoise-like. Information on what was happening in the field was slow to reach us in Detroit, and our directions were just as slow in getting back to the zone offices and the dealer body. This had all kinds of ramifications, none of them good. If compact car sales caught fire in the northwestern United States, we would probably be late in getting detailed and accurate information from our field about the sudden boom.

The gremlin in the works turned out to be the power of our nine regional sales offices. Each one of them had grown over the years to where their staffs were the equal in size of our sales staffs in Detroit. The regional offices were mini-empires. Unlike the rest of General Motors car divisions where these regional offices served as conduits of information to and from the field, Chevy's offices were originators of information. They accumulated, collated and interpreted information from Detroit for the field personnel and vice versa. A natural lag in our response time developed as this process took place. The regional sales managers, as a result, had huge staffs. They had their own marketing man-

In 1961, John Z. De Lorean, age 36 (above left), was named chief engineer of Pontiac Division. At age 52 (below), his hair dyed jet-black, he worked on his fledgling car company. By 1979, age 54 (above right), a naturally-gray De Lorean plans the introduction of his new sports car.

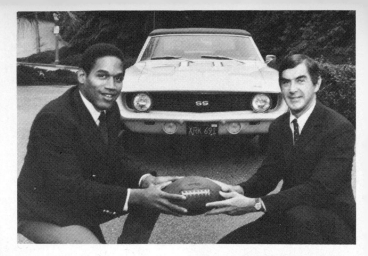

Photo by Ron Appelbe

At Chevrolet, De Lorean took personal interest in the division's far-flung operations and problems including marketing — with football star O. J. Simpson (above) who had just signed a Chevy promotional contract; public relations — at Soap Box Derby championship (below); and engineering — at Chevy engine laboratory (right).

De Lorean's life-style chafed his superiors at General Motors. On a movie set (above left) with actress Ursula Andress. At home (below) with his second wife Kelly Harmon, a top fashion model. Touring his 500-acre avocado and citrus farm in Southern California (above right).

Photo by Fred M.H. Gregory

His third marriage was to actress/model Cristina Ferrare (above). They have a son, Zachary (right), and a daughter, Kathryn (not pictured). Both children are named after De Lorean's parents. A third De Lorean "baby" is the DMC-12 sports car (below).

Photo by Andrew Sacks

Photo by Peter C. Borsari

agers, distribution managers, service managers, as well as a large staff of assistants and clerical help.

As I examined this problem I ran across a study prepared for Ed Cole by his staff, when he ran the Chevrolet Division from 1956-61, which recommended drastically cutting back the size and power of the regional sales offices to make the sales operations more economical and efficient. This problem, therefore, was not new to Chevrolet. It apparently developed at a time when Chevy was run almost independently of GM. And the problem grew as the business grew.

If the Cole study wasn't deemed appropriate in the 1950s, I figured that its time had certainly come in 1969. We started to move to pare back the size of the regional sales offices. The action met great resistance from the regions. I could understand the resistance. No one likes to see his power cut within an organization even if it can be demonstrated that the move will improve the business. There, too, was an undercurrent of suspicion in the sales organization that I was promoting revolutionary change and a wholesale purge of management. Nothing was further from the truth, but I couldn't convince them of this.

The sales staff at Chevrolet was a vainly proud organization. From its inception it considered itself a separate business within a business. In previous administrations the sales staff had been given carte blanche authority to run the division's sales and marketing efforts with little or no meddling from the general manager. As incredible as that may seem, that was the case. And I had a collision with this pride and power less than a month after I took over the reins at Chevrolet. It began when I took an active interest in the division's sales and marketing programs because while running Pontiac I had noticed that Chevrolet's advertising and marketing efforts were the worst in the industry. Knowing this, shortly after I arrived at Chevy, I asked General Sales Manager Lee Mays to show me the advertising campaign and marketing plan proposed for the 1970 models. He answered, "Anytime you want." But that was the last I heard from him.

Finally, in mid-March, after several attempts to see the program, I called him and said, "I want to see that program now. Let's set a time."

"I'll be right down to see you," he answered.

Mays office was on the second floor practically right above me, and it was only a minute or so before he came into my office, pulled a chair up in front of my desk and began to tell me how glad he was to have me at the Chevrolet division and how he knew that the two of us would work well together. But then he added the kicker: Chevrolet advertising and marketing were none of my business. It wasn't in an argumentative tone but more matter of fact. Mays, a hard-working executive, is a gentleman. But he said: "Mr. Roche gave me this job, and he told me that I would get absolutely no interference." I was shocked to hear this. It was like a general in the Army asking his captain to see the battle plan and being told, "That's none of your business, but you can come along for the ride if you want." I asked Mays to repeat what he had just told me and he did verbatim.

"If Mr. Roche told you that," I said, "then we'd better go have a conversation with him to get this straightened out." There was no way I could run Chevrolet properly and not have full control over all of the facets of the business, especially a facet as critical as the sales and marketing effort.

Mays left and I called Kyes, repeating for him the exchange that had just taken place in my office. "I want the two of us to meet with Mr. Roche," I said.

"Let me handle it, I'll get back to you," Kyes responded.

That was the last I heard from him on the matter. But two weeks later, in the first week of April, The Fourteenth Floor announced that Lee Mays was being promoted to head up the Buick Division. After quite a bit of squabbling, I got the general sales manager I wanted, Bob Lund, who had been an assistant sales manager in the division and knew the Chevrolet operations well. He was much more understanding about the problems we faced in the sales staff and more amenable to change. We began to redesign the sales staff, de-emphasizing the regional offices. It was a very tough struggle because there was field opposition at every step. The reorganization never was fully implemented. The regional offices were still too large as far as I was concerned when I left. Nevertheless, we smoothed out the process of communications between the field and headquarters in Detroit. And we came into closer and faster contact as a result.

The most confused and inefficient staff in Chevrolet was the engineering organization. Its structure hadn't changed one iota from the time Chevrolet was selling one car line and a few trucks. With a far more complicated business to deal with in 1969, it just couldn't handle the job.

The staff's management structure was very simple. One department designed the car body, another the chassis and components, and another did both jobs for trucks. The head of the engineering staff was sort of chief engineer for Chevy cars and trucks. The confusion developed as Chevy grew from one to five car lines with three or four models in each line. Trucks had a similar growth. Trying to manage this business turned into an organizational nightmare. As the product lines proliferated, the engineering staff added people and departments to the existing structure, instead of redesigning the structure to meet the new needs.

Therefore, in 1969 all of Chevy's car bodies were being designed in one department, all of the chassis and component work was done in another department. This was confusing because each car line was different in size, weight, style, performance characteristics and market. No department of engineers could be specialists in one car line. They had to be generalists for all of them. Furthermore, there was no coordination of engineering for each car line. It was quite common to have six different engineers working on the same car completely independent of each other and reporting to different department heads. Only in the office of the chief engineer for cars was each line brought together in total design and concept. The problems were similar for the vast truck operations. This process, obviously, overburdened the staff's two top engineers, one for cars and one for trucks. It is a wonder that they didn't blow their minds trying to keep track of hundreds of models of cars and trucks, engine combinations et al.

I asked Frank Winchell, an assistant chief engineer who had just returned to Chevy from the corporate engineering staff, to drop everything and make a thorough study of the engineering organization. Within a short while he completed this study and recommended that the engineering

141

operation be put on a project manager basis. This is a process giving one man total responsibility for each specific product. It is quite common in aerospace engineering but most prominently used in the marketing of consumer goods such as deodorants, soaps and cosmetics.

We implemented Winchell's proposals. Each car line, such as the Impala, Vega or Corvette, was put under a project manager whom we called chief engineer. Similar lines such as the Camaro-Nova and Chevelle-Monte Carlo were combined. The project manager had total responsibility for his car line. Under him were engineers in charge of every facet of design for that line—chassis, body and components. Truck engineering was organized in similar fashion within the categories of light trucks, heavy trucks and recreational vehicles. Within the engineering staff we also maintained large and separate departments for engineering overall components, engines, chassis and other parts of the car. Their function was to improve designs, develop new systems for use in our car lines, assist their counterparts in each specific car line and handle broad responsibilities such as certification of Chevrolet engines emission controls with the Environmental Protection Agency.

For the first time in years, engineering responsibilities were clearly defined. Thus when a problem cropped up in one of Chevy's manufacturing and assembly plants, the plant management had the name and phone number of a specific engineer to call with the problem. This helped us to stop product defects quickly and to produce workable solutions to these problems in the shortest time.

The organizational problems with the remaining Chevrolet staffs were relatively simple. In the finance operations there simply were too many people. We eliminated one layer of management and about 200 jobs. In the rest of the division we took out selected management positions and cut staff to shorten lines of communication and run the operation more efficiently. Within two years we eliminated about 2,400 salaried positions in Chevrolet while bringing the headquarters into better contact with the plants and offices in the field.

Almost all of these cuts were made without having to push people around unduly or resort to wholesale firings. Most of the pruning was done through attrition, leaving jobs vacant when their occupants retired or switching people into other areas of the corporation. What resulted was a much younger management team, dotted with seasoned, well-rounded executives who knew Chevrolet's operations well. While the average age of the chief engineers dropped from the mid-40s to the mid-30s between 1968 and 1971, the total organization still had talented older men such as Ralph Powell, a regional manufacturing manager and a very talented executive who trained many of the bright young guys in manufacturing. He was the kind of guy to whom others, even his superiors, felt free and comfortable about going to for advice. To me, this was a good blend of young, hard-charging executives and wise, seasoned, older veterans.

Controls

As we modernized the division's organizational structure, we also updated and in some cases completely replaced the management techniques being used. The most pressing problem was to get the division back into control, to examine in detail specific problems in all of the areas of the business and begin to remedy them.

Initially, we instituted relatively simple and fundamental mechanisms of control, such as tightening budgets, cutting out layers of management, firming up reporting channels and clarifying responsibilities. We moved to control the division's wild capital spending with several capital budget objectives—the main one of which was that capital expenditures (excluding cost savings projects which had immediate benefit) would not exceed 90 percent of the division's depreciation.

Capital expenditures are generally evaluated on their ability to increase a business' return on investment. If the return will improve, the expenditure is made. However, Chevy's expenditures were generally increasing from year to year from 1964 to 1969 while its return was decreasing, which meant we weren't getting our money's worth out of our capital expenditures. What we had to do was find out better ways to use our plants and equipment through better management. Cutting capital budgets would force managers

143

to use their facilities more efficiently. The figure of 90 percent was an arbitrary figure selected as a target to bring discipline to our expenditures.

The effects of this capital budget program were not too long in coming. The budget for 1970 was all but locked up when I got to Chevy. That year we spent $273 million. But the figure dropped to $138 million in 1971 and $125 million in 1972. Our rate of return on investment picked up because we were using Chevy's plant and facilities more productively.

Control of the manufacturing operations was impeded by the almost senseless proliferation of car models, parts and optional equipment which took place in the 1960s because of poor product planning. We began a study with the sales people to discover the effect of this proliferation on Chevrolet. It showed, for instance, that 67 percent of all engine combinations went into only one percent of the cars we built. So we could eliminate two-thirds of all of our engine combinations and face the prospect of losing only one percent of our sales potential. The study showed similar inefficiencies in all our product lines. We began to deproliferate.

Any piece of optional equipment which was ordered on 5 percent or less of our production was an immediate candidate for elimination. If a cost-benefit study on any piece of equipment, no matter how often it was ordered, showed that we were losing money on it, we either eliminated the part or found a more profitable way to build and sell it.

The results from the deproliferation program were dramatic. By 1972, with no apparent effect on our business, we had reduced the number of car models offered from 35 to 32, despite adding two entirely new car lines. Almost 50 truck models were dropped. Engine combinations for our car lines were reduced from 179 to 75. The axle selections were chopped from 142 to 68. The results in pruning our trucks were similar—a 73 percent drop in engine combinations and axles. One of the biggest reductions was in the dashboard clusters offered on our Camaro line. At one time there were an unbelievable 2,720 possible alternatives for Camaro dashboards. By 1972 that was reduced to 96, a drop of 96 percent.

When we had finished, not one part of our car and

truck lines had escaped the pruning knife, and we found the benefits to be dramatic and well worth our trouble. Manufacturing became far less complicated because our plants were building much less varied products. This improved quality and efficiency. Inventory levels also were reduced, which saved money. And the dealers found it easier to sell a more manageable range of car and truck models and optional equipment.

It also could be said, I suppose, that part of our manufacturing control problems were eliminated from 1969 to 1972 when the corporation transferred all 11 of our assembly plants to the GM Assembly Division, and one parts plant to the General Motors Parts Division. In reality, however, this gave us less control over these plants and created more problems for our division as we tried to make sure that these plants under their new management adhered to the lofty goals in control and quality that we were setting for ourselves.

Engineering's chronic case of "overbudgetitis" required special attention. It had been so long since that staff met one of its budgets that red-ink operations had become a way of life. I brought into engineering a talented manufacturing executive, John Debbink, and made him executive engineer for administration with specific instructions to get engineering staff back into the parameters of its budget. Debbink was a skilled cost controller and manager, talent well evidenced by his performance as a plant manager. He was given almost a free hand in whipping the engineering staff's costs into line.

The first thing he did was to set up a procedure for evaluating each project as it came into engineering and giving it a very specific, detailed budget. When a program for a new transmission, a new suspension system or even a whole new car or truck came into Chevrolet engineering, Debbink and his staff went over the project in every facet and prepared a budget. He then kept a constant monitor on the project to see if its costs were getting out of line. If they were, we quickly focused management attention on the problem to get the project back within its budget. This process was in marked contrast to the previous method in which project costs were roughly estimated and not monitored. Often it was six months after a project had been finished that the finance staff discovered a huge cost overrun. By then it was too late to do anything but pay the bills.

Second, Debbink implemented a manpower allocation system for the staff's draftsmen and engineering assistants corps. At the time, each department in engineering had its own draftsmen and assistants. When there was work for that department, these people worked hard. When there wasn't they drank coffee and sat idle. The cost of wasted manpower was tremendous. So we scrapped that system and in its place organized a manpower pool. No one department had its own corps of draftsmen and assistants. When projects came into engineering and were assigned to specific departments, those departments received the necessary talent to do their work from the pool. When the project was finished the talent went back into the pool and was redeployed elsewhere. This enabled us to cut staff without diminishing the effectiveness of the operations.

It didn't seem long under this new system of controls before the engineering staff started meeting its budgets for the first time in almost two decades. In 1971, it actually spent $10 million less than its $120 million budget—a remarkable reversal.

With most of the remaining staffs, solving control problems meant simply disciplining the organization to stay within its budget. We decided in staff meetings that we simply would not tolerate budgetary excess. If costs started to get out of line, I wanted to know about that immediately so we could analyze the problem and get back into the proper cost framework. It worked.

These relatively simple yet effective techniques would give us quick control over the division in the short term. But over the longer term we needed more sophisticated control, not just to run the day-to-day business but to handle the challenge of responding to a vastly more complicated and rapidly changing marketplace. Controlling budgets would surely have an effect on the division's immediate performance. What we had to do then was get control of the division in such a way that we could reduce the time lag between the new-car order and the day the customer drove it out of the showroom, and use the information coming into various parts of the division to react quickly to changing markets and product demands. Modern computer control was the obvious answer. And our almost instant assessment of Chevy's controls problems, bolstered by the start-up fiasco with the 1969 models the previous fall, was that nothing less than a totally new system of computer control would serve our needs. There was no way we could salvage the piecemeal program then at work in the division. We needed a new system which offered a master plan for controlling and connecting all of the division's operations. The benefits of this system, we would learn, exceeded our wildest imaginings.

A systems analysis department was set up within the finance staff and charged with looking into every facet of the division's operations to determine what we needed in a systems program and then to design it and install it. By late 1969 this department was the largest systems operation in the automobile industry, numbering about 400 people in Chevrolet alone with again as many people loaned to us from the corporation. Over 800 systems engineers and computer specialists were looking into every nook and cranny of the Chevrolet Division's operations, hoping to bring it into fingertip control. We wanted to improve the response time in every facet of the business: In manufacturing, to build cars quickly and more efficiently; in material control, to keep our plant inventories properly balanced and in conformity with production schedules and to provide our headquarters with an on-time account of the inventory in each of our facilities; in marketing, to permit us to respond quickly to sudden market spurts around the country and to anticipate the emergence of new markets; and in finance, to give us an accurate current assessment of costs and cost-variances throughout the operation, as well as a foolproof system for billing our cars. I never wanted to see the 1969 model start-up incident repeated in Chevrolet.

The systems team developed a three-year program for replacing the division's computer system piece-by-piece. As we did this, we set up the new system in parallel with the old one. When we had the bugs worked out of the new system, we replaced the old one. However, we didn't remove the old equipment and system until sufficient time had elapsed to give us unfailing confidence in the new program.

147

There was strong opposition to these efforts on two fronts. The Chevy financial staff management was reluctant to accept and approve the new program because its approval was an admission that its previous efforts had been a failure (which of course they had been). They also were out of sorts because, while the new systems team reported nominally to the financial staff management, it also operated somewhat autonomously, befitting its approach, which was pervasive and entirely new to the division. This ruffled the feathers of the financial executives which we tried to smooth out by keeping them informed of the team's progress and recommendations. But the program was going to be installed and the financial people knew it.

There also was strong opposition to this program from The Fourteenth Floor. If Kyes and his superiors were angry that I was not doing the same old things everyone else had done in trying to solve Chevrolet's problems, they were doubly mad when I started adding systems personnel at a time when all divisions were being ordered to cut staff. The auto industry was in the midst of a mini-recession, and staff cuts were ordered to lower costs.

The personnel cuts that our own reorganization was accomplishing would not surface for well over a year. So I was being badgered by Kyes and others for adding more people. I tried to explain to them that what I was doing would pay off handsomely in improved profits in the future. But that argument seemed shallow to them, and they remained unconvinced. Nevertheless, to its credit, management did not force the issue. Had it done so, I could have been removed for not following orders. What happened I think is that the magnitude of Chevrolet's problems and the inability of anyone upstairs to understand them, plus the historic autonomy Chevy operated in kept The Fourteenth Floor management at a distance. In addition, it was obvious by now that we were working hard as hell, which I am sure was reassuring to them.

The computer system took less than the three years we planned to install. It gave us great flexibility in managing the business, a vehicle for relating the various segments of the business to each other and the reins of control that heretofore were missing. When it was used along with the various efficiency programs which we were working into each department of Chevrolet, the results were dramatic.

For the first time, we were able to correlate material orders to the sales orders from our dealers. In the new process, we read each new-car order as soon as it came into the corporation. If it was incorrect, we called the dealer, made the necessary corrections and kept the order in its original place in the production schedule. From this order we could determine the parts and material needs for the assembly plant which would fill it. Parts and material ordering for all Chevy plants was switched to headquarters. A plant manager would now get a production schedule far enough in advance to prepare his operations. He would not be involved in the material ordering process, unless there was a snafu in the system. This eliminated the need for panicky last-minute calls to fill material shortages. Division headquarters had a constant on-time report on the inventory of parts, materials, cars in production, and of the cars in transit to dealers. When shortages did occur, we knew exactly where the needed parts could be located, and they were shipped quickly.

For the dealer, this meant he could get an accurate report on where a specific car was in the production process and when it would be built and delivered. Most important, the system cut the response time from new-car order to delivery from an average of six weeks to less than three weeks. We were competitive with Ford in order response and better than some other divisions in the industry.

The process also identified sudden booms in the marketplace and helped us get to those markets with the right cars faster than we had been. Through fast identification of new-car orders, we were also able to forecast material needs several weeks in advance. This eliminated last-minute scrambling to keep the lines running, also helped us to use our facilities more efficiently.

Within two years good results were beginning to show up in our manufacturing costs. By 1972 the results were impressive. Since 1969 our costs per vehicle for premium freight expense had dropped from a whopping $7.31 per car, or $15 million total in 1969, to $1.66 per car, or $4 million total in 1972. This saving of about $11 million went right into the division's profits. The cost per car of interplant

149

shipment of material and parts dropped from $1.66 a car in 1969 to 18 cents in 1972, which of course showed that we were getting the right parts and materials to the right plants on time.

Perhaps the most dramatic result, and by far the biggest saving, came in inventory turnovers. While in 1968 we were turning over our inventory about 16 times a year, by 1972 the figure was 25 times a year, a 56 percent increase. This freed up hundreds of millions of dollars, previously tied up in inventory, for use elsewhere in the business.

With a pervasive system of computer control and corresponding programs to deproliferate our product lines, we were able with the introduction of our 1973 model cars to introduce an entirely new, simplified system for identifying our parts. It was a system developed by Dave Hill, head of our computer systems analysis team. He had been preparing the program for a number of years on his own, and put it into operation. Now the whole division was on the same parts identifying system. This simplification reduced the size of the engineering parts list, as an example, from a book 19 inches thick, to one nine inches thick.

Planning

Along with the organizational and control changes we had to find an effective way to bring the divergent facets of Chevrolet Division together. We needed a vehicle to coordinate the operations of Chevy's staffs which had grown distant and isolated from each other as the division grew without direction or plan in the 1960s. Chevrolet was just too big and far-flung for the kind of informal communication we had at Pontiac. Nowhere was this isolation and lack of communication more evident than in the sales staff. It was a powerful and important function of the division and yet it rarely communicated effectively with the rest of the division. To a lesser degree, each of the other staffs was likewise uncommunicative. This didn't mean that personnel from the various staffs were not on speaking terms. It meant that one staff knew very little about what was going on with another. The sales staff, for instance, had relatively little to say in product planning. It simply took

150

the cars that were built, when they were built, with the instruction to "sell the hell out of them." This was the state of the business at a time when the sales staff's contact with dealers and our customers should have been providing valuable information for the rest of the division on matters such as what cars were selling well, how consumer tastes were changing and how these changes would affect the demand for cars and trucks.

Something was needed to bring all of the functions of the division together and to give the sales staff a much better input into the running of the whole division. The answer was the Planning Committee, a 46-member group which included the staff heads, their assistants and a number of other department heads. Frank Winchell was appointed chairman of this committee. It met at least once a month, sometimes more often, in the Chevrolet Engineering Building in the GM Tech Center. For half a day we brought together in one room all of the diverse aspects of the business. The meetings were broken into two different sections—current product appraisal and forward product planning.

During the current product sessions we discussed in detail every aspect of the cars and trucks we were selling—costs analysis, budget variations, production problems, potential costs savings programs. I wanted everyone in the division to know what was going on throughout the division.

The forward product sessions dealt, in as much detail as possible, with our entire range of future product programs and proposals, as well as prospective changes in the way we were running the division.

Everyone in these meetings was encouraged to express freely his thoughts and suggestions on anything in the division. There was some reluctance for one executive to talk about another's responsibility. And when such comments were forthcoming they weren't received well by others, at first. This was natural enough. Barriers to communication are not easily dismantled. Before long, however, the various staff and department heads felt less threatened by the openness of our conversation. They saw the wisdom of communicating with each other. It was also soon evidenced in a more smoothly run business.

Most important, I started to crack the shell around the sales staff as I insisted that we cover in detail the description and definition of current and future products from the marketing and sales standpoint. Anything that affected the consumer had to be discussed, thus giving the sales people an opportunity to comment. What this meant was that on the one hand we would not discuss the change in material used in a connecting rod, for instance, because the customer cannot see, feel or perceive the material of a connecting rod. On the other hand, though, if there were proposed changes in wheelcover design, the location of ashtrays or the material used in seats, these would be discussed. These were things which directly affected how customers perceived our cars. And I wanted the sales people to have a say in these matters. They were our experts at selling our cars, and we had better hear what they had to say on how our proposed product changes would affect those sales.

I wanted them in on our product decisions from the day of inception, instead of the day of production. As it turned out, every staff began to have early input into our product decisions, and that was good. It was a Planning Committee discussion that launched the deproliferation program. And it was the Planning Committee that guided the development of the new 1974 Chevrolet pickup truck line which I think was the finest American light truck ever built.

In the course of my tenure at Chevrolet, several executives headed the Planning Committee, which proved to be an excellent means of broadening our executives' experience.

Within 18 months after I went to Chevrolet, after an invigorating meeting of the Planning Committee, I got an excited feeling. "Dammit," I thought, "we're starting to get this monster under control." It was my first twinge of confidence that things were getting better at Chevrolet. We had no dramatic charts to show that a great turnabout was in progress, but the division's morale was obviously buoyant. People were communicating with each other as never before in the division. While a year-and-a-half earlier I was overwhelmed by Chevrolet's massive problems, I was now getting the fundamental problems under control and

152

beginning to see the less visible problems in each section of the business.

We were working diligently on product quality problems and dealer relations. Product simplification and deproliferation made this easier. Also, I took the quality control function out of the manufacturing staff and had it report directly to me. Having the director of Reliability report to the General Manufacturing manager was like letting a student grade his own tests. It didn't make sense to have the man supposedly riding herd on our manufacturing quality report to the head of manufacturing.

Next, meetings were set up between our divisional staffs and their counterparts in Fisher Body Division and the GM Assembly Division. We were losing the final step in our quality program, the building of the cars, to these divisions, so I sought meetings among all of us to solve our quality problems and to make them aware of our commitment to building much better Chevrolets.

Before we lost control of all of our assembly operations, I instituted a program for testing and repairing faulty cars as they came off of the assembly line, as I had done at Pontiac, and the results were phenomenal. The program cost about $8 a car, which drove The Fourteenth Floor up the wall. But I figured one way or the other we would end up fixing the defects or paying to have them fixed through recall campaigns or dealer warranty bills. If we caught the mistakes before the cars were shipped, we would get the reputation through the dealer body and our customers of building better quality products. The program worked well until GMAD took over the assembly plants and discarded the repair programs in an economy move. The Pontiac program was also discarded when I left for Chevrolet.

We also tried, at Chevy, to spot defects which escaped our assembly line inspections by placing quality control personnel in key dealerships around the country. When an inordinate number of customer complaints about certain product defects were received, they were quickly relayed to Detroit where we went to work isolating the cause of the defect and fixing it.

We closely watched the quality indices from each of our manufacturing plants. If they started to drop we focused attention immediately on the problem. In a couple of cases,

I closed assembly plants for a day or longer when their quality dropped. Kyes was livid, and the Chevy people were shocked, too, because nothing like that had ever been done before. It seemed to me that Chevy would have been much worse off shipping outrageously poor quality cars than it would be shutting down the guilty plants and correcting the trouble spots.

Chevrolet's quality problems were due as much to the use of cheaper parts and material as they were to outright product defects. Under pressure from the corporation to increase or stabilize its falling profit margins, Chevrolet management, from about the mid-1960s on, had taken quality out of its products as a cost-cutting measure. Some of this cost-cutting was in highly visible areas such as the interior appointments, exterior trim and size of tires. This directly affected the customer's perception of Chevrolet, how he felt inside the car, or how it rode. This quality cutting eventually caught up with Chevrolet. The resale value of its products dropped as did its sales increases relative to the rest of the industry.

The cost squeeze was not all of Chevrolet's making. In fact, a good part of the crunch was caused by a corporate program of standardizing parts across many divisional product lines. The corporation conducted a massive campaign to use similar engines, optional equipment and other parts on more of the company's cars. The program was designed to minimize tooling costs and increase productivity. It looked good on paper, but in application each common part had to be designed for the needs of the largest car lines using it. Chevrolet got caught in the middle. It was forced to put on its cars suspension systems, brakes and other parts and equipment that were designed for heavier Buicks, Oldsmobiles and Cadillacs.

Chevy's parts costs, therefore, went up, not down. In the case of the Chevelle's front suspension system the cost was $7 per car more than the system it replaced. The corporation spent $140 million standardizing this front suspension system which was used on the Chevelle and $200 million in a similar program for the rear suspension. The rationale was that this would cut costs. But for Chevy, when it was all done, the costs were higher. Thus, increased costs were forced on Chevrolet cars which could

154

not be recouped through price increases because such a move would have taken the cars out of competition in the low-priced end of the market and would have infringed on the markets of the other GM divisions. By 1969 the manufacturing cost difference between an Impala and an Oldsmobile Delta 88 was only $70, where once it had been several times that. Yet the Olds selling prices were still at least several hundred dollars more than Chevy's, as they always had been. So to try to eke more profit out of its cars, Chevrolet was cutting corners in visible areas, and the division's sales and image suffered because it was offering a cheaper car.

We decided that the only way to solve Chevy's quality problems was to put money back into the product line and try to improve our profits by other means—increased sales volume plus the various cost-cutting and cost-controlling programs at work in the division. We upgraded upholstery. We put on tires a size or two larger than the required minimum (for a few extra dollars per car here we could show dramatic improvement in the ride and handling). Outside trim was improved and new trim was added, where there had been none. On the 1972 Caprice, I had the designers and engineers spend a few more dollars per car in a new front grille assembly which gave the car a decidedly Cadillac look. It was the luxury, top-of-the-line Chevrolet, so I thought the new look was appropriate. The move made Cadillac Division people angry, but Caprice sales took off like a rocket. In our product decisions we were emphasizing quality first and cost second. We were looking elsewhere in the division to save costs and improve profits.

One as-yet-untapped resource for profit improvement was the pent-up innovative ability of Chevy's management which was all but unused under the old setup. As each manager tried feverishly to just meet the obligations of a day's work schedule, he didn't have the time to innovate or sit back to think how he could better run his operation. In cases where people did propose cost-cutting programs, their superiors were too busy to listen. I remembered the plant manager's complaint that he had discovered half-a-dozen ways to cut his manufacturing costs but no one would listen to him. So I set up a profit improvement program in which we would track down, evaluate and implement every viable proposal to cut costs and improve profits. The man appointed to head this function was a very talented executive named Lou Bauer. His story is an interesting one and a source of great pride to me because of the immense contribution Lou Bauer made to Chevy's turnabout.

Just before I got to Chevrolet, Lou Bauer, the divisional comptroller, was put on the corporate shelf. He was a seasoned GM man, quiet, kind-looking with his hair parted close to the middle and brushed back on the sides. But in the corporate financial staff management's stewing over Chevrolet's problems, it apparently had determined that he wasn't doing his job, a result no doubt of the growing cost squeeze on the division. Instead of moving him out of Chevrolet, they moved a man, Bill Gossett, from the corporate financial staff, into Chevrolet above Bauer in a newly created position of Finance manager. In essence, Gossett was now the top financial executive in the division. What Bauer had was a non-job.

It wasn't very long after I got to the division that I realized Bauer was a highly competent executive. In staff meetings, nine times out of ten whenever anyone had a question, Bauer had the answer. And it was the right answer. He could easily go back into his experience at Chevy and add important historical perspective to problems as they occurred, comparing the solution offered earlier to the one proposed now. He knew Chevrolet's vast operations better than any other executive in the division.

So I consulted often with Lou Bauer, and he became a father-confessor to me as I tried to grapple with the division's problems. He also was a divisional ombudsman helping to put out fires as they occurred in management ranks and providing liaison between me and the suspicious segments of divisional management.

It wasn't long before he was becoming intimately involved in the major programs we were instituting at Chevrolet. He was instrumental in the execution of our efforts to cut down the size of the regional sales offices. He was in on the conception and development of the Planning Committee. And one of the major programs, our profit improvement project, he managed himself. If any segment of the business, or any executive had a program for cutting costs and improving profits, Lou Bauer was the man to see. If a manufacturing engineer devised a new process for plating or buffing our bumpers, Bauer would study the proposal, analyze the process and make an economic judgment of capital investment required to institute the program versus profit potential from its use. He would then offer his recommendation. If it passed his analysis, we would most likely put the program into effect. After approval, Bauer would follow the project until it was working smoothly. I would say that in two years as head of our profit improvement program, Lou Bauer helped save Chevrolet division $140 to $150 million, an incredible feat for an executive who had been put out to pasture. Sadly, he died unexpectedly of a heart attack shortly before I left GM.

By the start of the 1973 model run in late summer of 1972, Chevrolet was showing signs not only of recovery but downright good health. Our recovery had been delayed by the national United Auto Workers strike against GM in 1970. Had there been no strike, I am sure we would have shown dramatic recovery in the 1971 model year. However, the 67-day work stoppage and the months of local strikes and contract settlement hassles which followed masked the internal work that we were doing. It also destroyed the introduction of the new Vega, lowered manufacturing quality (a common occurrence after a national strike), and for a while stopped the division's momentum.

Nevertheless, by late 1971 we had the Chevrolet machine running well once again. By the start of the 1973 model run in the fall of 1972, we had the statistics to back up our claim of the division's turnabout. The improved quality of our cars was evident when market studies revealed that once again Chevrolets were ahead of the field in resale value. By the 1973 models, a one-year-old Impala was selling for $264 more than a comparable Ford Galaxie 500. The internal corporation quality control audit revealed a 66 percent improvement in the quality of a Chevrolet coming off the assembly line between 1969 and 1973 models. And most important, warranty costs of our new cars were down substantially. Where in 1968 we had the second highest average car warranty costs in General Motors, by 1973 we had the lowest.

The efficiency of our manufacturing operations was evidenced by a saving of $14.1 million in our labor budget for 1972. Almost every Chevrolet staff was showing black-ink budgets where they had been nothing but red ink before.

Our sales were a record in the 1972 model year, when we sold over three million cars and trucks—an auto industry first. Chevy was once again firmly implanted as the industry's number one sales division, and we also retook the truck sales leadership from Ford. The division was in good shape, ready to set sales records in both dollars and unit terms for 1973, which it did. And most important, the division had turned around its profit picture. We averted the forecasted loss in 1970. We lost money in the 1971 model year, however, due primarily to the UAW strike. But in 1972 we were well in the black ink. Our return on investment picked up to a respectable 11.3 percent.

The dealer body's net profits, before taxes and bonus, which sank to a low of $126 million in 1970's strike year, rebounded to $355 million in 1971 and an all-time high of $424 million in 1972. They were happy and excited.

The Chevy divisional morale was as high as during the best days I knew at Pontiac. Executives, who in the past were working their rears off and getting chewed out for not doing enough, now were working just as hard and making money for the division, the corporation and themselves.

I, too, was becoming more at ease in the monthly Administrative Committee meetings on The Fourteenth Floor because our success was obvious. Chevy was once again under control. John Beltz, the head of Oldsmobile, was the first executive to recognize publicly our efforts at Chevy. During one Administrative Committee meeting he said for everyone else to hear, "Dammit, John. It sure is good to see Chevy with some black-ink figures."

Top management was never as vocal as Beltz. Public compliments are not in the nature of the system because you are considered a professional manager and your applause comes in your paycheck. In my case, that was quite evident. After the completion of the 1971 calendar year, I had the annual bonus discussion with my superiors, and was given a handsome bonus for 1971, with the explanation that "This is more money than the actual profit figures at Chevrolet would warrant. But we know the good job you have done in turning Chevy around, and this is our indication of that." My total salary and bonus for 1971 was $550,000. And with the division's outstanding performance in 1972, it totalled even more, $650,000. It was more money than I had ever earned before. But it was overshadowed by the personal feeling of accomplishment I had because our Chevrolet team had turned the division completely around. General Motors' biggest headache was now its showpiece.

CHAPTER NINE

Getting the USA To See Chevrolet

A substantial part of Chevrolet's overall problems in 1969, yet a problem all to itself, was the division's antiquated marketing effort. For all of the hundreds of millions of dollars the division was pouring into its sales and marketing effort each year, the return was minimal. Chevy was getting less for its sales and marketing dollar than anyone else in the industry. A study of Chevy's marketing problems was in fact a study of the corporation's marketing problems. The marketing efforts of both were dominated by the sales staffs, who, while adept at dealer relations, were woefully ignorant of the sophisticated marketing techniques in modern business management. In the final analysis, the success of GM's sales and marketing effort in the 1960s and 1970s was due to its strong dealer body. And the existence of that strong dealer body was rooted in a half-century of history.

When General Motors was being reorganized in the 1920s, Richard H. Grant, the head of Delco Light Co., a GM subsidiary in Dayton, Ohio, was brought to Detroit to direct the Chevrolet sales program by Williams S. (Big Bill) Knudsen, the division's general manager. Grant was a man of exceedingly good sales and business sense, and he guided Chevrolet sales through the booming '20s. Under him, Chevrolet surpassed Ford in sales and production,

161

and emerged as the industry's number one division, a position it holds today. Grant's forte was organization. At Chevy he developed "The GM Quality Dealer Program" which set for the division, and later the corporation, a scientific system for selecting and locating new-car dealerships in the major markets around the country. This program analyzed prospective sales territories for their current and potential sales volume.

We then selected dealers for their financial strength and business backgrounds and located them in these territories. Until Grant came to Chevrolet there was no sophisticated business formula for selecting and placing new-car dealerships in the burgeoning American automobile market. Anybody with a few hundred dollars and a vacant lot could become a new-car dealer.

As head of Chevrolet sales and later as sales vice-president for the corporation, Dick Grant systematically built the General Motors dealer body and the company's field sales organization, which served and directed that dealer body into the strongest and most respected sales force in the industry. Grant earned a reputation as the world's top salesman as he went about weeding out poor dealers, putting in strong ones and developing a strong and effective field sales organization.

With the help and approval of Knudsen and Alfred P. Sloan, Jr., and others, Grant did such an unbelievably good job that the system he installed at General Motors 50 years ago is essentially the same system the company used when I was there. The corporation was surviving on the momentum he gave to the sales effort, particularly in the perpetual strength of its dealer force. General Motors is more successful than Ford, Chrysler or American Motors (and these three admit it readily) today because its almost 13,000 dealers are more successful. The products which have been offered by the four companies are pretty much the same, and the manufacturing processes do not differ much. So the single identifiable reason GM dominates in the American automotive industry is its giant size as best expressed in the breadth and strength of its dealer body. Because of this, General Motors has fared much better than the competition in long industry sales downturns. Proportionately fewer GM dealers folded during the auto industry slump which began with the Arab oil embargo in late 1973, even though the markets most severely hit were for big cars which had been the backbone of GM's profit structure. The automaker which never showed a loss in the Great Depression, while others were losing their shirts, was the only domestic car maker to turn a profit in the troubled first quarter of 1975. The profit in 1975 was modest to be sure (only $50 million or about 20 cents a share), but it was a profit nevertheless. The financial strength of GM's dealers enables them to absorb large inventories of new cars—taking the inventory cost burden off the corporation—and still ride through periods of red-ink operations.

As the corporate tie with its massive dealer body, the sales organization in General Motors possesses enormous strength. It is run almost autonomously from the corporation and completely dominates GM's marketing effort. In exercising its power in the past couple of decades, the sales organization has resisted change to a fault. There is an obvious unwillingness to tamper with a seemingly successful program no matter how old it is. So at a time when a practical distinction is being made between sales and marketing, General Motors sees them as one and the same. Most American companies today see their contact sales effort as only one part of an overall marketing program. GM sees the sales program as the marketing program. Where modern industry prepares an overall marketing strategy which scientifically ascertains consumer needs, designs products to fill those needs and then merchandises these products to bring the need, the product and the consumer together, GM relied on little more than rah-rah sales pitches and hard-sell techniques.

The reason GM's marketing is the least sophisticated in the automobile industry and so dominantly direct-sales oriented is that it is managed by people trained and skilled in the field sales organization, not by professional marketing people who are trained in consumer psychology and the theory of consumer research. All of the important sales and marketing slots at GM are filled by men who worked their way up the corporate ladder through the field sales organization—first in a zone office calling on dealers, then in the regional office, on to the headquarters or divisional sales staff, and then back into the field as the head of a zone or regional office. The vice-president of Marketing in the corporation is generally a former divisional sales manager.

Therefore, the General Motors marketing effort is guided by men whose training in buyer psychology is no deeper than the Dale Carnegie course they all are required to take, and whose idea of sophisticated sales is having a few drinks with the dealers. Their credo, often given freely in public, is that "There is no such thing as a bad day. Some are just better than others."

"There is no problem," these people say, "that can't be overcome by a good sales pitch."

They believe that they could sell powerboats in the middle of Death Valley. True to form in the throes of the horrendous sales drop in the winter of 1974-5, GM management's solution was to send executives around the country telling the media and market analysts that the industry just had to "sell" itself out of the slump. That automakers were not building the kinds of cars that the American consumers wanted apparently had nothing to do with the problem.

Aiding the intransigence of GM's sales staff against changing its techniques is a corporate philosophy articulated by Sloan in his book, *My Years With General Motors*, which states that GM is reluctant to pioneer in the auto industry, rather banking on letting others pioneer new markets and following them up with a bigger and more aggressive sales effort. The logical result of this, when I was there, was that General Motors was usually late in the market with new products, slow to respond to quick turns in the marketplace because it didn't perceive them when they were happening, and the least effective in the automobile industry in its advertising programs.

Furthermore, and perhaps most tragically, the corporation did no sophisticated product planning, which is a vital function of any marketing effort. The little planning that was done took place in the styling department which had little feel for the practicalities of the marketplace.

These efforts to direct product planning from the styling department successfully thwarted product proposals which did not originate there. It was, in part, the styling department's objections to the smaller, lighter vehicle programs we proposed which played a prominent role in scuttling those efforts.

The number of times GM has been beaten to the marketplace, especially by Ford, is legendary and a subject that often provokes dealers to heated anger. One Ford coup in the mid-1970s was the luxury-compact car market. The Ford Granada and Mercury Monarch, which sport a somewhat European look and flair, came into the marketplace in the fall of 1974 at a time when lighter sedans in the European tradition were drawing increasing favor from American customers in the backwash of the energy crisis. Many felt their arrival was sheer luck in timing. However, development of the Granada and Monarch began in 1971 long before the energy shortage was on the minds of American consumers.

At about the same time, GM was planning the remodeling of its compact car line. However, what GM produced was not new and different but rather essentially restyled versions of the existing compact car lines. These "new" Chevy Novas, Pontiac Venturas, Buick Apollos and Olds Omegas looked remarkably like the cars they were replacing, even though GM spent hundreds of millions of dollars to style and tool them up. The result for Chevy was that its 1975 compacts were outsold by Ford Division's cars, although not by a staggering margin. The reason the Ford advantage was not more is the strength of the Chevrolet dealer body, which has been able to sell despite the product disadvantage.

It is not that GM has not had talented marketing executives. Grant was unparalleled in his time. Harlow H. Curtice, who was president from 1953-58, was considered an exceptional executive and a highly qualified marketing man. Bunkie Knudsen, Big Bill's son, has an outstanding marketing mind. In a way, these men made their contribution and helped the corporation. Nevertheless, despite their efforts, the corporation reverence for the traditional way of doing business, abetted by the power of the sales staff and a generally conservative philosophy of product development, continually dictated against the surfacing of new ideas and the changes that would follow these ideas.

When Ed Cole ran the Chevrolet Division, he introduced the rear-engine Corvair, which was an entry in the compact car field. Because the car was more expensive to produce than the competition, the Ford Falcon, the company drastically cheapened the interior of the car to make it price competitive in the market. The Corvair bombed. However, GM styling produced a sporty show-car version of the Corvair which was put into production and named the Corvair Monza. It was a market success. And many industry people felt that it was the precursor of the sporty-compact car market which was exploited several years later by Ford Mustang, introduced in April 1964. Ironically, despite the success of the Corvair Monza, GM missed the broad market that this car was signaling. When the Corvair became enmeshed in safety problems, the Monza went down with it, and the sporty compact market had to wait until Ford provided the Mustang.

The Mustang itself may well have had its roots in GM. In 1962, the Chevrolet Division, under Bunkie Knudsen, introduced a sporty, compact experimental car, a version of the Chevy II, at the New York International Auto Show. The car was an instant hit. People crowded around the Chevy exhibit asking questions and requesting detailed information about the car: When was it going on sale? How much would it cost? The flow and substance of the questions indicated more than just a passing fancy with the car.

In the crowd were Ford marketing research people, I was later told by friends at Ford. They, too, noticed the attention being given to the experimental car. Knudsen was delighted with the response and asked the corporation for permission to build and sell the car. He was turned down after several requests and told it didn't seem a good risk for the investment. In the meantime, Ford research people were preparing a detailed report on the emerging taste for sporty compact cars. The experimental Chevy II was used in the documentation of their conclusions. Ford went on to build the Mustang which set all kinds of sales records. Chevrolet, which had beaten Ford, first with the Monza, then with the experimental Chevy II, took two and a half years to react to the Mustang, responding with the Camaro in the fall of 1967.

In the markets where GM has appeared first, by accident

or design, it has done exceptionally well. The Pontiac GTO is one example. So is the 1969 Pontiac Grand Prix, which led the wave of personal luxury intermediate-sized cars, featuring such lines as the Chevy Monte Carlo, Oldsmobile Cutlass, Mercury Cougar and Chrysler Cordoba. Both the GTO and the Grand Prix put hundreds of millions of dollars of profit into the Pontiac Division and GM coffers. Unfortunately, their experiences were the exception rather than the rule.

Just as it has been slow to enter new markets, GM was slow in identifying sudden upsurges in established markets and translating that information into increased production and merchandising effort. Information from the field which is used to spot swings in the marketplace was often slow and fragmented in coming into divisional and central headquarters. Once there, it was subjected to relatively unsophisticated analysis, after which a production program was approved and put into effect. At the center of this operation is the marketing staff which ideally should be the corporate vehicle for the development and application of sophisticated marketing theory and technique. In reality, it was little more than a statistics-gathering operation, which uses the numbers of cars sold to project sales trends and develop production schedules. This means that what is selling well in the field is usually what is going to be built. There is little to determine sales potential. The marketing staff theory is essentially this: "If a car is selling well now and has been selling well, then it is going to sell well." The staff also coordinates the corporate and divisional advertising to make sure one campaign doesn't conflict with another.

The corporate marketing staff had a substantial input into the setting of production schedules. Until I got to The Fourteenth Floor, the general procedure followed was this: The car and truck production schedules for four months ahead were set once a month at the production scheduling meeting. In attendance were the Executive Committee of top corporate officers and two marketing staff executives. One of these marketing executives was a guy named Godfrey E. Briefs who conducted a production proposal presentation. What Briefs presented was essentially the result of the marketing staff's sales forecasts. In addition, members

167

of the Executive Committee were given written presentations from each of the car and truck divisions which included their own sales forecast and a subsequent production request for a certain number of cars and trucks. Most of the time, these meetings relied primarily on what Briefs proposed, and his power therefore grew far in excess of his position in the company—essentially a marketing analyst. This was, it appeared to me, because during the 1960s Briefs became the marketing confidant of James M. Roche, who was either president or chairman from June 1, 1965, through 1971. So confident was Roche of Briefs' expertise that he often interrupted marketing or product proposals from divisional executives with the question, "Did you check with Briefs on this?" If you had, then Roche generally went along with whatever Briefs recommended.

In the production scheduling meetings, therefore, Briefs' presentation was usually followed by approval of his proposals, car for car, truck for truck. Many times there wasn't the slightest variance from what he proposed. It became obvious at Pontiac that I was wasting my time asking Fourteenth Floor management to increase the production of certain models. What I really had to do was to get Godfrey Briefs convinced that I needed certain car and truck production mixes. Then they would be built. Since Briefs' proposals were compiled essentially by the marketing staff's rather unsophisticated techniques, this seemed to be a very poor way to decide what General Motors would build and sell. The system of forecasting sales was too simple and error-prone. There was too much power placed in the hands of one man. The process led to all kinds of interdivisional squabbles for production, produced inflated production requests and promoted a rush among division executives to get into the good graces of Godfrey Briefs. It seemed whoever did the best job selling Briefs, received the best production mix.

The troubles in this system were highlighted each summer when production schedules were being assigned to the new models. The divisional managements, mindful that their real market needs, as reflected in reasoned production requests, were not going to be met, always inflated their requests in excess of what they really needed. The hope among them was that, when the political machinations were through and the divisional requests cut back, they would be left with a sufficient supply of new cars to meet the opening-day demand. Therefore, each summer, the total of all the production requests equalled some outlandish figure like 140 percent of the corporation's assembly capacity. It was a ridiculous situation. When the final schedules were set, the inevitable happened. Some divisions received an excess of some models and a shortage of others. No one had submitted realistic requests, and generally no one got a realistic mix. There generally was not an accurate allotment of the hot-selling models among the five divisions.

In advertising, General Motors usually took a back seat to its competitors. When I got to Chevrolet we hired Gallup-Robinson, the polling firm, which did studies on advertising effectiveness and memorability. One showed that GM's car divisions occupied five of the bottom seven places in a study of 20 automobile advertising campaigns. Volkswagen was top in the poll with an effectiveness rating about seven times that of the General Motors divisional average. This meant that Volkswagen of America for its $40-$50 million a year ad program was more effective than General Motors, which spent about $250 million. In retrospect, who could forget the various VW campaigns centered around the ubiquitous Beetle? And, frankly, who can remember most of the advertising of any one of the GM divisions?

Therefore, what greeted me when I arrived at Chevrolet was simply a divisional version of the greater corporate problem in marketing—an inability to anticipate short-term and long-term trends, very slow feedback of information from the field, generally ineffective advertising and a confused overall program of marketing and merchandising which reported along with the sales force to the general sales manager of the division and not to the general manager.

My study of Chevrolet's marketing techniques when I was a competitor at Pontiac prepared me for the depth of the problem at Chevrolet. But I was not ready for the open hostility of the Chevrolet dealer body which was frustrated with years of poor marketing and inadequate products.

As I mentioned earlier, the first dealer council meeting

I held at Chevy was a verbally bloody affair, with angry dealers from around the country complaining about Ford's leads in product innovation and advertising. At the time, Ford's "Better Idea" campaign was in full swing, and Ford had been touting its product victories over GM, such as the three-way tailgate for station wagons, which contributed to the dealer anger. "You keep promising us things will get better, but they never do," snapped one dealer during the meeting.

So after that we developed a policy of never promising the dealers anything we weren't sure we could deliver. In many cases, programs that we promised were already in the works when we made the promise, which built up credibility with them. We then went to work on the fundamental problems in Chevy marketing.

After my run-in with the General Sales Manager, Lee Mays, and his eventual promotion to the head spot at Buick, I met with his successor, Bob Lund, and we mapped out a program to strengthen every facet of Chevrolet's sales and marketing effort. Lund knew well that we had to do some things differently in terms of how we measured our marketing information and how our marketing efforts affected the division. We decided to model part of our product approach after Ford in respect to the way it positioned its cars and trucks in the marketplace as well as researched new markets and developed and promoted products for these markets. It often was said at that time that the ideal automotive division would be Chevrolet's strong dealer body selling Ford's products, which covered the marketplace adequately without inundating it. We were trying to put together the ideal automotive division.

It was obvious that Chevy needed a much more professional approach to marketing; so I looked inside and out of the company for someone to bring that to our division. The ideal man was right in Chevrolet, Thomas A. Staudt, a quiet-eyed, soft-spoken wizard with a Ph.D. in business administration. A former Chairman of the Marketing and Transportation Department at Michigan State University, Tom Staudt was brought into the Chevy operations shortly before I arrived by Ed Cole, who also recognized the corporation's marketing deficiencies. Highly respected in the field of marketing theory and execution, Staudt also was familiar with the auto industry, which he had served as a consultant for many years. It was my understanding that Cole put him in Chevy for seasoning and then planned to make him GM's vice-president of Sales.

However, once at Chevy, Staudt was stuck in a corner of the sales department and made ineffective by the strong sales staff, which regarded him as a suspect and unwanted intruder. After a few conversations with him, it was obvious to me that Tom Staudt was the man we needed to professionalize Chevrolet's total marketing effort. He was made assistant general sales manager for Marketing, reporting to Lund. We used the time of his appointment to divide the confused sales department into three distinct sections—the field sales organization, which handled dealer contact, sales and assistance; the service organization, which was spun off of the field sales activity, thereby elevating it in size and importance; and the total merchandising advertising and planning functions, which were put under Staudt.

In the ideal marketing organization, the whole sales-service-merchandising effort should have been put under Staudt, since a full marketing program today should begin with the conception of a new product and carry right through to the final sales and servicing effort. In such a setup the contact selling force reports to the marketing director and not vice versa. This idea was in the back of my mind, and I thought that eventually I would do it with Chevy. But trying it then would have been impossible to sell to The Fourteenth Floor. And it would have been so vigorously opposed in the division that Chevy could have come to a standstill, wrecking all our other efforts to revive the division. Nevertheless, our actions broke the marketing-merchandising effort away from the rest of the sales operation and elevated it in both power and prestige within the division. The added benefit was that we now had in the division's marketing effort a complete team.

On the one hand, I had Robert D. Lund, the aggressive, highly motivated and highly motivating sales executive revving up the direct sales effort. Broad-faced and handsome, with wavy hair behind a slightly receding hairline, Lund was a hard-working executive with an infectious, positive attitude. (He now heads the Chevrolet Division.)

On the other hand, I had Tom Staudt, a quiet, contemplative and confident marketing theorist who devised marketing controls such as ad effectiveness tests; created purpose for our whole effort; and directed and laid out forward planning for our merchandising effort where there had been none before. And while my predecessor left the responsibility for the division's sales-marketing-merchandising programs in the hands of the general sales manager, I wanted to be intimately involved with this effort when I ran Chevrolet. I wanted to be sure that a new level of professionalism was brought into the division's marketing and I wanted to see the results.

Staudt began a systematic study of the sales operation in much the same way Winchell was studying the engineering operation. And, like Winchell, he recommended that our marketing function be organized according to the project-manager concept to simplify responsibilities and shorten and clarify the lines of communication. We began the project manager program in advertising. Each car line had a specific advertising manager assigned to it. His job was to know thoroughly this specific car line, its market and its competition. In the past, an ad manager handled several lines of cars such as the standard-sized cars, the intermediates and the compact cars. He was juggling so many balls that he had little control over the various projects. The customers who chose among these car lines were generally quite different in motivation, economic bracket and age. Asking one guy to be an advertising expert at once in all of these areas was asking too much. He either gave too little attention to every car line, or too much to one line and nothing to the others. With responsibility now for only one car line, such as the standard cars—Caprice, Impala, Biscayne—the advertising product manager could get deeply involved in specific knowledge of that market, its buyer characteristics, consumer attitudes and sales potential. He could direct advertising that was more specific to the needs of buyers of those cars. He also could analyze where we could outstrip the competition in these markets.

In a forward look to what I wanted to do with Chevrolet marketing, in general, we seized upon the introduction of the mini-car Vega as a pilot program for using a product manager for the entire marketing of a car line. Staudt

served as product manager here. He began by determining
the needs of the market this car was to serve and then devising advertising, merchandising and product programs to
push the car in that market. The thrust of Staudt's suggestions was to build and advertise the Vega as the quality
domestic small car, and upgrade the interior appointments
to bring this home to the owner. For reasons detailed in a
later chapter, "The Vega," not all of his well-prepared and
documented proposals were accepted by the corporation.

Nevertheless, Staudt built a competent, well-educated
and professional staff. His unobtrusive, confident manner
soon won over not only the skeptics in the sales department but others in the division who came into direct contact with him in the Planning Committee meetings. This
was good for both Staudt and Chevy, because within
months people from all parts of the business were coming
to him with problems that had the slightest bearing on
marketing. The sales people were especially willing to
consult with him, which made his programs more effective.
They saw him no longer as an intruder, but rather as a
vital cog in our new outlook.

One of his specialties was marketing research, an area
as yet undeveloped at Chevrolet. In product research
Staudt and his staff went several steps beyond the accepted
techniques of testing prospective products before controlled
audiences. His people not only expanded the types and
forms of research programs, they messaged the information differently. They wanted not only to know whether or
not people liked our cars, but why. They wanted to know
the effect these cars had on how the customers felt about
themselves and the division. Subtle perceptions are often
missed in product research, yet they can hold the key to
success or failure. We wanted to incorporate the latest
information with the most modern techniques to minimize
the risk of failure and maximize the sales potential of our
new products. If through modern marketing techniques we
could reduce the risk of failure, then in the long run we
could afford to be more pioneering, which, though contrary to the corporate philosophy, I felt was the only way
to solidify and improve Chevrolet's (and GM's) market
position.

In advertising, our research programs were entirely new

173

to the division. There had been very little testing of Chevrolet advertising by the division. This meant that the sales people became the division's experts in advertising. If the sales manager and his staff okayed a program, the ad campaign ran whether the audience liked it or not. And most often, from the studies we soon conducted, the audience didn't care much for Chevrolet advertising. I insisted that we pretest and post-test every commercial, especially TV commercials, to see whether they were effective. In the past, objections were raised to pretesting TV commercials on the grounds that it cost upward of $50,000 to prepare a TV commercial, too costly a venture to be scrapped if tests showed it would be ineffective. That was a dandy piece of circuitous logic, because the $50,000 cost was small when compared with the money Chevrolet was wasting on prime-time TV advertising with ineffective commercials. The cost in wasted advertising could be as much as a million dollars.

So we tested our advertising for effectiveness in all media—print, radio and TV. In the case of TV ads, we showed them to controlled audiences in storyboard form— a succession of slides strung together to simulate a film. This is a technique commonly used in consumer-goods industries. When tests indicated the commercial would be effective, we ran it. If not, we scrapped it or made changes to make it effective. Then we post-tested our commercials to discern exactly how effective they had been, how we could make them more effective and whether we needed to modify our pre-testing program to make it more accurate. Post-testing showed us that the Vega was being projected as a larger and more expensive car. We were able then to change the emphasis of our Vega advertising to point up the fun, happiness and economy associated with driving this mini-car. Similar studies told us that we had to concentrate Chevelle advertising on the car's comfortable overall ride and handling characteristics, which were not noticed by many of the intermediate-sized car buyers.

About the time we started work on the Chevrolet advertising it was close to being the worst in the industry, despite having the single largest auto division ad budget in the industry—$100 million-plus a year. Not only was it generally ineffective but there was no continuing theme. Rather, in the course of a model run, Chevy advertising would change themes several times. This, of course, destroyed continuity and left the customer confused or uninterested.

When I talked with Don Frey, the former head of Ford Division, I asked him how he had made his division's advertising more effective, because I remembered it showed substantial improvement under his leadership.

"It was simple," he replied. "I called our agency in and told them, if their advertising didn't improve, I was going to fire them."

"That's all there was?" I asked.

"Yep. That's all there was."

I wasn't sure I wanted to use that approach with our agency, Campbell-Ewald. I don't like to threaten people. And there was underway already a powerful campaign directed by Kyes to oust the agency, so my threat certainly wasn't needed.

Kyes had a dislike for Campbell-Ewald Chairman Tom Adams. The origin of his dislike I never knew, but in his attempts to fire the agency, Kyes ran into opposition from his Fourteenth Floor colleagues, many of whom were good friends of Adams and would have no part of an agency execution. So the cunning Kyes wanted to pick away at the agency's business a piece at a time. He suggested that I solicit outside presentations for the new Vega account. The little car was coming out in the fall of 1970, and his reasoning was that we could sell a switch in agencies for this business on the grounds that the Vega was going into an entirely new market for subcompact cars, heretofore unexplored. So Chevy needed new blood in its advertising to attack this market. The Vega business amounted to about $18 million out of a total division budget in excess of $100 million.

I reviewed the implications of such a move and the serious effects it would have in putting hundreds of people out of work; creating a difficult transition period for the division in taking part of its business from one agency to another; and complicating the administrative process by doing business with two separate firms. I decided against the switch because, after all, with the exception of a few outstanding people like Bill Bernbach, whom I've never met, most advertising people are the same. While Bernbach was probably the most creative ad man in the world, his agency Doyle, Dane & Bernbach already had the Volkswagen account and wasn't likely to abandon a $50-million account with VW for an $18-million account with Chevrolet. What's more, my conversations with the agency revealed Campbell-Ewald people to be certainly as competent as any in the industry, and I figured they could do better work with more guidance under a new, sophisticated marketing approach.

I sought a meeting with Tom Adams to go over our plans for Chevrolet advertising. We met in my office, and I told him I thought Chevy advertising needed drastic improvement. I asked him why it was bad and what he thought could be done to improve it. From our discussion, I quickly learned that there were fundamental underlying problems in the relationship between Campbell-Ewald and Chevrolet which were obstructing the agency's ability to perform creatively.

The foremost problem was a cumbersome process of approving the agency's advertising proposals, which let divisional management nitpick campaigns to death, making them ineffective. A second problem was that Campbell-Ewald was providing some additional services for free to Chevy, which other agencies did not provide free to their clients. To pay for this added expense, the agency had to skimp on its creative costs in preparing Chevy advertising.

Under the existing approval system, Adams explained, Chevrolet advertising was approved first by the advertising manager, then by the regional sales managers, the assistant general sales managers, the general sales manager, the divisional general manager and a similar set of management levels in the corporate marketing staff before going to The Fourteenth Floor.

At each level, especially in the division, the advertising was picked apart with specific changes recommended or ordered. I think a lot of the Chevy sales people felt that it was their job to make changes and suggestions, even though the process usually emasculated the division's advertising campaigns. To adapt to this practice, the agency switched its priorities from preparing advertising which it thought would be effective to devising campaigns it thought could get through the approval process. Chevy's advertising became what the sales staff thought it should be and not necessarily what the market needed.

In this respect, Chevy was not unique. Auto advertising is a lot like auto design in that everyone in the company thinks he is an expert, but few really are. More than one car was designed a certain way and built because a top executive thought it was a nice car, despite numerous market analyses that dictated a different approach. It is the same with advertising. So it is not unexpected that a lot of the auto advertising prattle which goes out over the air-waves today has the harsh, brassy ring of a showroom sales pitch. This is exactly what one would expect of advertising approved and sometimes directed by a salesman. The criticism is often offered that much of Detroit's advertising talks only to itself, crowing about its sales conquests or telling a customer what he or she needs rather than telling how this product fills his or her needs. That is because it means a lot to the sales staff that its division is number one. But that doesn't mean much to the customer who wants to know, "What have you got for me? How does this car fit my needs?"

At Pontiac we had a somewhat similar problem which I eliminated by making Pontiac advertising my special concern. This was going to be the same approach at Chevrolet. I asked Adams: "What do you think we should do?"

He responded: "Let's eliminate this complicated approval procedure. Let's get to the point where you just tell us you think the advertising is good or bad. If you don't like it, we'll do it over."

"Fine," I said, "we will all meet in one room at the same time and look at your proposals. If the consensus is that it is good, you will get our approval. If not, we'll reject the whole thing, but we won't get into a process of picking the campaign apart, saying the car should be bigger in this magazine ad or that the tune should be different in this TV ad. We will try to give you guidance without trying to be the guys who design the advertising."

This was not easy to do because it took away much of the power of the sales staff which had grown accustomed to more or less tailoring the division's advertising to its personal tastes. But we did shorten up the approval system as well as the time it took to process an advertising campaign. Also, at Staudt's suggestion, we set objectives with the agency, which represented our goals for Chevy advertising, and against which we could measure the effectiveness of our advertising. In the past, the division had let the agency set its own objectives, which were sufficiently vague as to be easily met each year.

I was surprised when Adams told me that Campbell-Ewald was cutting cost corners because it wasn't making much money on the Chevrolet account. Everybody in the business thought the Chevrolet account with its big budget was the plum of all auto advertising. Industry people assumed that Campbell-Ewald was making big profits on the account. I asked Adams what things his agency was doing for free that other agencies were not. He listed certain special studies, odd research programs and about a half-dozen other things. "We have to pinch in other areas where we might be able to do a better job for you," he said.

I asked Chevy's auditor, Lou Kemp, to look into the Adams claims, study their books and then check with the other GM divisions and their ad agencies to see what services were being paid for compared with Chevrolet. Sure enough, when Kemp came back he said that Chevy was asking more of its agency than the other GM divisions. So we began paying for all of these services, which put over $1 million into Campbell-Ewald profits. This freed up other funds for more creative advertising and, I am sure, made the agency an attractive prospect for the merger which took place with the Interpublic Group of Companies. Instead of just being a marginal operation, the agency was once again profitable. I was accused by Kyes of using my position to help my friend Tom Adams. I've often helped my friends in the business, but I've always demanded better performance.

Later in 1971, I tried to revise the compensation program with the agency to equate their revenue with the effectiveness of their advertising. Most advertising payments then and now are based on flat fees and a percentage of the total cost of the advertising media space. My idea was to change this and relate it to how well the agency did its job. After all, advertising is a form of selling, and most salesmen are paid on how effective their

178

selling is, not whether they just make the necessary calls. If the agency did a good job, it would make plenty of money. If it did a poor job, it would just break even. I proposed that we begin with a pilot program using a small series of ads in one medium, say magazines. Staudt, his staff and the agency could work out the details of measuring the effectiveness of the advertising, perhaps simply using one of the reputable polling companies to determine the results. And the financial people could work out a sliding scale of payment for the advertising based on its effectiveness. If it worked in one medium, then we could expand it until it was a program covering all of the division's advertising.

The idea caused several near heart attacks in the agency and General Motors because it was revolutionary. The corporate people opposed it because the financial staff said that we could not develop an adequate method of payment for the agency's work. And the agency opposed it on the ground that it could create effective short-term advertising which was harmful to the division's long-term objectives. Both excuses were a gossamer in front of the real quarrel, which was with anything that upset the current way of doing business. I could not even get a pilot program approved.

It was not too long after we started to pay close attention to Chevy advertising and to introduce new techniques to predetermine the effectiveness of our campaigns that better results started showing up in our ratings. By 1972, we had improved Chevrolet's advertising effectiveness. A Gallup-Robinson poll, which showed Chevrolet advertising to be in the bottom seven in the industry in 1970, showed that in 1972 we had jumped into the top ten in a field of twenty. We were a far cry from VW, to be sure, but we were considerably better than before. We had the most effective advertising in GM. We were getting more for our money.

Giving the agency a freer hand in its creativity spurred it on to better efforts. We also sought to establish a single unwavering campaign theme at the beginning of each model run to carry through the whole year. This is the most effective way to keep yourself in the public memory. Dodge advertising was well known for its campaigns, such as the Dodge Rebellion. Ford's Better Idea campaign was so effective that it lasted for years. We did exhaustive studies to determine the best central theme for Chevrolet advertising. As a result, we discovered that Chevrolet more than any other car in America, except Ford, enjoyed a status with the American motorist that transcended mere commercial aspects of the business. Over a long time, Chevrolet had become closely identified with the building of America from a small to a large industrial nation. I think this was in part because of the role of Chevrolet trucks in the growth of commerce and construction in the United States during the '20s, '30s and '40s. It was American to buy a Chevrolet. Our cars were an American tradition. I wanted to try to reaffirm that relationship in our advertising.

At this time, the country was split in the midst of the Vietnam conflict which had forced Lyndon Johnson out of office and was making the road tough for his successor. The country was, and still is, racked with racial conflict. The institutions of the United States, including big business, were under fire. There was a tremendous amount of criticism being focused on America and the American Way of Life. Much of it was justified. But in addition to this, there seemed to be so much guilt and negativism surrounding the American Way that we wanted to reaffirm our position in the minds of American consumers by building our image around the good aspects of this country and the good aspects of our cars.

We discussed this approach with the agency, and it developed a campaign around a theme that said, "We live in a great and beautiful country and our car with its instant availability gives you the opportunity to get out and see this beautiful country." If there is one thing that America has, it is fantastic and diverse topography, from the Grand Canyon to Pikes Peak; from the geometrically-shaped wheat fields of the plains states to the sleepy Smoky Mountains of Tennessee; from craggy Maine seacoast to soft bluffs of Southern California. We put our cars in these beautiful settings alongside clean-cut, middle American families with whom just about everybody could identify. There were no curvaceous blondes lying prone on our car hoods, or adjusting five-speed gear shifts while clad in mini-skirts. We were not pushing the hard sell. The dealers could do that. We were trying to build a warm, friendly feeling around our cars and our division.

The nostalgia craze was coming, so we dipped into Chevrolet's past to resurrect the popular Chevy tune "See the USA in your Chevrolet," which had been closely identified with the old Dinah Shore TV Show on Sunday nights. Then we incorporated the song's jingle, Chevy's identification with the building of America and the good things about American Life into the slogan for our 1973 advertising: "Chevrolet—Building a Better Way to See the USA."

The campaign was a resounding success. Not only did the division's image and sales pick up, but we got widespread approval for the theme of the campaign. We got letters from the President of the United States, senators, congressmen and the general public lauding Chevrolet for promoting the positive and good aspects of this country. Chevrolet was obviously enhancing and cementing its favored position with Americans. My plans were to keep that theme each year, adding to it and modifying it as we built up to a massive Chevrolet-America campaign during the Bicentennial celebrations for the United States.

But a tangential feature to this advertising campaign got me into hot water with The Fourteenth Floor. One objective of this theme was to avoid any unpleasantness in our advertising similar to that associated with the traditional loud, clanging, fast-talking, auctioneer-type babbling which typifies much of today's radio and TV auto advertising. We felt that our advertising should not contribute to the blight and pollution on TV and radio and in print. It occurred to me that in a broader sense we were part of the blight, however, with our billboard advertising which was cluttering the countryside. If we were going to stress the beautiful aspects of the country we lived in, we had to do our part to make it beautiful. So I ordered that all Chevrolet billboard advertising be dismantled. This order got tremendous negative reaction from the agency and some top corporate people. One of the points of great pride in advertising is the positioning of billboards. People boast about having the billboard right at the Triborough Bridge in New York City, the one at the turn in Lakeshore Drive

181

in Chicago or one right by the Los Angeles International Airport. The agency objected, but I insisted that we were not going to contribute to the pollution of the great countryside we were promoting in our ads by keeping these billboards. We took down Chevy advertising from 250 permanent divisional billboards and thousands of others which were being used temporarily for the new-car introduction period. I thought that our size and importance to the American economy would draw sufficient attention to this action so that others would follow suit. But The Fourteenth Floor wouldn't let me publicize this program. The Marketing Policy Group said this publicity would reflect adversely on the other GM divisions, some of which grabbed up our key billboard spots practically the moment we vacated them.

Nevertheless, as we examined and improved Chevrolet's marketing techniques, we exposed practices which, though time-tested, were not fundamentally sound in a business sense. One such practice was the "strike-while-the-iron-is-hot" method of advertising which essentially dictates that, when business is good, more money should be spent on advertising. And when it is bad, less should be spent. This practice, as best I could see, was an outgrowth of the finance staff's method of costing out GM products. When production volume determinations were made at the beginning of the year, a certain amount of money was assigned to each car for advertising. So advertising expense was a budget variable based on volume, irrespective of market needs. If the volume was up, then you got more advertising money. If it was down then you got less. If, hypothetically, $100 a car was earmarked for advertising on a projected volume of one million units, the ad budget was $100 million. If production turned out to be 900,000, however, then the division only spent $90 million.

From a marketing standpoint, that seemed to be backwards. It seemed reasonable that in bad times you should spend more in advertising to go out and reach the customers, and you should conserve some in good times when there is consumer willingness to buy. With Staudt's guidance, we devised a program to test this theory during a slump in car sales one year. Three very similar markets were picked for the test. In the first, we did nothing in the way of extra promotion and advertising. In the second, we put more money into a special promotional campaign directed from Detroit. In the third, we instituted the same special campaign, except that we brought the dealers into the promotion effort with showroom placards, banners and their own supplemental programs. The test lasted several weeks. The results were dramatic. As I recall, the second test area showed something like a 25 percent sales increase over the area which had no new promotional effort. The third area showed around a 60 percent sales increase over the first area. We were ecstatic. "We really have something here," I told Staudt and his people. As I recall, we showed the results to the Marketing Policy Group. The hope was to sell the corporation on the idea of banking some of our advertising dollars in good times, then spending them in bad times. Our enthusiasm was quickly dampened by the cordial but uninterested reception Staudt and I received from the Marketing Group. The committee members listened politely to our presentation, asked a couple of perfunctory questions and thanked us for our efforts. That was the last we heard from them except for the fact that we weren't permitted to use this method of allocating our advertising budget on a division-wide basis.

Perhaps the most exciting marketing development while I was at Chevrolet involved our attempts to devise a system for reducing response time to sudden changes in the market and spotting these changes in advance of the competition. We figured our improved product, our revamped marketing programs and better dealer relations could coalesce in a mighty sales effort if we could get to the market with the right cars quickly and anticipate which models would boom next. The only way to do this and incorporate the valuable sales information we had available in the field was with computers.

As part of the overall systems analysis effort, James P. Wallace, a very bright computer-scientist, was eventually brought into Chevy from the marketing staff. With him, Wallace brought a computer program, called Marketing Information System (MIS), which he had developed for anticipating market demands. It was predicated on the accepted axiom of the automobile business that very few things happen in the marketplace overnight. With the exception of the Arab oil embargo and attendant gasoline shortages (which actually compressed into a few weeks a sales pattern which would have taken several years to develop), history has shown that trends in the automobile business develop slowly. Evolutionary change, the industry calls it. The consumer switch to smaller cars is an example well documented in the growth pattern of the car industry since 1965. While everyone was crying, "The consumer has suddenly switched to smaller, better-mileage cars," after the embargo hit, the records show that he had been switching since 1965. From 1965 until the record sales year of 1973, the industry as a whole grew 25 percent, while the domestic manufacturer's share grew only 10 percent, mostly in the compact and subcompact car markets. Imported car sales, however, grew 122 percent. They were offering smaller cars with better gasoline mileage. This was a dramatic growth but not an overnight occurrence. It took seven years. The trend was easily documented in annual car sales and the gradually increasing penetration of foreign cars into the American marketplace.

It was Jim Wallace's contention that seemingly sudden changes in the marketplace on a short-term basis were similarly documented in the mass of sales data that the auto companies had on hand. But predicting short- and long-term trends from this data required much more sophisticated assimilation than just adding the sales figures every 10 days. Wallace's program incorporated not only trended sales analysis but also the circumstances around those sales: Where they were occurring, what inventories were in relation to sales and, perhaps most important, what were the dealers' gross profits on the cars they were selling. Gross profits are a good sign of things to come because they indicate the willingness of customers to pay top dollar for a car. When hot new cars are introduced, such as the 1969 Pontiac Grand Prix or the Cadillac Seville, dealer gross profits are almost unbelievable—$1,000 a car and up ($3,000 on the Seville). When those grosses start to decline, even though the sales rates are seemingly high, this indicates that customers are not quite as enthused about the car. They are bargaining more with the dealer. This is a sign that the car is starting to fade. If the decline continues, inventories are going to build up and production may have to be slowed. For the same reason, when gross profits on a car increase, it indicates that demand is up and inventories are going to shrink unless production is increased.

Wallace developed this program for Chevrolet's use, but it incorporated the rest of the GM lines as well as the lines of our competitors. While gross profit figures were not available for competitive makes, we used all the other sales information that was readily available. We put the program to work at Chevrolet in November, 1971, and it worked.

When it indicated that Chevelle sales were going to drop off in May, sure enough, about May 1, Chevelle sales would start to slip. If it indicated that sales of the Ford Galaxie 500 would tail off in November, then in November we would start seeing lower sales of the Galaxie 500. Each month people from the various departments in the division sat down with us and went over Wallace's report. It was in printed form with about a ten-to-twelve-paragraph summary in the front followed by tens of pages of graphs, curves and statistical charts which supported the summary. The report was about four inches thick and somewhat dull to read. But the information it contained was invaluable to our marketing effort. Knowing which car-line sales were going up, and which were going to drop, we were able to adjust our production schedules. We were able to give increased merchandising support to the models gaining momentum, and we were able to focus management attention on the models which were starting to decline.

At Chevrolet, we began to feel that we were getting a better hold of our business by responding faster to changes in the marketplace which we now could see in advance. Our ultimate hope was to get corporate approval of this program and use it to produce production schedules which represented the art of the real and the possible in terms of properly allocating products to the divisions according to their needs and the corporation's ability to build. This would be a computer program analysis replacing the less sophisticated system which resulted in Godfrey Briefs' production recommendations. Doing that was an ironic goal because at one time Wallace's operations reported to Briefs, who tried to get the program disbanded early in 1971. And it was at this time that we acquired Wallace with his Marketing Information System for Chevrolet.

When I moved to The Fourteenth Floor, naturally my horizons widened and I expanded Wallace's program to include all of the GM car and truck divisions. We then held monthly interdivisional reviews with top divisional management and some corporate brass. After I left the corporation, the effectiveness of the Marketing Information System was so well demonstrated that the program was further improved and revised to give it capability for all of GM's operations worldwide. As far as I know, it is in use today in varying degrees, although the dynamic force behind it, its creator Jim Wallace, left General Motors to set up his own business.

CHAPTER TEN

The Vega

General Motors was genuinely embarrassed and irritated by Ford's dominance in product innovations during the 1960s. So the auspicious occasion of the opening of the gleaming, white 50-story General Motors Building in midtown Manhattan was chosen to make the corporation's most dramatic product announcement of the decade.

On October 3, 1968, Chairman James M. Roche told an audience of dignitaries, reporters and employees that in two years GM would introduce a new sub-compact car designed for American tastes and developed to counterattack the growing trend toward foreign cars. It was a bold announcement for a corporation which usually refuses to talk about future products for fear of hurting the sales of those already in dealer showrooms. (Current Chairman Thomas Murphy's announcement to shareholders in May of '75 that GM would build a sub-sub-compact car, the Chevette, in 1976 was the only similar departure from tradition since Roche's speech in 1968.) And Roche went one step further. He predicted that the car, code-named the XP-887 and later named the Vega, would weigh less than 2,000 pounds, be priced at the level of the Volkswagen Beetle— less than $1,800 then—and feature the most automated assembly process known to American automotive technology.

Roche's announcement was a coup for General Motors. It sent Ford scrambling. While the Number Two automaker had been pondering a mini-car of its own, which became the Pinto, it was now only rumored. General Motors, the gigantic car manufacturer, had beaten Ford to the punch in Ford's own field—smaller cars. The auto world and the nation's millions of car enthusiasts were excited by the prospect of a GM small car. Importers privately cringed while maintaining public postures of quiet composure. To many, GM's announcement simply meant that the American automotive industry finally had decided to get serious about competing in the small-car market. Led by General Motors, the giant domestic auto industry was going to flex its muscle and swat the pesky fly of imported cars off its shoulder. Future tantalizing revelations about the XP-887's all new aluminum engine, fail-safe sophisticated marketing research and highly automated assembly technique built an image around the car that said, "This is a revolutionary change from a company and industry that heretofore have stressed slow, evolutionary change." That staid, conservative, down-the-middle-of-the-road General Motors was leading the way told critics in government, the consumer movement and the general population that Detroit was mending its ways. This was going to be the first car that consumers told GM they wanted to buy and not vice versa.

This two-year rush of decidedly favorable publicity prior to the introduction of the Vega was to be the only continually good publicity the car would ever get. Behind the flag-waving publicity push leading up to the introduction of the car in September 1970 existed a confused and diffuse program of development for the Vega which raised serious questions about the viability of the car. This program also produced a hostile relationship between the corporate staffs, which essentially designed and engineered the car, and the Chevrolet Division which was to sell it.

A study of the conception and gestation of the Vega reveals not a lesson in scientific marketing and development, but rather a classic case of management ineptitude.

In the early and mid-1960s, Chevrolet and Pontiac Divisions, conscious of the growing appeal of smaller, foreign-built cars, were working separately on futuristic small cars.

At Pontiac we developed our small car mindful that Chevy would probably get first crack at such a new market. But we wanted our own version just in case we got lucky and either beat Chevy into the market or were allowed to come in quickly afterward. The Chevrolet staff also was fast at work on its mini-car. Ed Cole, who was executive vice-president of Operating Staffs, was working on his own small-car project using the corporate engineering and design staffs. He took this program with him into the president's office in 1967. When the corporation started talking seriously about a mini-car, Cole's version was chosen. It was chosen mainly because of Cole's corporate position and the forcefulness of his personality and salesmanship. The proposals from Chevy and Pontiac were rejected. Pontiac eventually was entirely cut out of the small-car development meetings. The new mini-car was Cole's baby, and it was to be given to Chevrolet to sell.

While the early announcement of the Vega was a break with GM tradition, so was the manner of its development. The guiding corporate precept of centralized policymaking and decentralized decision making was totally and purposefully ignored. GM tradition dictated that The Fourteenth Floor would decide that a new market, such as small cars, should be developed (policy) and then would assign the responsibility for producing a car for that market to one of the five car divisions (operations). However, with the Vega, not only did corporate management make the decision to enter the mini-car market, it also decided to develop the car itself. This was to pave the way for many of the Vega's troubles. It was a corporate car, not a divisional car. Ed Cole was the chief engineer, and Bill Mitchell, the vice-president of the Design Staff, was the chief stylist. It was being put together by people at least one step removed from the marketplace. There was no system of checks and balances. The divisions reported to The Fourteenth Floor. But The Fourteenth Floor reported only to itself.

When Roche announced the car, his information came from statistical abstractions. Not one prototype had been built or tested. There was no model to point to because the car existed only in financial statistics and blueprints derived from a consensus of the existing sub-compact cars, all of them foreign and some of them built by GM overseas. The engineering blueprints were costed out by the central financial staff in conjunction with the Chevrolet finance staff. Their work was to be proven shoddy and haphazard. All of this information provided a weight and price class for the car that became the foundation for the chairman's startling small car announcement. Shortly thereafter, the first prototype was delivered from the central staff to Chevrolet.

The first indication that this was an unwise way to build a GM car was not long in coming. Chevrolet engineers took the prototype Vega to the GM test track in Milford, Michigan. After eight miles, the front of the Vega broke off. The front end of the car separated from the rest of the vehicle. It must have set a record for the shortest time taken for a new car to fall apart. The car was sent to Chevy engineering where the front end was beefed up. Already the small, svelte American answer to foreign car craftsmanship was putting on weight—20 pounds in understructure to hold the front end intact. Thus began a fattening process of the "less-than-2,000-pound" mini-car that would take it to ponderous proportions in weight and price compared to the original car described at the opening of the new GM building in New York City.

From the first day I stepped into the Chevrolet division, in 1969, it was obvious that the Vega was in real trouble. General Motors was pinning its image and prestige on this car, and there was practically no interest in it in the division. We were to start building the car in little more than a year, and nobody wanted anything to do with it. The Vega was an orphan. Chevy's engineering staff was disgruntled because it felt it had proposed a much better car (and it had) than the one it was given by the corporate management. It was going through the motions of preparing the car for production, and that was all. Engineers are a very proud group. They take immense interest and pride in their creations, but they are very disinclined to accept the work of somebody else. This was not their car, so they did not want to work on it.

Other complaints were surfacing about the car from inside the division. While it looked similar to the Fiat 124, the division executives felt it could have been more contemporary European with a greater use of glass. Work that was proceeding on the car revealed that the central staff had completely misgauged the weight and cost of the car they designed. Simple items such as side door crash protection beams were left out of the original drawings even though they were in the plans for all future GM cars. To be a viable product on the road, the Vega was going to arrive on the market heavier and costlier than the company's target because it was already close to 200 pounds heavier than planned, and production costs were running way above estimates. These miscalculated costs were pervasive: The estimated body costs were wrong; the chassis costs were wrong; and the tooling costs were wrong. So it was obvious that the Vega was going to miss the market in weight and cost, and it was feared that Chevrolet people who didn't want the "corporate car" were going to bear the blame from the public.

The biggest objection from the division, specifically the engineering staff, was reserved for the Vega engine. In their own small-car program, Chevy's engineers developed a neat little short-stroke, four-cylinder engine with a cross-flow hemispherical cylinder head. It was made of cast iron and fit easily into the sub-compact car body. The Engineering Policy Group, however, discarded this engine along with the Chevy-designed mini-car in favor of the engine pushed by Cole and the corporate engineering staff which featured an aluminum cylinder block with a cast iron head.

The industry had fooled around for a couple of decades with aluminum engines. Each of the auto companies at one time or another had an aluminum engine, GM most recently in the early 1960s. And each in turn rejected their aluminum engines primarily because they cost too much to build. The lure of aluminum is its weight. It is one-third as heavy as iron. If this much weight can be taken out of the engine, it means more weight can be taken out of the car's structure which supports the engine weight—suspension systems can be made lighter and brakes can be made smaller. Weight is all-important in building small cars, to keep them small, lower in cost, and light in fuel consumption.

The disadvantages of aluminum compared with the iron are that it does not wear as well and is distorted easier during the heat of operation. To improve the wearing

191

characteristics of aluminum engines in the past, iron sleeves were put into each cylinder and used with standard aluminum pistons. The costs of doing this in a small engine exceeded the cost saving from the lower-weight material. So aluminum engines for smaller cars were generally rejected. The heat distortion problems of aluminum engines have never been fully solved.

Reynolds Aluminum Co., however, kept working on the various problems with these engines and, in the late 1960s, developed a longer wearing material—aluminum with a 17 percent silicone content—for the die-cast engine block. This proved compatible with iron-coated aluminum pistons and was a fairly simple production process. Ed Cole fell in love with it, even though this method was still more costly than the time-proven cast iron engine process. He was hooked on the Reynolds idea. In addition, the corporation engineers decided that the aluminum engine needed a longer piston stroke, and a bigger, iron cylinder head. The longer stroke (distance traveled by the piston) approach was chosen to better control engine emissions. And the iron head was needed to withstand the pressure of combustion.

Now during the '60s, the auto industry became enamored of short-stroke, high-speed engines for their compactness and performance. Chevy's engineers felt that emission problems could be worked out within the framework of such a short-stroke design for the Vega. But the corporate engineers, instead, went the route of a longer stroke engine which was traditionally less polluting. So while they were going for an innovative production process in using aluminum, they were relying on an old basic design for the engine. What resulted was a relatively large, noisy, top-heavy combination of aluminum and iron which cost far too much to build, looked like it had been taken off a 1920 farm tractor and weighed more than the cast iron engine Chevy had proposed, or the foreign built, four-cylinder iron engine the Ford Pinto was to use. Chevy engineers were ashamed of the engine. With the start of engine production rapidly approaching there were still several major engineering problems to be solved such as excessive wear of the valve lifters and the camshaft. Yet Chevy engineers were almost totally disinterested in the car.

The most important problem for me with the Vega, therefore, was to motivate the hell out of the division to get this car into as good shape as we could before introduction. So we made the final development of the Vega the first project of the new Planning Committee and gave it top priority with the revised marketing department. Then I told each and every staff of the division: "It does not matter now that you had an argument over the nature of this car and lost. Like it or not, we are going to be building and selling this car. Any way you look at it, this car is going into the market as a Chevrolet. We can't put a little notice in the glove box saying, 'We didn't design this car, Central Staff did.' It's a Chevrolet, and we are going to be responsible to the public for how good a car we build and sell."

The reaction was surprisingly positive. A genuine effort was constructed in the division to put life and spirit into the Vega project. As the Lordstown, Ohio, assembly plant was converted to Vega production, we also introduced an intense program for quality control with the target of making the first cars off the assembly line the best quality cars, from a manufacturing standpoint, ever built. As the starting date approached we put tens of additional inspectors and workers on the line and introduced a computerized quality control program in which each car was inspected as it came off the line, and, if necessary, repaired. As the defects in workmanship showed up during inspections, they were typed on a keyboard on the spot and immediately displayed on a screen in the area where the defective work was being done. This quickly told workers where the defective work was occurring, that a problem had developed. Generally this information stopped the defect after only a handful of cars had been built, where previously the defect often went uncured until later after as many as four weeks worth of defective cars had been assembled and sometimes even sold to customers. We also test drove the first 2,000 Vegas built and a sizeable proportion of the others thereafter. The corporation gave us strong support in approving the additional manpower and expenses we needed to improve the quality of these cars. I was able when the car was introduced to brag that it was the best quality car we'd ever introduced. I'm thankful no one asked me if I thought it was the best designed and engineered car ever introduced.

The marketing problems with the Vega were substantial. By late winter 1969, it was well known in the corporation that the car was far above its original estimates in weight and cost. The Fourteenth Floor was pretty damn shook up about this. The big question was: "How the hell can we promote a car that is going to be bigger and cost more than any car in the market in which it is supposed to compete?" Mr. Roche said the market target was the small foreign cars and the price would be in "the ball park" of the VW Beetle. How could we explain the variance from that?

Tom Staudt and his staff attacked this problem vigorously. They initiated a raft of background tests and evaluations to determine how the car was going to be perceived and, thus, how we should sell it. They tested the car as a stripped down model and as a fully equipped luxury model. They researched a long list of potential names. In all they spent more than half-a-million dollars in marketing research. The Chevrolet Planning Committee discussed and explored all aspects of the mini-car. The marketing people made recommendations for selling the car based on its higher price and heavier size. They advised that we abandon the cheap end of the mini-car market, spend a few more dollars on trim and appointments and sell it as a premium small car. Since, as yet, a name for the car had not been chosen—we were still using the code name XP-887—they advised that we call the car the Gemini.

Specifically, the marketing people argued that since the cost of the car was going to be too high to price it head on with the Beetle or others like the Toyota Corolla, we should add about $12 to 15 more cost to the car in chrome stripping, interior trim and a larger tire size to give it a real quality, semi-luxury motif. Then we should sell it for the higher price we were going to need to make any money on the car. The recommendation struck a familiar chord at GM. The corporation has always been very good at selling its cars as the "best version" in a specific market class. Moving customers into more expensive cars, and selling the best quality product in each market was a concept at the heart of Sloan's marketing philosophy from the time Chevy was reorganized in the 1920s to better compete with Ford. We presented this recommendation to the Engineering Policy Committee and received its enthusiastic but tentative approval to develop a plusher mini-car than the others in the market.

Naming the car was a matter of serious concern for both Staudt and me. A good name can "make" a marketing program simply because of the image it conjures in the customer's mind. A bad name can make marketing a new product a difficult chore. The studies that we conducted showed that one name stood head and shoulders above everyone—Gemini. It had a kind of magic not found often in car names. Since the NASA space program was constantly in the public eye, the name Gemini was instantly familiar and it sort of imparted some of the aura of excitement around the space program to our car. What's more, we learned from the tests that the public instantly identified the phonics of it. When pronounced, it almost said "G-M-ini." At the bottom of the list of preferred names was Vega, which had very little automotive connotation to it. It sounded like a disease or a fungus. But modern, scientific marketing tests notwithstanding, Ed Cole liked the name Vega and so did top corporate management who threw our test results out the window and named the mini-car the Vega. We were told that corporate management was afraid that we would overdo the GM association by using the name Gemini.

That was a tough battle to lose. But an even bigger and totally unexpected loss came a short time later, just before the public introduction of the Vega on September 10, 1970, when the Pricing Review Committee on The Fourteenth Floor completely countermanded the tentative okay from the Engineering Policy Group giving us approval to upgrade the Vega. While they kept our recommended selling price, they took out most of the additional interior and exterior trim we'd added and knocked back the standard tire for the car by one size. The saving on the tire change was about $3 a car, but the loss in appearance, ride, and fuel economy to the customer was much more than that. If customers wanted a plush Vega, they were going to have to pay for it through the optional equipment route. They were not going to get it as part of the basic car package.

195

The Pricing Review people obviously wanted to extract the last dime of profit from the car even if it meant hurting the car's image and our marketing program. The incredible thing to me was that the members of this group were almost exactly the same people who sat on the Engineering Policy Group. What they were giving us with one hand they were taking away with the other. In a sense they were contradicting themselves. I still can't figure how they could do that. And I never did get a satisfactory answer to my questions about it. I guess in the final analysis the corporation was more cost-profit oriented than it was product-marketing oriented.

Ford management which earlier announced the base Pinto price as $1,919, I suspect to give us an indication of what they thought the price level should be, must have been gleeful when we introduced a plain-Jane Vega with a basic sticker price of $2,091. This put the car $172 higher than the base Pinto, $311 more than the VW standard Beetle and $192 more than the Super Beetle. It was literally priced out of the market. It weighed 382 pounds more than the Beetle and 161 pounds more than the Pinto. We had earlier forecast that 400,000 Vegas would be sold our first year, taking 100,000 of those sales from VW. But I was now privately suspecting that our targets were too high.

The timing of the price announcement for our 1971 cars couldn't have come at a worse time for me. The media got hold of them in time for a lunch I was hosting in connection with our national new-car press preview. As general manager of Chevy, I was called on to explain the unexplainable. How could we call our car "competitive" when it weighed almost 400 pounds more, and was priced more than $300 above the intended foreign competitor? What happened to the car Mr. Roche announced two years earlier? It was an embarrassing experience for me and highlighted a problem I had all through the publicity build-up for the Vega. While I was convinced that we at Chevy were doing our best with the car that was given to us, I was called upon by the corporation to tout the car far beyond my own personal convictions about it. There was a moral conflict in this. In press releases, I was praising the name Vega when I knew it was one of the worst we could have chosen. And now I was justifying the price and weight of the car when I knew well that a better-designed and engineered car would have weighed less and cost less to build. The realization that hundreds of thousands of jobs, the health of the national economy and my job depended on the sales of Chevy cars gave some justification for this and similar actions hyping some of our products. But this conflict never did resolve itself fully in my mind and was one of the many factors that precipitated my departure from the company.

At this particular press conference, however, I said that the new car was different and more American than the Beetle and that, viewed in this context, the price and weight were fully justified. I said with a clear conscience that it was a quality car, which it was because we road-tested the first 2,000 off the assembly line and spent millions of dollars to reinspect and repair each vehicle. The press was not happy with my answer, however. One particular exchange sticks in my mind. In reply to a question on whether the Vega was in the "ball park" with the Beetle, as Mr. Roche had promised, I answered, "When you consider the car we are talking about, equipped as it is, I think it is in the ball park." I thought to myself: "Well, now I've worked around that problem pretty well."

Then Dan Fisher of the Los Angeles *Times* fired off the zinger. "Would your boss accept a ball-park estimate of your anticipated expense budget at Chevrolet for the next year that was a plus or minus 25 percent?"

The question struck right at the heart of the problem with this car. The Vega had missed its mark in almost every respect because it was poorly managed from the very beginning. In the past we all knew of management foul-ups, but this knowledge was kept internally. With this car, however, management incompetence was out in the open for everyone to see.

I cringed at the question, then rattled off an answer telling Fisher that he missed the point, that the Vega represented good value for the money to be spent. All of which was true. But we still didn't have an answer for the imported car popularity which their increasing sales figures later proved.

After lunch, I went back to my Chevrolet office and

thought, "What a helluva lousy way to kick off a new car." But these problems were purely academic by midnight when the United Auto Workers struck General Motors. The 24,000 Vegas we had on dealer lots or in transit were all we were going to see for two-and-a-half months. The strike ashcanned the '71 Vega for all intents and purposes. Our dealers didn't get an adequate supply of the cars until well after January 1, 1971. In the 1971 model year we sold only 245,000 of the mini-cars, compared with Ford's Pinto sales of 316,700. GM lost money on the Vega that year.

We regrouped and decided to make a second major effort with the car for the 1972 model year which began in September of 1971. There were several things in our favor. President Nixon's economic actions on August 15, 1971, abolishing the 7 percent excise tax and putting a surtax on imported-car sales—which then were taking 20 percent of all car sales in the U.S.—made us competitive with the Beetle and its foreign friends. The decision to let the dollar fluctuate vis-à-vis other currencies soon resulted in the upward revaluation of the German *deutschmark* and the Japanese *yen*, which eventually gave the Vega a pricing advantage over the foreigners. We were also able to take about $20 of cost out by using lighter-gauged steel in a few places on the car. And there was still plenty of public interest in the automated assembly line at Lordstown, which had giant Unimates spot welding our cars, and a seemingly happy work force which was cranking out almost 100 cars an hour. The Vega design was intended to last for at least five model years, so we had very little new to do to the car except bring it up to the 1972 safety and pollution standards. We got off to a strong start for the 1972 model year, with substantial stocks of cars in the hands of our dealers. It looked like the Vega would get off the ground (albeit a year late), challenge the Pinto and take a swift kick at the imports. That was too hasty an assessment.

On October 1, 1971, a most unfortunate occurrence took place. The corporation transferred the last three car assembly plants under our jurisdiction to the GM Assembly Division (GMAD). It completed a management move giving the tough GMAD almost complete control over the company's assembly operations. The rationale for the move was that one assembly division in the place of several produced a more efficient and coordinated production operation. The plants we lost control of were the Ypsilanti, Michigan, Nova plant; the St. Louis Chevelle and Impala plant; and the Lordstown Vega plant. Chevrolet now had control only over its Flint, Michigan truck assembly plant.

When each car division assembly plant was turned over to GMAD, so was the accompanying Fisher Body Plant (traditionally in GM, Fisher Body Division had built all car bodies and transferred them to nearby assembly plants where the body was joined to the rest of the car). In each case previously, a GMAD takeover resulted in huge union squabbles and many local strikes. The combining of each body plant and assembly plant under one management, where there had been two, eliminated the need for two separate union locals which had dealt with the two separate managements. So problems developed as two union local leaderships tried to out-muscle each other for representation of the new, single local.

Once this matter was settled, the new leadership began to bargain with GMAD for a single local contract where there had been two. In these negotiations, the union tried to incorporate the features of the old contracts which were best for the workers, and the company tried to incorporate the features that were best for itself. Natural eruptions resulted. In addition, GMAD had a tough reputation among unionists for trying to eliminate jobs and extract more work from each worker. This technique was evident practically from the day GMAD took over the Lordstown plant, when it fired 700 workers, many employed in quality control areas. The division also took out the computer quality-defect feedback system. The company said the move by GMAD was just to eliminate extra jobs that had been created to ease through the problems of starting up an entirely new assembly process. They said that no one was being asked to work any harder. But the union people didn't buy that reasoning one bit. They are no dummies. They can count. And they knew that when you took 700 people off the assembly line, you were going to work the butts off the ones who remained. The UAW balked. GMAD remained firm on its firings; the union wasn't going to tell GM how to run its operations.

199

The brewing trouble in Lordstown attracted national news media attention, especially after a couple of reporters touring Lordstown noticed a few long-haired youths on the line and in the union halls. The stories started flying fast and furiously out of this little central Ohio town that a monumental sociological struggle was taking place as the young, militant workers rebelled against the mindless system of mass production. This struggle was called "the Lordstown Syndrome." It captured the imagination of young Americans, the very people to whom we were trying to sell new Vegas. The stories completely misplayed the situation. Sure, young workers were rebelling against the system in America. But not at Lordstown. What was taking place was a classical confrontation of union and management over the oldest issue in the history of auto-labor relations—a work speed-up. The company was trying to do the same job with fewer workers, and the workers were refusing to go along. In February of 1972, UAW's Lordstown local struck the Lordstown assembly plant, and a bitter three-week work stoppage resulted. The second start-up of the Vega was halted only months after it began.

In the battle between the company and the UAW, which was being waged in the press, once-happy workers at the Lordstown plant charged that the company was so productivity conscious that the workers were being forced to push cars along the line that were little more than "pieces of junk." The company countered that the workers were sabotaging the cars. That feud left the unfortunate conclusion in the minds of consumers that both sides felt the Vega was of poor quality. That impression gained the status of fact when the company was forced to recall 132,000 cars for defective carburetors, which had caused fires.

Later, when the heat distortion problems inherent in aluminum engines surfaced, Vega engines started to burn out when excessive thermal expansion forced water out of the cooling system. Once the water was forced out, the engine's ability to cool was impaired. The little engines overheated and eventually were severely damaged or completely burnt out.

These problems led to the recall of thousands more Vegas with engine trouble. Chevrolet, trying to overcome the engine's poor public image, later introduced a 60,000-

mile warranty which was a very costly burden to the division and the corporation.

By the end of the Lordstown strike, the once bright little mini-car from GM was held in disrepute by a growing segment of the market. The combination of the Lordstown strike, its erroneous "young-worker-against-the-system" theme and the real and apparent quality problems the car was experiencing just about ruined its image and our marketing program. The strike ended, but the 1972 Vega was shot. Consequently, two years after its dramatic introductions, the Vega was in deep trouble. The recall campaigns of themselves may have been weathered. But the combination of quality-sociological-labor problems was too much for the car and company. We went back to the drawing board to correct our quality problems and prepare another marketing program. This was launched with the introduction of the 1973 models, and by the 1974 model year the Vega was finally selling close to the Pinto, largely on the sheer strength of the Chevrolet dealer force.

Nevertheless, the decision to turn over the Vega plant to GMAD was devastating to our program for the car. A year later might have been a much better time. And the car itself, like the camel which was a horse designed by a committee, arrived on the scene vastly different than planned in weight and cost, primarily because it was designed on The Fourteenth Floor, far removed from the practical demands of the marketplace. I hope the Vega lesson was learned well by GM management and that the knowledge gleaned from this lesson is applied in the development of future products. As for the Vega, it was discontinued at the end of the 1977 model year.

CHAPTER ELEVEN

The 1970 UAW Strike

It was late August, 1970. I was heading up to The Fourteenth Floor for a meeting with the chairman, James Roche, and the president, Ed Cole. The subject of our meeting was the growing probability of a national strike against the corporation by the United Auto Workers Union.

My concern was that a long strike would kill the momentum we'd been building for a year and a half in turning Chevrolet around. We were pointing to the 1971 model year, which began in mid-September, to put it all together and begin to harvest the fruits of our labors. The signs that the division was becoming vibrant once again were beginning to appear: Our profits were picking up; we'd avoided a loss for the 1970 model year; the division's market penetration was improving. We had the business coming under control, and we were working hard on our weaknesses. The new "mini" Vega was being introduced in less than a month, and in this car we had our first entry in the import-dominated sub-compact car market. What made us so sure that the 1971 model year would be a big winner for Chevrolet was that our programs for turning the division around were coming on stream at the same time the national economy was working its way out of a long recession. The combination of the two would be dynamite for Chevy.

In the way, however, was the prospect of a long and

tortuous UAW strike. All the signs pointed to GM as the strike target. Complicating the usual economic tensions surrounding auto contract negotiations was a unique situation. The union was in political turmoil following the death of its leader, Walter Reuther, and the selection of his successor, Leonard Woodcock. The company was totally unsympathetic to this problem and quite possibly looking to use this turmoil as a bargaining tool to forge a more-than-satisfactory three-year pact.

Reuther, the nation's most forward-thinking labor leader, had died with his wife in a plane crash May 9, 1970, on the way to the union's Educational and Recreational Center at Black Lake in Northern Michigan. His death shocked the union. It couldn't have come at a worse time. The battle plan for the triennial contract talks with the automotive Big Three had been drawn up several weeks earlier at the UAW convention in Atlantic City. Reuther, who designed the plan, was the general leading his troops into battle. He had the consolidated union support behind him. His death wrecked everything. As the shock of his death faded, the union was rocked by political scrambling as the 25-man Executive Board chose his successor. The vote was 13 to 12 in favor of Woodcock, who headed the union's GM bargaining team, over Douglas Fraser (now President, succeeding Woodcock), who headed up the Chrysler negotiations team. It hurt the union politically and emotionally.

It was public knowledge that the union was split as a result of the vote favoring Woodcock (who is now United States Ambassador to the Peoples Republic of China). The depth of this conflict, however, was not widely known. I learned how serious a problem this was for the union from an official of a UAW Chrysler local with whom I worked out a couple of times a week at a Vic Tanny gym near the GM Tech Center. The local official was a physical fitness nut like I am. We met while working out together during the lunch hour. We talked about the union and the company and the auto business and became friends. It was during a workout in midsummer that he told me: "Woodcock is under tremendous pressure from inside the union to strike General Motors because Ford and Chrysler have been previous strike targets and there is a large faction in the union which wants to prove that he doesn't have the nerve to strike GM."

I told him that I didn't think Woodcock lacked the nerve to strike anybody but that I always had the impression, from afar, that he was more constructive than strike-oriented. He'd rather find a different way to get a fair, good contract for his workers than to put GM's 400,000 workers out on the street, drain the union's coffers and sock it to the national economy. The official agreed but added that Woodcock needed a way out. He appeared to have no alternative to striking.

So I asked for a meeting with Roche and Cole, who were directing the bargaining efforts of the labor relations staff, to tell them what I knew. As I recall we met in Roche's office, and I related to them what the UAW local official had told me and the devastating effect of a strike on Chevrolet's efforts. Then I offered a solution: We should quietly ask the President of the United States to come onto the scene, without interfering with the actual give-and-take bargaining, and simply tell both parties that because the country was just coming out of a recession it would be in the best interests of the country if the company and the union forgot about a strike for 60 to 90 days and continued to bargain to settle on a contract. It would keep our GM assembly lines running. It would keep the Chevy turnabout in high gear. And most important it would give the union a way out of its political turmoil. With a Republican as President, and the UAW's expressed opposition to Richard Nixon a matter of public record, however, I was not sure Woodcock would buy this solution. In fact, both the industry and the union traditionally eschew government intervention in their bargaining. But it seemed to me the only way to avoid a costly strike. Woodcock could simply turn to his detractors and say, "Look, I'm not afraid to strike, but the President has asked us to continue bargaining in the best interests of the country and the national economy." From a strictly business standpoint, it appeared to me to be a sound proposal.

But Roche and Cole rejected it immediately. Their answer was essentially: "We don't want the government running our business." They missed the point entirely. This was not an invitation to government control. It was a way

205

to avoid a costly strike. It was a sound business proposition. But there were more than business factors at work in the decision. For one thing, GM executives are almost paranoid about even the suspicion that anyone but themselves is in control of the business. They bristle at the thought of government influence in car building, even though that influence has become vast and prominent in the 1970's. At a time when some developed nations, such as Sweden and Germany, are giving the working person a say in how the company is managed, GM executives and their counterparts at the other domestic auto companies discard the idea out of hand. In fact, among all layers of management at GM, there are those with outright contempt for the working person. To them the worker is devoid of integrity and purpose. It is deep-seated. Its psychological roots may be in the fact that many GM managers came from working-class families in the Depression, and now that they have "made it," they reject this past and its contradiction with the present. Not all feel this way, but enough do that it affects the company's union dealings.

On one occasion, for example, the company was having labor difficulties with a major Fisher Body plant which was vital to all of the automotive operations. The labor relations people were trying to negotiate a solution to the workers' complaints. Eventually, the problem worked its way up to The Fourteenth Floor. At one of several meetings discussing this problem, Dick Terrell looked up from his place at the table, and said, "Well, the hell with it. We'll just close the plant and move all of the work somewhere else." Practically everyone at the meeting was shocked to hear a top executive say something like that, even if he felt that way. This was no way to run a business, this was robber-baron psychology. It was going back to the goon squad days of auto-labor relations. Things just weren't done that way anymore. What Terrell was implicitly saying, it seemed to me, was that, "If they won't toe the line, we'll just shut down that plant and put the work someplace else." A Chevy executive who was with me at the meeting, said, "Can you believe that guy saying something like that in this day and age?"

On another occasion, in 1971, we were growing concerned about the intrusion of foreign cars into the American car market. Not only sales but jobs were being lost as the importers sold more and more cars in this market. So Norm Ellis, Chevy's director of Personnel, set up a meeting between our division management and the UAW's GM bargaining people to talk about the whole matter of foreign car sales and what we and the union could do to combat them. The union group was headed by Irving Bluestone, who succeeded Woodcock as head of the UAW's GM unit. He brought along his assistants and several union specialists in this area. We had an exciting dialogue about the whole problem of product cost, productivity and the loss of jobs. I was really impressed with the union's grasp of the problem and understanding of the automobile business. I consider Irv Bluestone to be one of the most intelligent men I've met. The union had set up seminars and conferences on the problem. We had no ulterior motive in getting together other than to share our views of the problem of increasing foreign car sales and what we thought could be done to combat them. However, shortly after the second meeting, Ellis got a call from the labor relations staff: "Tell De Lorean to stop the meeting with the union." Through him, I was told to keep myself out of any labor areas. I was to run Chevy. The labor relations staff would handle union matters.

That was generally the same attitude which greeted me in management's rejection of the idea for avoiding a UAW strike at GM. I stewed over their refusal. September came, and the union announced in Detroit that GM and Chrysler were chosen as twin strike targets. Everyone in the world knew, however, that, if it came down to a strike, the union would shut down GM. With less than a week remaining before the strike deadline, I went back and petitioned the corporate management again to consider my alternative proposal. By this time, the guys at Chevy were sick with the thought that the whole damn operation was going to be closed by a strike. What made it seem especially worthless was that the two sides were not really far apart on the economics of a contract settlement. Once again, management refused my request to ask President Nixon to intervene.

I went back to my office downstairs and brooded. "This strike," I thought, "isn't going to be caused by a huge difference in the settlement proposals. It is really going to be caused by the internal politics of the union and the stubbornness of General Motors management who refuse to see the union's side of the issue and the chance we had to help it out." It also seemed tragic that America would be thwarted in its efforts to come out of the recession. The real losers would be working Americans. In distress, I did the unthinkable. I sought to get President Nixon involved in my own way.

I did not know the President, so I called up Max Fisher, a prominent American and international businessman, who had been a big Detroit fund raiser for the 1968 Nixon campaign. I told him about the problem in the union, GM management's willingness to let a strike occur and my proposal to stem the strike. Fisher knew full well the implications of a GM strike on the national economy. He agreed to call the President. He couldn't get hold of him because the President was in a meeting. So Fisher talked with a Nixon adviser, who said that the President's office, surprisingly, was unreceptive to White House involvement and felt that a GM strike wouldn't have much effect on the economy, an incredible position, I thought.

I had no contacts there, so I practically begged Fisher to call the White House again. He did. I am not sure whom he talked with, but within a short time someone at the White House called up GM management, either Roche or the labor relations people, and asked, "Do you want our help in the negotiations?" The response from The Fourteenth Floor was, "Hell no! We don't want any government help here. We know how to handle these things ourselves." That ended my plan. I was reprimanded for meddling in matters outside of my purview as head of Chevrolet. Several days later, a bitter 67-day strike of GM by the UAW began. It put a 5 percent dent in the Gross National Product and held back the nation's recovery from the '69-'70 recession by up to half a year. The union's GM strike fund went broke, and the UAW had to borrow $30 million, using as collateral its Black Lake facility, the Union's Retiree Center, and its headquarters, Solidarity House. Thousands of workers lost their savings. Chevrolet's full recovery was pushed back two years. The Vega fell on its face at the start of the model year because we had only

208

24,000 cars to sell for two-and-a-half months. We blew millions in our original Vega introduction advertising campaign and then we had to spend a like amount in a second introductory campaign after January 1, 1971. The division wasted about $12 million in advertising in the October-December quarter of 1970. All this was caused by a strike that I think didn't have to be.

CHAPTER TWELVE

Pushing Small Cars in a Big Car Company

General Motors' forte historically has been selling big cars. Its large profits have come from bigger, more expensive cars. It is in the intermediate and full-sized car markets that GM has dominated. This has been a corporate objective. American car customers, historically, have been willing to pay hundreds of dollars more for a few extra pounds and inches in their cars. The returns to the company are obvious. When I was with GM, a $300 to $400 difference between the building costs of a Chevrolet Caprice and a Cadillac DeVille, a bigger car, was small compared to a $3,800 difference in the sticker price. The difference in profit to General Motors on the two cars is over $2,000. Within the Chevrolet itself, the Caprice, a full-sized car, generated about $200 more profit per car on the average than the Chevelle, an intermediate, and about $400 more than the Nova, a compact.

Ford Motor Co., which has been strongest in the small-car market, recognized the fact that "big is more profitable than small" in the mid-to-late 1960s. It committed $800 million to a program which redesigned and revamped the corporation's big cars, especially those offered by the Lincoln-Mercury Division. The investment paid off well. During the 1970s, Ford set sales and profit records, in large measure due to the increased sales penetration of the Lincoln-Mercury Division in the big car markets.

Nevertheless, any auto analyst who studied the domestic car market during the 1960s knew well that the growth of the auto industry from about 1965 on was in smaller, lighter-weight and more fuel-efficient cars. The dramatic rise in imported car penetration from that time forward proved the trend. By late summer 1971, imports were accounting for one of every five new car sales in the United States. The aforementioned Presidential surtax on foreign car sales and the currency revaluations around the world escalated imported car prices and their penetration began to drop.

But not for long. Soon Americans started buying these cars in increasing numbers once again because their appetite for small cars had never subsided and it was not being satiated by the domestic manufacturers. When the Arab Oil Embargo was enacted in October of 1973, the American interest in small cars jumped appreciably. Big cars fell out of favor overnight because they were inefficient and wasteful. In some respects, it became un-American to drive a big car. The domestic manufactuers, especially General Motors, which had ignored the sales charts when they clearly showed the trend to smaller cars, were now faced with a market demanding products they did not have. The industry was forced to begin plans to slim down all of its product lines because of the demand for better gasoline mileage and the soaring costs of materials. They also began to develop plans for entries into mini-car markets where they were not represented. This changeover would take time and money. In the interim, the domestic automobile industry plunged into a severe recession in part because the domestic manufacturers failed to heed the call from the marketplace as early as the mid-1960s.

This was a particularly unfortunate occurrence for the country because the rising imported car penetration contributed a substantial portion to the United States' balance of trade deficit—three or four billion dollars a year. The auto recession stymied the American economy's attempts to recover from the '74-'75 general recession, kept unemployment figures high and put the sting of poverty into hundreds of thousands of American homes.

Much of this trouble need never have been. There were several programs with which I was associated during the 1960s that proposed to management that General Motors move into smaller car markets and take size and weight out of its successful big cars to meet the future demands of the marketplace. Most of these proposals were turned down. These rejections became classic examples of decisions which were made for the short-term benefit (record profits of $2.16 billion and $2.4 billion in 1972 and 1973, respectively) but hurt the company longer term. (The burden of the 1974 and 1975 recession might have been lessened if GM could have offered more fuel-efficient cars.)

While I was running Pontiac, we put together a sprightly, low-cost, two-seat sports car that incorporated the Pontiac overhead cam, six-cylinder engine and a fiberglass body. It was an exciting little car that would have given competition, at that time, to the growing number of foreign sports cars, such as the Triumph Spitfire and Austin-Healy Sprite, and later the Fiat 124 and the Datsun 240Z. We made our presentation to the Engineering Policy Group and it was turned down, I suspect because it would have been a low-price competitor to the Chevrolet Corvette which was given corporate exclusivity in the sports car market.

Mindful of this experience, I sought Chevy's participation in a lighter-car program Pontiac developed in 1967. The program was developed because our big cars were losing their spirited performance and youthful appeal as all GM full-sized cars gained in weight and size during the 1960s. I felt we needed to do something soon to recapture the "Pontiac feel" for these cars. We decided the best way was to reduce the weight and size of the full-size car lines, such as our Catalina. We proposed to do this by building these cars from the same components that we used in our intermediate cars, such as the LeMans.

It was not difficult to lengthen the intermediate body and chassis a little to keep the full-sized cars distinctively bigger, while preserving the lighter-weight and overall smaller-size characteristics of the smaller car. Such a car would enable the corporation to cut its production costs without lowering its prices. We further proposed that GM spend a few extra dollars inside of the car in upholstery and appointments to give it a quality attractiveness. (Unlike the corporation's

213

standardization programs of the '60s and '70s, which sought to "commonize" the parts on existing car lines, this program proposed to "commonize" by designing the standardization into completely new car lines. By doing so, we thought we could make the cars much smaller.)

Pontiac people built several models and we showed them to executives around the corporation. They were amazed at what we had done. They could not tell the difference from the regular full-sized Pontiacs and the new ones built from intermediate components.

I knew that Pontiac could not justify such a complete changeover for the big cars on our sales volume alone, so I showed the smaller full-sized car to Pete Estes at Chevrolet and also the Fisher Body management. They were excited by the program and agreed to go along with Pontiac in the project.

The next step was toward the corporation. We presented the proposal formally and informally to the corporation brass. They agreed that the cars looked exceptionally good and that this was a sound program. But we could not get anyone upstairs to make a final decision on it. They delayed and in the end wound up giving us approval only for a scaled-down version of the project. We were permitted to switch the Grand Prix model from a full-size to an intermediate body. That was all. This was done on the 1969 model Grand Prix and the results were dramatic. From the day we introduced the car in the fall of 1968, its sales soared. The Grand Prix quickly became the hottest car in the industry. It was selling at the full sticker price which was in the area of $4,000 with optional equipment. The dealers were making more than $1,000 per car profit. Because we had taken about 360 pounds out of the car between 1968 and 1969 models, the company's profit on the car rose markedly. The Grand Prix was returning about $1,500 a car to the company compared to an average $600 a car profit for the intermediate car lines. The success of the car pushed the auto industry into a whole new specialty-luxury car trend in the intermediate car class. Our car was followed by the Chevrolet Monte Carlo, a year later, and then the Ford Elite, a bigger Mercury Cougar, the Dodge Charger and the Chrysler Cordoba.

Despite The Fourteenth Floor's refusal to accept the

broad program for making full-sized cars with smaller car components, I figured the success of the '69 Grand Prix, especially in its ability to improve the profit levels of the car, would make the corporate management more receptive to a program we were working on at Chevy to lower the size and weight of all of our intermediate and compact cars.

All domestic car lines grew in weight and size during the 1960s. By the end of 1969 the combination of the surge of imported cars in the small-car market, our inability to generate substantial profit from our smaller car lines and the steady rise in production costs seemed to me to make this program necessary for the corporation. We called this project the K-Car Program, which simply was the letter designation of the new body size (GM gives all of its body sizes letter names. The full-sized cars are either B or C bodies. The intermediates are A bodies. Compact cars are X bodies.)

The K-Car program proposed a common body and chassis for all of the GM cars in the intermediate and compact car classes. On the Chevrolet lines alone this meant building the Chevelle, Camaro and Nova, which at the time varied greatly in weight and dimensions, from essentially the same components. Like the similar program for big cars, this proposal was aimed at taking weight and cost out of these car lines and improving their fuel mileage. The Nova alone was scheduled to lose 600 pounds as its weight dropped from 3400 pounds to 2800. The equivalent savings in the intermediate car would be 800-900 pounds. In addition, we proposed a substantial change in the looks of these car lines. They would become more compact, higher and shorter, which would enable us to make more efficient use of the passenger compartment. European car makers had been doing this for years while GM's top stylists had fallen in love with the longer, lower, sleeker look. The low look had reached the point of diminishing returns. For the sake of style, car designers were building domestic cars in the intermediate and compact classes which had very little back seat room. The K-Cars were designed to have more comfortable rear seats with plenty of luggage space in the trunk.

The single most important aspect of the program, I felt,

215

was that it would give General Motors greater flexibility and versatility in meeting the vacillating demands of the marketplace. Since these car lines were being built off the same body, they could be built on the same assembly line. This gave the company the ability to easily switch from one model production to the next. If the market demand switched from compact Novas, Venturas, Omegas or Apollos to intermediate Chevelles, LeMans, Cutlasses or Skylarks, we could switch from one to the other almost overnight. As separate bodies, however, the switch would take months, which was one reason GM was slow in responding to suddenly booming markets.

We proposed instituting the K-Car program with the 1973 or 1974 models. We even discussed prices to the extent that we felt a bottom-end Nova at that time should be priced in the area of $2,600. This would have put it solidly in the lower end of the imported car price range. It would be a very tough competitor for the pesky foreigners, indeed.

This program was presented to either the Engineering Policy Group or the Advance Product Planning Subcommittee four different times starting in late 1969. Each time we gave this presentation, the corporate executives generally agreed that it was a good program. But each time, they would hold up final approval until we made additional changes, or provided more information such as additional cost details. We held private presentations, in addition, for President Ed Cole showing him full-scale models at the Tech Center. His support varied. When he was in our camp, things started happening, and the program gained corporate favor. When he was not, the corporate interest waned. The delay in giving us final approval for this program was puzzling to me.

I later found out that the K-Car was getting substantial opposition from the GM Styling Department, especially the Vice-President of Design, William L. Mitchell. The main objection from this quarter was that the car was taking the corporation into a more utilitarian design and away from the longer, lower and sleeker look. Also some of the stylists were irritated because the program was "not invented here." Oddly enough, we had worked hand-in-glove with the advanced styling section of this department in preparing the

216

program. So styling was an integral part of the project. Nevertheless, the department now was opposing the program.

Eventually, the K-Car proposal was "improved to death." It was the victim of an old corporate game of continually sending a program back for more information or refinement until its backers are just plain worn down. Without Cole's support and with opposition from the styling department, two strong voices in the corporate product decisions, we had no top-flight corporate backing. As divisional management we were not allowed into all of the corporate meetings which discussed our program. We had no group or executive vice-president strong enough upstairs to push constantly for this project—opposing Cole and the styling people, if necessary. Our last presentation to Fourteenth Floor management was in late 1970. The K-Car program died quietly thereafter. It never was formally turned down, just permanently shelved.

Had management approved the program in the latter part of 1970, GM would have had the lighter, smaller, fuel-efficient cars it needed when gasoline prices soared in late 1973 after the oil embargo and when Americans went storming into the marketplace demanding small, economical cars. A portion of the program was taken off of the shelf in the wake of the fuel crisis and put into effect, resulting in the 1975 Cadillac Seville, which was essentially a very heavy, beefed-up Nova.

A fourth program which I promoted in the early 1970's, the "Italian Vega," found its way into production. It was a sporty European looking sub-compact built off the Vega body. Ed Cole supported the program when we agreed to put the Wankel engine in it (the Wankel was replaced by a conventional engine in this car). It was this program which gave GM something new and small to introduce in the fall of 1974, in its '75 lineup, as a parital answer to the demands for smaller cars. Chevrolet, Oldsmobile and Buick each got a version known as the Monza 2 + 2, Starfire and Skyhawk, respectively. The cars sold well and brought credit to their divisions.

CHAPTER THIRTEEN

GM in Substance and Form

In the great expansion in General Motors between 1918 and 1920, I had been struck by the disparity between substance and form: Plenty of substance and little form. I became convinced that the corporation could not continue to grow and survive unless it was better organized and it was apparent that no one was giving that subject the attention it needed. . . .
—ALFRED P. SLOAN, JR.,
My Years With General Motors (1964)

The breadth of the General Motors Corporation today is due to the imagination and courageous mind of William Crapo Durant, the founder of General Motors, whose expansionary philosophy put substance into the corporation and set a precedent for growth after his departure. Indeed, it was Durant's appetite for growth which led to his downfall.

After a successful career as the nation's top manufacturer of horse-drawn wagons and carriages, Billy Durant yearned to enter the burgeoning market for horseless carriages. He found his chance in the floundering Buick Motor Car Company in 1904. He reorganized it and within four years piloted it to the top position among all motorcar

219

producers in the United States. Durant's sights were on something much bigger than a single, small auto company. On September 16, 1908, he formed the General Motors Company. Two weeks later, he brought Buick into GM. A month-and-a-half later he added Oldsmobile, and in 1909, Cadillac and Oakland (Pontiac). Within a year, four of the eventual five General Motors car divisions were inside the organization. By 1910, Durant enlarged General Motors Company to include 25 smaller companies which, for the most part, built automobile parts and accessories. They were loosely organized, each company practically running itself. The parent firm served as a holding company.

However, Durant's eye for expansion took in more than he could afford, and more than his limited administrative abilities could control. He was overextended in his commitments. GM plunged into a financial crisis. Two years after he formed General Motors, Durant was forced out of active management by a group of investment bankers who injected $15 million, through a five-year note, into the failing automobile company. Under the bankers' conservative management, GM revived and by 1915 it was healthy.

Undaunted by the turn of events in 1910, Durant teamed up with inventor Louis Chevrolet, who wanted to build a lightweight, somewhat less-expensive car than was generally being offered. The two formed the Chevrolet Motor Company, and by 1915 their firm's operation spanned the United States and Canada. By offering Chevrolet stock for General Motors shares, Durant slowly worked his way back into General Motors, until on June 1, 1916 when Bill Durant was once again running General Motors as its president and chief executive officer. The Chairman was Pierre S. du Pont, a sound financial mind who was president of the du Pont Company, and had purchased GM stock in 1914 as a personal investment. Shortly thereafter, the General Motors Company became the General Motors Corporation, and Durant was off and running once again.

The next four years, especially from 1918 to 1920, produced a whirlwind round of acquisitions and expansion which added Chevrolet, Sheridan (later phased out) and General Motors Trucks to the automotive products. The company acquired a 60 percent interest in Fisher Body and bought a host of smaller companies which built axles, gears and crankshafts. To Durant's perceptions of the need for a variety of automotive products with an integrated manufacturing facility was added the desire for diversification into non-automotive areas. This, he apparently felt, would provide a suitable profit hedge against the vagaries of the automobile market. General Motors entered the agricultural equipment business through the purchase of the Samson Sieve Grip Tractor Company, the Janesville Machine Company and the Doylestown Agricultural Company. The purchase of the Guardian Frigerator Company (Frigidaire) put the company into a whole new field for "iceless" iceboxes. Through the acquisition of the Dayton-Wright Airplane Company, GM was able to transport people in the air as well as on the ground. New businesses were started, including General Motors, Ltd. of Canada and the General Motors Acceptance Corporation which financed wholesale and retail sales of General Motors vehicles. (The corporation's overseas operations were developed beginning in the mid-1920s.)

An entrepreneur in the strictest sense of the word, Durant wheeled and dealed like an inveterate gambler as he expanded GM's horizons. His manner though broad in scope was sometimes capricious, which left his associates concerned and confused. Sloan told an interesting story about the day Durant chose the location for the giant General Motors Building. The story typifies the hyperactive Durant's manner.

Durant wanted to build a headquarters in Detroit. Several sites were under consideration, including a spot on Grand Circus Park in downtown Detroit. Sloan suggested he look at a site farther north on Grand Boulevard which was near the old Hyatt Bearing Building (a company Sloan brought with him into GM in 1916). The two went to the location. Durant sized up the area and stood on the corner of Cass Avenue and Grand Boulevard, then walked a number of paces west on Grand Boulevard past the old Hyatt Building, stopped suddenly and said to Sloan, "Alfred, will you go and buy these properties for us, and Mr. Prentis (Meyer L. Prentis, GM's Treasurer) will pay whatever you decide to pay for them."

When the purchase was concluded, Durant decided he wanted the rest of the block which Sloan then bought as

221

directed. That was the simple manner in which the location and size of the General Motors Building was determined.

Under Durant's leadership, General Motors operated with no central control to speak of. His technique was the extreme example of decentralized management, and one suited to his talents because he was not an adept administrator. The business was so informally managed that there was no formal accounting performed in the corporation until after Sloan urged that an annual, certified audit of the corporate books be conducted.

While his management methods presented the potential for getting the best out of his managers, who had free rein to manage and innovate, they provided no central guidance and direction for the corporation. There was no orderly growth plan. So once again General Motors under Durant grew too fast for its resources. When the recession of 1920 hit, GM was overstocked in inventory and overbuilt in product for the slowing marketplace. The company's stock dropped precipitously. A cash crisis developed. The various operations were having a hard time paying their bills. General Motors was out of control and had to borrow $83 million in short-term notes to meet its current obligations. Under pressure, William C. Durant once again resigned from General Motors on November 30, 1920.

He later launched into new automotive ventures which met with only fluctuating success. The most famous of these ventures was Durant Motors Company, which he started only six weeks after leaving GM. Durant Motors built several cars, including the Durant. It fell on hard times during the Depression and was liquidated in 1933. In the process, Durant squandered a fortune and declared bankruptcy in 1936. He died, as he was born, practically a pauper, on March 18, 1947. His last working days were spent managing a bowling alley in Flint, Michigan. It was typical of Durant that in these last business days he wasn't so much occupied with running the bowling alley as he was in laying plans for 50 bowling centers to be built across the country.

In the panic and reorganization that followed Durant's resignation, Pierre du Pont accepted both the presidency and chairmanship of the troubled company. By his own admission, du Pont was not a product- or operations-oriented man. He was a financial manager. But it was financial control which General Motors needed most at the end of 1920.

Du Pont's top lieutenant was Alfred P. Sloan, Jr., who, amidst the turmoil, was displaying the talents of a sound operations executive, as well as a competency in financial and organizational matters. His business logic was keen, developed no doubt from his training as an engineer. It was a perfect complement to his easy grasp of the broad picture of the corporation. As GM was floundering in 1920, Sloan studied its problems and prepared the *"Organizational Study"* which was a program proposing a new organizational structure and business philosophy to be super-imposed on General Motors to give it control of its far-flung operations.

Sloan said that the objective of his plan was to preserve the best features of decentralized operations while introducing a measure of financial control and interdivision communication which would maximize the efforts and efficiencies of this diverse and integrated company. The proposal had two principles:

1. *The responsibility attached to the chief executive of each operation shall in no way be limited. Each such organization headed by its chief executive shall be complete in every necessary function and enable [d] to exercise its full initiative and logical development.*
2. *Certain central organizational functions are absolutely essential to the logical development and proper control of the corporation's activities.*

As Sloan pointed out, the two principles are contradictory. If an operation head was given complete and full control, then there could be no central control and vice-versa.

And yet, at the heart of this contradiction lay the success of GM's organizational system of decentralized operations and coordinated control. A delicate balance was to be maintained between the freedom of the various operations to manage their businesses, competing internally as well as outside of the company, and the controls necessary to coordinate these operations in the best interests of the corporation's growth and performance. At the time, the various car operations in GM had carved out definite niches for their products because of their independent ability to analyze the marketplace and build products for it. But at the same time, their power over the corporation resulted in a "How-much-do-you need? We'll get it" attitude by the corporate officers when the divisions asked for funds for expansion. The divisional money requests were rarely questioned with respect to the effect on the whole corporation. The divisions grew almost as they saw fit. To this substance of a wide and diverse company, Sloan was proposing to add the form of an organization which could achieve a coordinated success for the corporation.

The *"Organization Study"* laid down a definite format for the shape of General Motors. It separated the operations into groups of related activities, assembled central advisory staffs and determined that the control exercised at the corporate level should be through the imposition of overall policy within which the operations could freely run their businesses. This policy was to be decided by the two top corporate committees: the Finance Committee, which laid down the financial policy for the corporation, and the Executive Committee, which determined the operational policy. Later, in May of 1937, these two functions were combined into one committee, the Policy Committee; and a new committee, the Administration Committee was formed which was composed of the top corporate officers and the top operations executives. It was given the responsibility of carrying out corporate policy. As the business grew more complex, the Policy Committee grew overburdened. In 1946, it was split into its two original parts, finance and operations. These committees today are once again known as the Finance Committee and the Executive Committee. The Administration Committee carries out the policy of the Executive Committee.

Assisting the Executive Committee are nine committees called policy groups which are formed in such functional and operations areas as engineering, marketing, personnel, public relations and overseas operations. These groups were devised early in GM's history to recommend policy decisions to the Executive Committee. These groups are closely aligned with the related central staff functions—for example the Engineering Policy Group with the engineering staff—and are composed of the members of the Executive Committee, the group vice-presidents and the heads of the appropriate corporate staffs or operations.

From this somewhat complex committee structure came the often-used term for the General Motors system—management by committee. In theory, then, the system as set up was to operate in this manner—general managers of each operation (division today) ran their businesses by themselves within the framework of financial controls and general policy set by the corporation. The policy was decided by the corporate executives who were freed from the day-to-day chores and therefore had the time to look after the greater good and growth of the whole company and to see how the various operations fit into the broad corporate picture. The administration of corporate policy was communicated and exercised through the Administration Committee, which brought policymaking executives and operations executives together. In addition, as a practical matter, corporate executives in charge of the various product groups (such as group vice-presidents) also administered policy application.

Besides separating policymaking and operating decisions, another feature of the *"Organization Study"* was that the company was split into two parts—finance and operations. A strong financial staff and Finance Committee was set up to provide strict guidelines within which to promote orderly growth of the company while maximizing the profit potential. The financial emphasis was in reaction to the 1920-22 crisis period which developed because the company was out of control. The chairman of the board became the top financial officer of the corporation. (Only once was this not the case. When James M. Roche was chairman, he was not the top financial officer because he did not come up through the financial ranks.) Each of the company's operations had its own financial staff, which reported both to the head of the operation and to the corporate financial staff.

The top executive of the operations side of the business was the president, who was a man trained and accomplished in the operations of General Motors. The relation at the top between the two sides of the business as the company developed was this: The president was the chief

225

executive officer, the top official in the corporation, entrusted with the development and guidance of General Motors. He came up through the operations ranks and had a much broader view and background than the chairman who was essentially trained strictly in finance. Nevertheless, considering the importance of financial controls, the chairman held a powerful position in the company.

The limitations of the typical chairman's outlook was perhaps best evidenced in a reply of Richard C. Gerstenberg to a senate subcommittee question concerning a technical aspect of a GM product. He was vice-chairman at the time of the hearing, but clearly marked as the next chairman. Said Gerstenberg in reply: "Gentlemen, you are talking to Gerstenberg the bookkeeper. I am not an engineer."

The imposition of financial controls and the placement of a financial executive so high in the corporation was done not to stultify the flare and creativity of presidents such as Durant, Sloan and later Bill Knudsen and Harlow Curtice, but rather to harness their abilities within the perspective of the money available to build the business and therefore maintain a constantly good return on investment.

This system worked best, Sloan said, where cooperation among the various parts of the business was stressed, where management moved through persuasion rather than command, and where decision making was forced to the lowest level at which it could be made intelligently. He was quite specific about keeping the decision-making demands on the president to a minimum. The purpose was, he said, "To limit as far as practical the number of executives reporting directly to the President, the object being to enable the President to better guide the broad policies of the corporation without coming in contact with problems that may safely be entrusted to executives of less importance."

The *"Organization Study"* was adopted as the new form for the General Motors corporate philosophy and management structure. Sloan later lauded its flexibility, saying that "The new policy asked that the corporation neither remain as it was, a weak form of organization, nor become a rigid command form."

On May 10, 1923, Pierre du Pont, realizing his own limitations in the operations and product development areas of General Motors, and recognizing the blooming talents of Alfred Sloan, relinquished the title of president to the author of the *"Organization Study"* who also became chief executive officer.

From that point through most of its corporate existence, General Motors was run by an operations man, the president, who was both chief executive officer and chief operating officer of the corporation. Through his unique abilities as both an operations man and a keen financial mind, Sloan kept the job of chief executive officer when he became chairman in 1937, and William S. Knudsen was elevated to president. But even Sloan relinquished the chief executiveship in 1946 when he gave the responsibility back to the corporate presidency in the person of Charles E. Wilson. The uppermost power in the corporation resided in the presidency through the tenures of Wilson and his successor, Harlow H. Curtice, who was chief executive during the last years of Sloan's chairmanship.

When both Curtice and Sloan's successor as Chairman, Albert P. Bradley, retired from General Motors on August 31, 1958, the modern General Motors Corporation took a dramatic change in its course. Frederic G. Donner, a strong-willed, loyal servant of the financial staff who'd risen steadily through the financial side of the business, was elected chairman and chief executive officer. It was the first time since Pierre du Pont relinquished the presidency and chief executiveship in 1923, that the top officeholder in General Motors was not a man well-schooled and experienced in the operations of the corporation. Donner's only experience was in financial management. He never ran a division. His hand-picked president was John F. Gordon, an engineer by training but an executive with a lackluster business career.

Though it was not recognized inside or outside of the corporation at the time, the delicate balance at the top of the world's largest industrial corporation was starting to tip toward the financial side of the business, and in the process, the substance of the organizational system so thoroughly thought out by Sloan was beginning to dissipate. I doubt that Sloan himself realized what was taking place. To his death in 1966, he touted the Donner team because, I suspect, he like many others at the time was blinded by the financial successeses of the Donner administration which culminated in records for sales and profits in 1965. What was happening was a predictable result, however, when the control of a consumer goods company moves into the hands of purely financial managers. Short-term profits are dramatically improved, but a lack of sensitivity for product, for markets and for customers also sets in, which is usually detrimental to the long-term strength of the corporation. Therefore, those lauding GM's management in the 1960s could not see the organizational fissures developing as they looked at the bright figures appearing on the corporate cash register.

CHAPTER FOURTEEN

Work To Be Done on Fourteen

It was widely speculated throughout the Corporation during the summer of 1972 that I was going to be promoted from general manager of Chevrolet to a group executive job heading up GM's far-flung overseas operations. I don't know how the speculation started but my emotions on the whole thing were mixed. I didn't want to leave Chevrolet because we still had work to do with the division. But if I had to leave, the overseas operation was where I wanted to go.

It was the only part of the business with which I was not familiar. It would expose me to all GM automotive and non-automotive operations outside the U.S. and Canada. While the overseas business in total was not as large as Chevrolet, it was much more diverse—manufacturing cars in Germany or refrigerators in England or road-building equipment in Brazil. Besides the challenge of managing diverse businesses in different countries with their widely varying customers and people, GM's overseas operations presented a business challenge similar to the one I encountered at Chevrolet. Like Chevrolet, when I took over, the overseas operations was disorganized and deteriorating.

General Motors has never done as well overseas at it has

in the United States and Canada. Its dollar volume has grown as the overseas markets have grown. But its automotive sales penetration overseas is only about 9 percent today. It is second to Ford outside North America. The combination of the dwindling growth rate of the American automotive market with the increasing growth rate of markets overseas, in which GM has a much smaller share, seemed to portend a decreasing importance of GM in the world automobile industry. In 1969, vehicle sales outside the U.S. and Canada exceeded those inside for the first time in the modern automobile industry. Throughout the rest of this century and into the next, the greater growth in the automobile industry will take place overseas. Thus, the problems with GM's overseas operations took on greater significance when matched against the potential for growth in those markets.

Like the Chevrolet problem, it appeared to me that no one in GM quite understood what was wrong overseas or how to remedy it. I certainly didn't have the background to tackle the overseas problems that I did to tackle Chevrolet's troubles.

Nevertheless, I had made some preliminary observations about GM overseas. One was that GM made very little use of foreign nationals in managing its multi-national operations. It had no foreign nationals on its board of directors, or among upper management, despite the background and perceptions of overseas markets that such people could bring to the corporate board room. Because of this, while overseas operations were run autonomously, they were always headed by an executive promoted from the domestic side of the business. And his general management philosophy was, "This is the way we do it in Detroit, so this is the way we are going to do it in Rio, Tokyo, Stuttgart or Sydney."

I have heard the complaint from multi-national automotive suppliers and other companies in other industries that GM executives are unsophisticated and unknowledgeable in the ways of international business. The "way we do it in Detroit" won't do overseas, where tastes, lifestyles, provincial habits and the perceptions of cars are different than in North America. The cars are generally smaller and more

230

efficient overseas because the roads are narrower and the cost of fuel is much higher than in the U.S., even with today's inflated price of gasoline. The manner of doing business differs from country to country. In some countries, for instance, once you hire a worker you practically marry that worker. Layoffs are almost unheard of, so you pay employees whether the plant is running or not.

If I got the overseas job, I decided one thing I was going to do was rely more on what the nationals had to say should be done in their home countries and less on "what we do in Detroit."

My interest in the overseas post proved to be a false hope, however. I never got that job. Instead I was promoted to group executive in charge of domestic Car and Truck Group. Despite my growing quarrel with the system and what I thought were insignificant assignments and endless meetings on The Fourteenth Floor, I set out to do what I thought a group executive should be doing—making policy decisions and leaving day-to-day operations to the divisions. From my sixteen-year experience in the automotive operations dealing with The Fourteenth Floor, it was not difficult to isolate the areas I felt were most critically in need of management attention: planning, marketing and customer satisfaction.

Planning

It seems incredible, but sound, long-range and comprehensive business planning was almost non-existent at General Motors when I was there. The management form for planning was there. Committees were constantly being set up, usually stacked with financial types, to study the dimensions of the industry ten or fifteen years ahead. And they usually came back to management with a presentation of growth trends and capital investment requirements. But on the whole these studies were heavily weighted with financial data. They lacked depth and a sensitive feel for the market. In the end, management usually did not act on this information but instead reacted to developments in the marketplace as they occurred.

So there was no planning in GM similar to that which we instituted in Chevrolet where we got all the various facets of the operation together in one room to discuss the total business—product, costs, marketing, manufacturing and such outside influences as government standards or consumerism. The short-range effect of such planning at Chevrolet was complete coordination of efforts in the day-to-day operations of the business. The long-range effect was that all the parts of the business were explored for new ideas and then coordinated to bring those ideas from concept to the market.

Without sound planning and coordination as a guide, the decision-making process on The Fourteenth Floor was slow and cumbersome. There was also, as I mentioned earlier, an almost paranoid fear each year of what the competition was going to introduce. So product decisions which were slow enough in the making often were held up longer until management got an idea of what Ford was going to introduce. By this time there was nothing GM could do anyway. But top management, particularly in the last years I was there, insisted on waiting.

The results were devastating to divisional managers' morale and hurt corporate profits. Executives who worked furiously to get product proposals up to The Fourteenth Floor with sufficient time to be easily implemented watched those proposals sit before management until their deadlines passed. Once top management gave its late approval, the divisions had to scramble to get the programs implemented on time and often bore the blame when these programs overran their costs, were late on the market or produced poor quality products. Fingering Chevrolet for the Vega cost overruns was a typical example of management saddling a division with a problem and then blaming it for the results of that problem.

Studies we conducted at GM showed that year-in and year-out we were substantially slower to effect new-product decisions than Ford, Chrysler or American Motors. Our lead time for building new-model tools was much less than that at Ford or Chrysler. This meant that our competition sent its engineering drawings and die models into the tool shops as much as six months earlier than GM. So the other three domestic automakers would often have their tool preparation done on a straight time (no overtime) cost basis. In addition, the lead time difference between GM and our competitors gave them sufficient time after final delivery of the tools to test them before launching full-scale production. On the other hand, General Motors typically would get into the tooling shops much later, spend millions in all-out overtime costs and then rush the tool into production without sufficient testing. Our testing was done on the first cars built. Often when we started production, the dies hadn't been tested and smoothed into working order. So on the first cars off the assembly line fenders weren't in line with doors, fillers weren't in line with bumpers and fenders and bumpers were rough-edged. The problem was most acute with entirely new models. If you got a GM car built in the first sixty days of production, it often was a quality disaster.

One of the worst cases I remember involved the 1971 model full-sized cars, called B-bodies, of Chevrolet, Pontiac, Olds and Buick. Approval of the tooling for these cars was not obtained from The Fourteenth Floor until forty weeks before production was slated to begin. This was little more than half the time needed to build and test the tool and dies properly. The divisions put the B-body program before top management far earlier than the deadline. But the program was subjected to interminable meetings "upstairs."

A dispute developed between top management and the divisions over the ventilation system of the new B-bodies. The corporation management wanted to use a system designed by the central engineering staff. The divisions were unanimous in their opposition to this ventilation system because it added ten dollars cost to the car and leaked cold air into the passengers' compartment, making the passengers uncomfortable and the car difficult to heat. The opposition from the divisions was stronger and more united on this matter than I had ever seen. When our objections were ignored, we petitioned our group executive for an appeal of the decision. But he overruled us.

After endless meetings and foot dragging, the program was sent into the tool and die shops less than 10 months before production start-up. Because the shops were almost filled with work from Ford, Chrysler and AMC, they charged GM excessively for the straight-time work. Then 56- to 70-hour work weeks had to be okayed just to meet the production deadlines. GM had to pay over $1 billion for a tooling bill which should have been less than $750 million. That was a waste of over $250 million due to management indecision. Even with the overtime rush, we were late getting into production with the 1971 models. When our plants went down on September 14, 1970, with the UAW's national strike, GM dealers were so short in their supplies of the new B-body cars that they missed hundreds of thousands of potential sales. We at Chevy lost almost 100,000 potential sales of the new cars, which cost us dearly in profit.

Once the B-body cars got into customer hands after the strike, complaints poured into our offices about the ventilation system, which was leaking cold air into the passengers' compartment and making it impossible to properly heat the car. We had to fix these cars at our cost. The cost of putting the system on the cars was about $24 million for the 1971 model run. With the repair costs, the total loss attributed to the ventilation system which the divisions didn't want was at least $50 million pre-tax profit to the corporation.

There were even worse ramifications. The delay in getting this program approved, followed by a panic program to remove the ventilation system from the 1972 B-body cars, kept our attention off the intermediate-sized cars (the A-bodies), which were supposed to undergo complete remodeling for 1972. When we did turn our attention to the 1972 model intermediate cars, it was too late to get them into production. Even with all-out overtime, the earliest these cars could have been introduced was November or December 1971, two or three months late. So the new 1972 model intermediate cars were delayed a year until the 1973 model year, which started in September 1972. Management indecision was responsible for the delay in 1972 A-body cars, but instead the 67-day UAW strike against the corporation became the scapegoat. GM brass blamed the UAW strike for the delay of the 1972 A-body cars, even though Ford Motor Co. with a longer strike in 1967 didn't miss a beat in its product program for the next year. The reason, as I saw it, was that Ford planned better.

The case of the 1973 model safety bumpers is another example of the effects of poor planning and coordination on executive row. We knew far in advance that the federal government would require that 1973 model cars be out-fitted with energy-absorbing bumpers which could with-stand a 5 miles-per-hour hit in the front and a 2½ miles-per-hour hit in the rear. It was quite obvious to anyone that we had to meet the law. So we should have just given the engineers and stylists the problem and let them work it out. Instead, The Fourteenth Floor engaged in endless debate over how to meet the standard. At one point, one of the top financial executives, I think it was Oscar Lundin, suggested that we exceed the requirements of the standard, among other reasons, because GM has a large insurance subsidiary, Motors Insurance Corporation, which could benefit from reduced damage in low-impact collisions. When the costs were worked out later, it became obvious that it would cost too much to exceed the standard. So the idea was abandoned. Nevertheless, new discussions devel-oped.

While there were no new proposals forthcoming, the bumper decision was put off until it was almost too late. Suddenly, management found itself in the spring of 1971 a little more than a year away from the introduction of the 1973 models and therefore exceedingly late in getting the bumper program into the tool and die shops. Once again, GM had to pay a premium tooling bill and authorize 56- to 70-hour weeks to get the parts built. Chrysler and Ford in the meantime were having their bumper work done for the most part on regular time, eight-hour shifts, five-day work weeks. For some of their models they were eight months ahead of GM in getting to the tool and die shops. We barely made production start-up and had to scuttle plans to begin building the new models a week early. Our costs to tool up for the bumpers were 40 percent more than Ford. The extra tooling cost was $30 million for Chevrolet alone and about $80 million for the whole cor-poration. The crowning insult came when The Fourteenth

Floor criticized the divisions and the central engineering staff for "not being able to start on time."

The slow decision-making process "upstairs" was not a recent development. It was something I witnessed throughout much of my career. In fact, from 1965 to 1972, when I was general manager of either Pontiac or Chevrolet, I prepared 18 proposals to corporate management to improve our lead time and save billions of dollars. And there were others in the corporation who pushed for similar programs and got the same results as I did: a response generally arguing that it was a marketing advantage to see the competition's products before we made our final decisions. The car divisions when I was at Chevrolet tried to get our lead time lengthened without corporate help. That proved a futile effort because ultimately any program of this nature required Fourteenth Floor sanction and participation.

The result was that GM became a much less efficient manufacturer of cars and trucks than Ford. Corporate studies during the 1970s, often quoted by our Chairman, Dick Gerstenberg, showed that Ford tooled up for its new cars for $45 less per car than General Motors. The reason was that Ford planned its new-car programs with more care and diligence than GM. Ford set strict deadlines and then met them. The profit advantage we had over Ford lay entirely in our dominance of the medium- and large-car segments. In the 1973 calendar year General Motors earned $2.4 billion on sales of almost $36 billion, for a 6.7 percent return on sales. Ford that year earned $907 million on sales of $23 billion, for a return on sales of 4 percent. Yet our internal studies showed that if GM's market mix was distributed more proportionately to smaller cars as was Ford's, our profits per car would have been less.

The difference between Ford's and GM's costs to build cars is best evidenced in a comparison of small-car programs during the 1960s which was prepared by GM's financial staff. From 1959 through 1969, Ford introduced four all-new small cars, which were interrelated—the Falcon, Mustang, Maverick and Pinto—with a total developmental cost of about $350 million, according to GM studies. With the Falcon and Mustang, Ford clearly beat GM into new markets. In that same time, GM introduced four small cars which were almost totally unrelated—the Corvair, Nova (Chevy II), Camaro and Vega—at a total developmental cost of $850 million, or half-a-billion dollars more than Ford's. Ford's four small cars in their lifetime outsold their GM competitors in the only real head-to-head test of the product planning and management competence of the two companies.

The lack of adequate planning also must be blamed for General Motors' inability to change over its manufacturing plants from one year's product to another's as fast as its competitors. During the '50s and '60s, the annual shutdown for new model changeover was a four-to-six-week ritual as widely accepted as the new-model changes themselves. The industry stopped dead in its tracks from mid-July to late August, and Detroit, in turn, slowed to a crawl. However, as numbers of models were reduced in the late '60s and early '70s, and manufacturing technology improved, the industry began a process of weekend shutdowns and running changes. Ford, Chrysler and American Motors were able to change tools and dies on the run, or handle the whole process in little more than a long weekend. Only entirely new models took longer. In the hot selling years of 1972 and 1973, such short "down times" meant that these automakers could run the production of the current models longer into the summer or start the production of the new ones faster, which gave dealers a favorable supply of new cars when they went on sale in the fall. The quick changeover meant hundreds of millions of dollars in increased sales and profits.

GM, however, was unable to reduce substantially its down time for changeover. There was no concerted management effort to seek a solution to this problem and any individual proposals that were made were talked to death "upstairs." We did a study in the early 1970s which showed that one year Ford switched from one model to another with a total of 42 plant days of down time. The same process took an incredible 460 days at General Motors. If GM could have saved up to 400 of those down days, it could have produced enough cars to equal the addition of two assembly plants. Ironically, in the midst of its slothful attitude toward new-model changeovers, during the production boom of 1972-3, GM announced that it would build two new assembly plants, in Memphis and Oklahoma City, which would cost about $800 million dollars. Had management been able to effect faster changeovers, it could have generated the new capacity from within its existing plants and saved the $800 million. As it was, plans for these plants were abandoned in the industry's huge sales slump after the Arab oil embargo crisis in 1973-74. The Oklahoma City plant has since been built.

In planning for the move to Fourteenth, I felt that my initial function would be to develop a three-year product program with the divisions, set specific deadlines for management approval, then force these programs through the maze of executive decisions by constantly pushing for quick answers. I began work on a program that emphasized not only faster tooling decisions and other manufacturing imperatives but also promoted a process for an orderly switch to fast changeovers at new-model time. I prepared it in concert with Harlan Heinmiller, a talented and understanding executive in corporate forward planning and scheduling, who knew the problems well.

Marketing

Ford's dominance in product innovation clearly proved that it had a decisive management team much more oriented to market innovation than GM. This advantage was never denied by GM management. In fact, in the early and mid-1960s, Bud Goodman, a member of top management, continuously reminded his colleagues that GM had not produced a significant, major automotive innovation since the hydramatic automatic transmission (1939) and the hard-top body style (1949). Ford pioneered in practically every major new market while Chrysler produced the significant technical innovations, such as power steering, power brakes, electric windows and the alternator.

What marketing suggestions General Motors had were confined to the divisions, but their efforts were often emphatically ignored. There were numerous examples to prove the case against GM's marketing efforts. In late winter, 1970, when I was running Chevrolet, we were ordered by the corporate management to reduce the manufacturer's suggested retail price of the Nova by $150. We paid for this move by deleting some standard equipment—such as going to a lower quality tire—and lowering the dealer's potential profit per unit. Bob Lund, general sales manager, and I opposed the move on business grounds: Chevrolet dealers were selling all the Novas they could get their hands on and our plants were working overtime to keep up with orders for these compact cars; and on moral grounds the move was fraudulent because it appeared as if GM was cutting the price and its profits when in fact the cut was coming from dealer profits and product quality.

The order might have made good business sense, if not moral sense, had the Nova been in a sales slump. A price reduction could have stimulated sales. But this was not the case. We were selling all we could build. I never learned the origin of the order from Fourteen, but Chevrolet's opposition was completely disregarded. The Nova price was lowered. The move, as we expected, did not increase Nova business because we couldn't build any more cars than we were already doing. It did, however, cost Chevy about $10 per car profit on the equipment which was previously standard and now was optional. Our dealers were livid because we reduced their profit potential on a hot car while not touching our own margins. Their anger increased when previous 1970 Nova buyers interpreted GM's "price-reduction" announcement at face value and stormed the dealerships around the country demanding a $150 rebate. To fend off this onslaught, the dealers told the irate customers what had happened: GM reduced the Nova price by seemingly fraudulent gimmicks. No one came out ahead on this Fourteenth Floor decision. Almost everyone lost—the previous customers, the division, the dealer body and the corporation.

It was this kind of capricious, almost mindless, marketing decision which I thought we could eliminate "upstairs" by bringing a new marketing awareness to the group executive job. If I made improving our marketing my personal concern on Fourteen as I had at Chevrolet, perhaps the power of my corporate position could pull wholesale changes and new programs through the system. I figured that an urgent program of comprehensive planning could be combined with a push for more sophisticated marketing to create a new corporate awareness on Fourteen.

Once again, my Chevrolet experience was the prototype for my corporate activity. The idea was to develop future product proposals in such a way that management could not refuse them. I had learned the corporate art of killing programs during my experiences with our smaller car proposals three years earlier. This experience could be used to design future programs that were unassailable from any corporate corner.

It was an ambitious venture because it flew into the teeth of the GM system as I knew it. But the way it looked to me and to the marketing and engineering people in the divisions, we could develop a product idea, test it in the consumer arena with sophisticated marketing tools, thoroughly cost it out and then present it to the corporation so that the power of our arguments was strictly in the facts. If the facts were assailable, we would scrap the proposal. In this way it seemed there would be no room for personalities, or "this is my opinion" objections from the corporate brass.

Customer Satisfaction

Customer satisfaction is inextricably interwoven with product quality, service and speed of delivery. I felt we could effect an immediate improvement in quality by better planning, which would give us more time to test out tools and dies as well as the first products built before full production began in each new model year. Other problems, though similar to those at Chevrolet, were more complicated and would have to wait for our attention until we tackled the pressing problems.

Order response time was an immediate problem. Ford Motor Co. was able to deliver a car as much as 14 days faster than GM. This necessitated speeding the process from a dealer's order to the actual manufacturing of that order as we had done at Chevrolet. At the same time, I was going to get the sophisticated, computerized Marketing Systems Information program at Chevy implemented on a corporation-wide basis.

Dealer service was a complicated problem related to the corporation's emphasis on sales as well as some basic inefficiencies in general dealer operations. Studies show that poor service is often related to poor business management in the back shop. Just as we worked with dealers in solving their sales problems, we now needed a corporate program to help dealers solve service problems, impressing on them the need for a good service facility and helping them better manage the back shop. There were good profits to be made in the service departments, and we had to show them this.

I decided to occupy my time on The Fourteenth Floor in studying the corporation's problems in automotive planning, marketing and customer satisfaction, and in preparing programs to cure these problems. To me this was a proper activity for a top GM manager—planning the direction of GM by developing policy and seeing that it was enacted. I sought the approval of my superiors to work on these new ventures, and I was told, "That's your job. Go do it." But when I petitioned them for relief from the oppressive piles of paperwork and the endless meetings I had to attend all day, their answer was similarly: "That's part of your job, too." And the paperwork just kept coming.

A study I did with the assistance of the financial staff while at Chevrolet indicated that we could add $550 million to General Motors profits immediately by getting our tooling programs into the shops on time, effecting back-to-back new model changeovers and improving our new product order response time by 14 days. This $550 million saving was at the heart of efforts I made on Fourteen to speed decision making and improve production and market response timing.

But I could not get management to move in these directions. Aside from the personal quarrels I was having with the system by then, my efforts "upstairs," from a purely business standpoint were becoming repeats of my earlier efforts to sell the corporation on building smaller, lighter

241

cars. The difference was that now the frustration was an all-day, every-day proposition. In a division I at least had the inherent fun of running my own operation to counterbalance the frustration with the corporate system. But once "upstairs," there was nothing. On Fourteen, as I have explained, I was left without the protection of my own abilities because there was no objective criteria for judging my performance, no factual measure of my competence such as operating profit, quality indices or overall efficiency. The only criterion for my performance in top management was how my superiors thought I performed as a "team-player" in the system. On that basis, I knew I was failing miserably.

In the final analysis, my efforts on The Fourteenth Floor were plainly fruitless. I blame part of this on top management's (excluding Ed Cole) inexperience in the actual operations of the automobile business, and its devotion to perpetuating the system rather than achieving sound business results. There was a fundamental lack of understanding of the importance of the programs we were designing to speed decision making, develop better market response and improve dealer service. A number of the people in important decision-making positions on The Fourteenth Floor learned about General Motors through the financial staff or in the non-automotive or parts operations. They didn't grasp the pertinence of these proposals which were not glamorous programs with catchy phrases, but rather simple, basic solutions requiring nothing more than well-coordinated hard work.

At the same time, I must also blame myself for my failure on The Fourteenth Floor. To me the decisions that had to be made, just like the switch to smaller cars, were so conspicuous and so obviously important to the future of General Motors that I should have found some way to communicate this to my superiors. If the corporation could be sold on programs such as the Corvair or the huge Wankel engine effort, with their questionable potentials for good results, I should have been able to sell my programs which were so fundamental in nature and important to the corporation.

Looking back now to the changes that have taken place in the auto industry, it is even more obvious that I should have managed somehow to get the job done on The Fourteenth Floor. But I didn't do it. And I consider that to be the biggest failure of my business life at GM.

CHAPTER FIFTEEN

General Motors' Decline

At the corner of West Fort Street and Cass Avenue on the fringe of Detroit's financial district, the staid Detroit Club was quiet as usual. Gray-haired businessmen wrapped inside of high-backed leather chairs read the *Wall Street Journal* and puffed on cigars. From the back, you couldn't see their heads, just the occasional clouds of smoke from their cigars. One of the most exclusive clubs in the Motor City, the red-brick Detroit Club was the site of many retirement dinners for General Motors brass. This mid-October retirement party in 1967 seemed no different than any of the dozens of others I had attended, except that the honored guest was Frederic G. Donner, the finance man who had dominated General Motors for over nine years. He was ending his official term in office, which was the third longest of any GM chairman, ranking behind only Sloan and Pierre du Pont, and second longest of a chief executive officer, behind only Sloan. Like his two revered predecessors as chairman, Sloan and du Pont, Donner had left his indelible imprint on General Motors.

This party was quite typical of the others I had attended and of the ones I would attend in future years. The affair began with a cocktail party at a side bar on the second floor. All the company brass from around the world was there, from the vice-president level on up, in a commanding show of force. The atmosphere was stiff, almost formal. It never was conducive to a friendly exchange in which you could let your hair down, slap a guy on the back and say, "It was nice working with you." In some respects, it was almost like a stand-up committee meeting with drinks. The guys in the corporation who were heavy drinkers—some had definite drinking problems—were always on their good behavior, nursing a drink or two through the whole night.

After an hour of conversation, drinking and posing with the honoree for the corporate photographer, the assembly of 30 to 40 executives passed from the bar into a large adjoining room for dinner and the after-dinner program.

A soup course was followed by salad and a fish appetizer. The entree was either sirloin steak or sliced roast sirloin, with side orders of green beans and au gratin potatoes. Wine was served with dinner although most who were still drinking opted for another order from the bar. Dessert of pie a la mode or ice cream and coffee preceded table clearing and the official "good-by" program which was conducted by the chairman or, in this case, his successor, President James M. Roche.

Most retirement programs, I felt, were pappy, almost patronizing. You can praise a guy just so much and then he's got to start wondering whether these effusions are really coming from the hearts of the guys giving them. The program began with a film prepared by the public relations department, which supposedly summarized the honored executive's life and accomplishments with the corporation. It usually bore little resemblance to fact. No matter how good or bad a job the guy had done, the film always came out about the same. After the film came speeches of praise and loyalty to the departing executive, usually by the chairman and president, after which a few of his close buddies might hang around for a few extra drinks while the rest hurried home so they would be at their desks on time early the next morning.

The party for Roger Kyes several years later was more realistic than most because the film and the after-dinner speeches kept hammering away at what a hard-nose he was. He almost burst his buttons in pride as he watched and listened to his program.

The party for Donner was proceeding predictably. The film was shown, and he seemed pleased. The after-dinner speech by Jim Roche gushed with praise and admiration. The next speaker was Jack Gordon, Donner's hand-picked president in 1958, who had retired two years earlier. He was rambling on about the virtues of the outgoing chairman to whom he owed his corporate rise. But he wasn't satisfied with just praise for Donner. Gordon went farther and began a vicious verbal attack on his own predecessor, President Harlow H. Curtice. The exact words of Gordon's blast are difficult to remember, but his zingers went essentially like this:

> When Fred and I took over this corporation in 1958, it was in trouble. Executive morale was low. People were horribly depressed. We were coming apart inside. It was like that because Harlow Curtice let it get that way. He almost wrecked this company.
>
> Fred and I recognized these problems and by busting our rears with hard work we were able to turn this company around. We got GM going. And our record sales and profits ($20.7 billion and $2.1 billion, respectively) of 1965 proved that.

Most of the management present was caught between modest surprise and downright embarrassment by this uncalled-for, vituperative attack on Curtice. It was the first time I had ever heard a General Motors executive openly criticize another one, past or present, in front of corporate management. There were grumblings by one against another in the privacy of an office, or a quiet lunch, as there always are in any corporation. But this was the first blatant, gloves-off attack in front of everyone that I'd seen or heard.

Gordon had hardly sat down when the last speaker, Donner himself, rose and, as I recall, continued the castigation of Curtice, repeating what Gordon had said and adding his own shots. Those present who weren't embarrassed by Gordon's attack were now shaking their heads and looking puzzled. They knew, as I did, that the attacks were unfounded and vicious. They couldn't have been further from the truth. Harlow Curtice was an accomplished and successful executive when he ran GM. He was one of the few to work at the divisional level in both the finance and operations sides of the business. He was controller of AC Spark Plug Division at one time and later general manager of the Buick Division. His rise to the top of General Motors included experience in most of the company's operations, where he established himself as a sound product man with an exceedingly keen marketing sense.

Curtice was GM's last dynamic leader, a man whose mere presence would command attention and stop conversations when he walked into a room. Red Curtice was revered internally almost as a father figure by many of the younger General Motors executives. And on the outside he was a respected spokesman for the company and the industry. While my personal contact with Curtice had been limited, since I was only an engineering executive at Pontiac when he ran GM, I grew to know him at corporate functions after he retired and through the corporate talent he developed. It was ironic that under Curtice General Motors launched and completed a billion dollar expansion program which enabled the sales and profit successes achieved under his two detractors, Gordon and Donner. He ran the company with foresight, as had Sloan.

But apparently, when Curtice was in command, great resentments built up toward him in the financial side of the business because it felt it had no control or power. Even though Chairman Sloan, and Bradley after him, exercised the traditional financial influence over a strong president, the finance side of the business felt left out. In the person of Fred Donner, the financial side had the strong-willed leader it needed to muscle its way into control of the corporation. It was not going to let an operations man dominate as Curtice had done. The selection of Gordon, who was not a particularly strong president, over more obvious choices established that objective. These castigations and the personal vindictiveness expressed against Curtice at Donner's retirement party affirmed in my mind the motives of the financial side of General Motors in moving into control. That control signaled a shift in the balance of management power at the top of General Motors Corporation.

Since Donner's rise to power, General Motors Corporation has sufficiently curtailed the responsibilities of the president's office to insure that the authority in the corporation rests with the chairman and the financial staff. Since the retirement of Harlow Curtice, the strongest personality to occupy the president's office at General Motors was Ed Cole. When he came to power in 1967, as president and chief operating officer, however, Cole found a job stripped of much of its clout. For one thing, his presidency did not include responsibility for the vast overseas operations, which are vital to the future growth of the corporation. Cole was actually chief operating officer for North American Operations alone, which put him on a par with an executive vice-president at other large industrial corporations. For another thing, in practice, Ed Cole's contribution was strongly confined to product areas alone. Terrell's statement that Cole was "just the chief engineer of General Motors" contained a measure of truth.

Cole's chairman and chief executive officer was Roche, who, though not a finance man in the strict sense of the word, was certainly under the influence of the money side of the business. But when Roche was absent, Cole was not the top corporate officer. The power passed from Roche to a new position, vice-chairman, a financial man, who also eventually had responsibility for overseas operations. Thus, the power of the presidency in 1967 had reached an all-time low in General Motors. While it had been the number one slot for most of GM's nearly 70-year-history, it was now the number three slot, behind the chairman and vice-chairman. And that was the way it was when I left.

It is ironic that the financial side of GM tried to explain away its rise in power in the corporation since Donner in terms of producing a "balance of power at the top," because there is no balance of power at the top. Today, the company is clearly in the hands of the financial side of the business. And that dominance plus Donner's personal effect on the process of management selection has directed the company off the course planned and charted in the 1920s. While the "form" of Sloan's *Organization Study* for the most part is in place, the "substance" has been dissipated. The results have not been good for General Motors. GM when I left was clearly not the company it was under Sloan.

A weakened presidency had taken from the top the emphasis on sound, broadly viewed operational policymaking and intelligent planning in product and organizational areas. When I left, as I've noted previously, there was little long-range planning at General Motors. Management, instead, reacted from one crisis to another.

A promotional system which stressed "loyalty to the boss" more than performance put into top management executives who, while hard-working, nevertheless lacked the experience, and in some cases the ability to manage capably or guide the business. The preoccupation on The Fourteenth Floor with the appearance of working—putting in long hours, going through the motions of the job, occupying time with minutiae—is a direct result of management's inability to grasp the scope of its job and grapple with the problems that arise.

While the organizational structure instituted by Sloan is still basically in place and management constantly points to this as an indication that the system has not changed, the philosophy of management has changed. In the place of sound policymaking, much of the time of upper GM management is being occupied with the day-to-day business. In this respect, GM is much more centralized. The divisions are more under the operational control of corporate management than at any time in the peacetime history of the corporation.

From what I had observed, neither Donner and Gordon nor their successors had the sense of history and understanding of the General Motors system necessary to manage the business effectively, which is why they steered the company away from, or let it drift from, its original course.

A man trained and skilled only in financial control, who has no direct operational experience, simply lacks the understanding necessary to run the business. Pierre du Pont understood this, which is why he quickly relinquished the presidency and chief executive officership to Sloan in 1923. Too strong an emphasis on cost control can actually hurt a company. I can remember Gerstenberg, when he was chairman and the industry was being inundated with costly federal controls, saying "We cannot spend money on product changes anymore. That's all there is to that. We cannot afford the luxury of the things we've done in the past."

He was right in his assessment of costs. They were increasing. But in the narrow view of a cost cutter, he never questioned the impact of a decision to cut product changes in half, and he never looked to another alternative. It mattered not to him that the automobile industry had spent 50 years convincing the American customer to trade in his car every two or three years for a newer model (a practice itself which some of us questioned); that this something new by the 1970s was nothing more than a styling change; that GM became the great success it was in large measure by urging the customer to "buy up"; that the heart of buying up was offering better styling and more car to move up to. All that mattered was that the costs said no more styling. It was all there "in dollars and cents." Ironically, the decisions to forego the annual model change, though based on the wrong premise, turned out all right for the corporation. This is because the changing consumer taste, ignored or unnoticed by management, was demanding longer-lasting body styles with more emphasis on utilitarian aspects. This trend coincided with the corporation's push for cost savings through longer model runs.

A similar set of circumstances today is forcing General Motors to build lighter, smaller cars. While management rejected most of our programs to develop these sizes of cars in 1969 and 1970, it has been forced to reverse its position today because of the drastically rising manufacturing costs and the federally mandated fuel mileage levels. The decision to go small is based on costs and government action, pure and simple. Nothing else.

Unfortunately, not all GM decisions from the top in the past 20 years of financial dominance have turned out as well. The excessive emphasis on cost cutting has permeated the organization as the first, and sometimes the only, precept of management. It has produced an aberrant method of evaluating performance. At one time, the assembly plant in Tarrytown, New York, year in and year out, produced the poorest quality cars of all 22 GM U.S. car assembly plants. In some instances, Tarrytown cars were so poorly built, the dealers refused to accept them. At the same time, it had the lowest manufacturing costs in General Motors. So the Tarrytown plant manager was getting one of the biggest bonuses of all the assembly-plant managers while building the worst cars in the company.

The creation of the GM Assembly Division (GMAD) to build almost all GM cars in North America was explained as a move to build cars more efficiently, at less cost. But the "down time" experience, when the division "got tough" with the union locals in each plant it took over, cost the company more money than it would make up in savings for as long as a decade.

The company's heavy-handed cost squeeze often forced the parts divisions to push out inferior parts. At one time, the car and truck divisions refused to accept some of these parts because we at least had responsibility for the cars built in our home plants (GMAD built the rest), and we were trying to build them with the best quality possible. The assembly division, however, had no receiving inspection, and so it accepted some of these parts and put them in cars which, unfortunately, went out with our division names on them. On numerous occasions when touring our parts plants, I saw huge shipments ready for delivery and marked "do not ship to home plants." We wouldn't have accepted them. GMAD did.

On these occasions, the narrow view of cost cutting actually was costing the corporation more in warranty expense, additional preparation charges, lost sales and consumer ill will.

As I noted earlier, the corporate program for maximum standardization of parts across product lines was a knee-jerk cost-cutting reaction to the incredible proliferation of models, engines and parts which took place in the uncontrolled and unplanned boom of the 1960s. However, the program was not intelligently thought out. It was not thoroughly analyzed for its actual effect on the company. On paper the concept looked good and seemed like a sure way to save money. In reality it wasted money. The car divisions rebelled at various stages of the standardization program. Their cries were unanswered. When Chevrolet rebelled against using the new corporate U-joint, opting to keep the one we already had, Kyes told me, "Use the corporate one or I'll get someone in Chevy who will."

We used it, at an investment of about $16 million in tooling, and our costs rose $1.40 per car. In addition, the corporate design failed in use and Chevy paid out about $5 million extra in warranty claims.

Instead of saving money, the standardization program at GM wound up costing the corporation about $300 million extra per year. It also was in part responsible for raising Chevrolet costs, which we were not able to recover with appropriate price increases. To do so would have taken us out of our lower-priced car market.

The last straw came in 1972, however, when management asked us: "Why is the cost of building a Chevrolet $70 closer to Oldsmobile today than it was in 1964?" The question from the top was offered in the usual "you aren't doing your job" manner. The irony was incredible. The very people who forced us to accept these corporate standardized parts with their accompanying cost increases, were coming back and asking, "Why are your costs up?" To me, this displayed a fundamental ignorance of our business and our company by the financially influenced top management. The program of standardization was an example of a centralized operating decision made over the objections of the divisions. If top management, instead of directing the program, simply declared it corporate policy to maximize commonality between all car lines while preserving the marketing integrity and profit structure of the corporation, the divisions would have done much better jobs because it is there that operating decisions are made most efficiently and effectively, as Alfred P. Sloan said. The Company would have saved money, not wasted it.

However, as operating decisions were brought into corporate headquarters and centralized on The Fourteenth Floor, simplistic concepts, such as standardization of parts, were grasped as the answers to complicated problems and put into effect without a thorough analysis of those problems. The engineering and design of the Vega by the central staffs is a perfect example of a "corporate" operational decision which was fouled up. And it proved the growing trend toward the centralization of operating decisions at General Motors.

One simplistic concept practiced is what I call "management by task force." In a sense, it replaced "management by committee" because it seemed that, every time a problem was brought before one of the corporate committees, a "task force" was formed to look into it. We had task forces on everything: new-model start-up, material cost increases, management-labor problems. It got so ridiculous that one time Terrell organized two separate task forces to work on the same project—new-model start-up problems. One was formed under the direction of GMAD and the other under the manufacturing staff. Each task force required the divisions to answer essentially the same questions. Our Chevrolet people were so tied up just answering the same questions from two different sources that we had to work overtime to get our own production into shape.

When the reports were prepared and submitted by the two task forces, the divisions were called in for the results. What we heard was just a playback of the information we had given them. In other words, they asked us how we were doing in our plans for start-up and then called us to central headquarters for a meeting to hear them tell us what we had just told them. This was not the first time this had happened. And it wasn't the last.

After one of these task force reports, John Beltz, Oldsmobile Division general manager, stood up and said:

> *You know, this is really an asinine thing we are doing. You guys (corporate management) make us give you all of this information and then you bring us down here and read our information back to us. Hell! We understand we've got to start production on time. That's what we are paid for. And we are working as hard as possible to do it. But we waste all of our time getting ready for these meetings, giving you data and then coming down here to listen to it played back to us.*

I admired him for telling management what most of us felt inside. To many of us, task force management was a sign of management weakness. Task forces are effectively used to solve emergency problems, such as rebuilding a plant gutted by a fire. But the wholesale use of task forces to manage the business is quite another thing. It is a sure sign of failing management. It says that you cannot get the job done within the framework of your management system. Yet management often boasted inside the company

254

and out that, "We've got a task force working on that problem." To me, that was nothing to be proud of.

It was shocking that task force solutions were constantly offered to fundamental and complex problems alike. To me, task force management was a copout brought on by a top management which apparently lacked self-confidence, and was saddled with a system that simply did not work. And in any system where inexperience and even incompetence exists in the upper reaches of management, lower-echelon executives become demoralized and dissatisfied. They see a system which impedes rather than enhances decision making. Their own jobs become frustrating. Divisional managers reporting to a group executive who is uneducated in their businesses must literally try to teach the business to him before getting decisions from him on their proposals. We often waltzed our bosses on The Fourteenth Floor through a step-by-step explanation of each program proposal—what it meant, how it related to the rest of the business and what it would do for the company. Even after this, their judgment most often was based on what GM had done before. Budget reviews, for example, usually went through without a hitch if you were proposing to spend no more money than you did the previous year.

One review I especially recall took place with a Fourteenth Floor boss. I was with Chevy at the time, and I always gave the divisional management exposure to Fourteenth Floor meetings, as part of their management development. For this review, Bill Gossett, Chevy's Finance manager, and I took along several other Chevy executives to show them how a division works out its new budget with top management. We were not far into the review when it became quite obvious that the boss wasn't too sure about what we were telling him. He understood the numbers all right, but from the questions he asked it was plain that he was not familiar with the various aspects of running an automotive division. That was to be expected because he never had run one. But it was embarrassing to me to have my managers see the basic, fundamental approach we had to take to explain our business to our boss and get his approval for our budget. After the meeting, Gossett said to me: "I don't think he knows what we are talking about. That's the saddest, most pathetic budget review I've been

255

through in my life." I thought to myself: "I wish we'd gone to this meeting alone."

One of the most demoralizing meetings on The Fourteenth Floor took place when all of the divisional general managers were called downtown to meet our new vice-president for Car and Truck, Body and Assembly Operations, Kyes's successor, Richard L. Terrell. To a man, we had had such unpleasant experiences with his predecessor that we all were anxiously awaiting this meeting and hoping that the successor would be a welcome change. We knew little about Terrell because his life had been spent in non-automotive areas.

There were the usual pleasantries and handshakes preceding the meeting, and when the meeting started, we expected a wide-ranging discussion of each of our operations, our problems, objectives and perhaps to hear from Terrell his initial goals for the total domestic automotive operation. Instead, Terrell launched into a discourse on "foreman training." We were all thunderstruck. He was telling guys like Jim McDonald of Pontiac, and George Elges of Cadillac, who grew up in manufacturing, how to train foremen. He was presenting such a narrow view of his job that we never talked about the business. The performance was disheartening to all of us. We left the meeting depressed.

Increasingly, group and upper managers seemed to look upon their jobs in such narrow terms that it was impossible to competently direct broad corporate policy. Often misplaced, unprepared or simply undertalented, these executives filled their days and our committee meetings with minutiae. After one particularly frustrating meeting of the Administrative Committee, John Beltz and I were picking up our notes when he looked down at the far end of the conference table at the corporate management and said to me, "I wouldn't let one of those guys run a gas station for me." It was a bitter and sad indictment of our top management by one of the then young, truly bright lights of General Motors management.

Perhaps most frustrating was the realization that there was (and is) in General Motors no vehicle for change. For the most part, a top executive by the time he works his way through the system is a carbon copy of his predecessors. If the men in place cannot do the job, there is no reason to believe that their handpicked successors can. There never was, in most of my days with General Motors, an attempt by management to analyze previous corporate decisions to see if they were right for the company, and to use this information in perfecting the management process of the future. No one questioned whether General Motors should be moving more toward centralization and standardization during the '60s and '70s. No one in upper management seemed to be concerned with those questions. When they were raised on the outside by the press or various corporate critics, instead of taking the matter seriously and studying it, management vehemently denied that the process set up under Sloan had changed in the slightest. For all I know, it may well have believed this, even though the facts didn't support it.

It was impossible to raise meaningful constructive dissent. This is a reflection of the personality of Donner. He was a totalitarian. He would not tolerate opposition. Donner was the singular boss. Under him each management level had its boss, and the word of this boss was final. Whether it made sense or not, there was no questioning it. When we were having a problem with poor valve wear on our engines due to a switch to unleaded gas, we proposed to top management that we spend $600,000 to modernize and expand our Flint Chevrolet engine plant to accommodate a valve-plating process which would cure the wear problem. I asked Terrell for permission to submit the project. He refused. I explained that by spending this money we would actually be saving money because it would cost much more to have the plating done on the outside. He responded with authority: "Look. We are not building any additional floor space. Even if it is just 5,000 square feet."

That was it. There was to be no further discussion of the matter. So we went outside to have the work done, and it cost us $3 million per year instead of $600,000 for one construction project.

Criticism from the outside is generally viewed as ill-informed. General Motors management thinks what it is doing is right, because it is GM that is doing it and that the outside world is wrong. It is always "they" versus "us." The press is viewed in a Nixonian sense as constantly carrying out a vendetta against the corporation.

257

When a reputable Harvard management professor, Peter Drucker, in 1946 wrote *The Concept of a Corporation*, which dissected and analyzed General Motors, the public regarded the work as decidedly pro-business and pro-GM. But the corporation didn't. Drucker noted in an epilogue to that book, written in 1972, that GM became very unfriendly to him because he suggested that the company had to reappraise its organization, objectives and business structure in the post-World War II years. He was resoundingly criticized within the company for daring to question the organization of the corporation.

Criticism from the inside is looked upon almost as treason. After reading Robert Townsend's book, *Up the Organization*, I decided to have Chevy management read it. While, some of it was light, shallow, glib—almost a wiseacre's kind of thing—part of it contained good, terse, and concise observations about the business world. I felt that just about any guy could read it and perhaps improve his business perspective. So I ordered 600 copies of *Up the Organization* and sent them to every one in Chevrolet who was classified as a manager. A few months later, the corporation somehow found out about this and it went through the ceiling. One of the executives above me at the time made a big thing about it, "How could you ever go out and buy this book by a guy who was critical of General Motors? That is just one of the most unforgivable things you could do, to give credence to some guy who criticizes the system. That's just unheard of around here," he remarked.

I said, "Hell. That's silly. Everyone on the outside is reading it. It's a best seller. These guys might as well know what somebody is saying about them."

Unable to accept criticism inside or outside, totalitarian in its exercise of management authority and thin at the top in the broad-based understanding and experience needed to manage the business, General Motors also was the victim of business developments that have been plaguing hundreds of large companies in many industries.

For one thing, there are fewer "owners" of the major businesses of this country. By "owners" I mean people in management with very substantial holdings of the company stock. In theory, this is not bad because it would appear to make business more democratic by spreading the ownership. More democratic ownership should make companies more responsive. In truth, this is not happening.

The big individual owners of GM, like Sloan or du Pont and others, who owned hundreds of millions of dollars worth of the corporation's stock, had long tenure. Their decisions were biased as much in favor of the long-term growth and health of the company as they were in favor of the short-term profit statement. When they managed the business, sound planning was a fundamental aspect of management because that was the only way the company could grow and prosper. Their tenure gave a continuity to management.

There are no great owner-managers at General Motors today. Thirty-thousand or 40,000 shares are considered a large position of stock. But that is almost insignificant compared to the 250-million shares that have been issued. Much of the corporate stock, however, is controlled by institutions of one sort or another. These organizations are usually short-term and results-oriented, and they do not take an active hand in management. When they are dissatisfied with the company's performance, they just sell the stock.

The people running General Motors today tend to be short-term, professional managers. They are in the top spots only a short time, less than 10 years. In a sense, they just learn their job, about the time they have to leave. So the concern at the top today is for the short-term health of the company. These professional managers want to produce a good record while they are in office. They do not have the perspective and incentive that a long-term owner with a large financial position in the company has because they are in a top spot for only a short while and then gone. They are running the business for themselves.

Several times in the late '60s and early '70s, outside board members asked management why we weren't getting into small cars. Management brushed aside their inquiries and never gave the questions serious consideration in running the company. Sloan or du Pont wouldn't have stood for this.

Furthermore, management is isolated from its business. At a time when customers are crying mightily about poor car quality, service problems and the unpleasantness often

259

associated with buying a car, top managers probably haven't purchased a car for themselves or sat in a line outside of a dealer's service garage in 20 years. Part of the entrapments of high office include "company" cars which are serviced daily in the company garage. The closest reference an executive has to the marketplace is usually through his own family, which hardly lives the life of typical car buying Americans. GM executives' jobs never take them into contact with the real world. And their free time is spent socializing with other General Motors people and their suppliers.

By 1972, it was obvious to me that the degeneration of GM's management system not only was seriously hurting the company's performance—even though our sales and profits were strong, they could have been much stronger—but was undermining executive morale. Chairman Dick Gerstenberg grumbled loudly when it became obvious that Ford's operations and return on investment were improving relative to General Motors. So, with the assistance of Gossett, his finance staff at Chevrolet and the central corporate financial people, I quietly prepared a study which assessed our failings vis-à-vis Ford, proposed a profit improvement program that could add $1.3 billion to GM's profit, and critically analyzed what I felt were serious management failings. It was a rare study because I garnered help from the financial side in a report that was critical of the financially dominated management of the company. None of them, including Gossett, would sign the completed report, and I certainly could understand that under the circumstances.

In the first draft, my growing bitterness with the system was too obvious in the harsh language I used. Gossett pointed out that such a report would not be effective. So he toned down the language, although it remained strongly worded. A 14-page, single-spaced final version was prepared.

It talked frankly:

> *It is obvious from the Ford comparison that real problems exist within General Motors. To hide behind our comparative absolute profit rates, when this is due primarily to our relative strength in the*

*medium- and high-priced market is foolhardy. . . .
Today General Motors' management morale and
efficiency are at modern-day all-time lows. Everyone has misgivings and vague feelings of uncer-
tainty. Various levels of GM management are openly critical of one another. . . . First and most importantly, there are a great many incompetent
executives on The Fourteenth Floor. . . . Most of
our management mistakes today are not mistakes of
commission, they are errors of omission. Missed
opportunities—things left undone. . . . In General
Motors, with the exception of a small group we are
now building in Chevrolet, we have virtually no
marketing expertise. Contrary to Mr. Sloan's teach-
ing we do not use the best information available to
make decisions. None of the modern marketing
tools are used regularly or extensively. When they
are used the results are generally disregarded. . . . We
seem to forget that a cloistered executive, whose
only social contacts are with similar executives who
make $500,000 a year, and who has not really
bought a car the way a customer has in years, has
no basis to judge public taste. . . . We no longer
have a highly motivated team and the team spirit
that built GM. . . . Our present group management
so little understands this problem that they have
evolved simplistic solutions that will accomplish
nothing. . . . As John Beltz pointed out, General
Motors as a corporation today has a poorer image
than any of our divisions—again because we react
rather than act. . . . Our inability to compete with
the foreign manufacturers is more due to management failure than anything else. Past managements
spent our lush advantage extravagantly. . . . The
system and management are stifling initiative.*

It pointed to problems and the results of these problems:

Management inexperience or incompetence

*When you have a serious business problem who
do you go to for help and advice? During the last*

seven (7) years there were only two (2) years that either the Group or the Executive Vice-President of the Automotive Group had the ability to run a car division themselves, much less help a floundering general manager. This has led to an attitude that floundering executives should be replaced—instead of helped. Sacrificing one of GM's main strengths— deep mutual loyalty. If I had a serious problem— who would I talk to? Certainly not Don Boyes (group vice-president), or Roger Kyes or even Ed Rollert. Today, no division manager would ever really think of getting advice from Rube Jensen or Dick Terrell (except as a courtesy). Both are great guys but the largest business either of them has ever run was smaller and much simpler to manage than one of our engine plants, and neither has ever solved a major business problem—or is known for success. They absolutely have no automotive knowledge or competence. Even the simplest discussion with them is hopelessly complicated—because you must explain the whole thing from the beginning and how it relates to the business. Even then, judgment is based on what you did, or spent in previous years, or what other divisions are doing. Leadership and innovation are impossible. . . . Not only are these people of no help, most of what they do is wrong.

The lack of planning

People who do not know and understand the automobile business could not possibly give it direction. We have no constructive corporate direction in solving any of the many very obvious major problems that have greatly reduced our return on sales and investment. GM is without direction operating management-wise.

Absence of good management development program

A prime example of corporate non-feasance, and a tragedy, is that we have not brought along more trained automotive people. There is no way a man without fifteen (15) or twenty (20) progressive years in the automotive side can manage a car division much less be a senior automotive executive. The only way a division can prosper under this kind of management is through a competent experienced staff—in which case the staff is managing the business, not the manager. (My GM training was quite short by most standards.)

People from the financial side seem to be good at keeping score—but we are yet to see one man who can play the game himself. When I came to Chevrolet, I was given four (4) major financial staff analyses of Chevrolet's decline in volume and profits —not one (1) showed the least depth of understanding of the real problems. A manager trying to work from them (I guess Pete Estes did) would get absolutely nowhere (which Pete did).

Obviously, we have not fulfilled our obligations to the stockholders. We are primarily an automotive company, but we have not developed executives capable of insuring the future success of General Motors' automotive business. There is a genuine concern for General Motors' future. GM has an unbelievably great potential—but it is not being realized.

A program for profit improvement: (Annual basis)

Potential

1. *Better management, management motivation & morale* .... $ 200,000,000
2. *On-time tooling programs & better planning* 250,000,000
3. *Least cost, non-standardization (of parts and cars)* 300,000,000
4. *Back-to-back start-up* 200,000,000
5. *Reduce cost components-or-assembly to lowest level in GM today* 100,000,000
6. *Competitive motivation of all suppliers, car divisions and allied (divisions)* 200,000,000

263

7. 14-day improvement in order response,
one-time profit *100,000,000*
DOMESTIC POTENTIAL $1,350,000,000

*If we accomplish these things—and they could
be done in as little as three (3) years with real management direction, we could improve our profit-
ability by at least $1 billion a year.*

The analysis was finished in mid-June of 1972, and I
waited for an opportune time to present it to Chairman
Dick Gerstenberg. The reverence in which the chairman is
held in GM is such that you don't just call him up and say,
"Hi, Dick, I've got a plan that will make one point three
billion dollars for you." There is decorum to be maintained. And although the company says that everyone's
door is always open to anyone else, and that there is freedom in communications from one management level to
another, in general practice an executive at my level had
to keep his boss informed of his activity, especially if he
wanted to call on the chairman. Since my bosses were
implicated in my critique of the company, I wasn't about
to show the report to them. So I waited. But an opportunity never came up. I relied instead on the financial side
of the business to get the report (unofficially) into his
hands. The dual responsibility of the financial people often
had them bringing divisional secrets and reports to their
financial bosses at the corporate level. And I am pretty
sure this report got to the chairman in this manner.

Eventually, I used it as my operating plan when I went
to The Fourteenth Floor the next fall. But instead of helping the company out, as I hoped, it put one more nail into
the lid of my corporate coffin.

In October 1973, about six months after my resignation,
I mailed a copy of the report to Gerstenberg with the accompanying letter:

Dear Dick:

*In going through my files I came across this
memo which was written April, May and June of
1972. The final version was completed on June 13,
1972. The financial figures were put together and*

the language toned down by Bill Gossett, Chevrolet's finance manager, and his staff. Recognizing Mr. Gossett and his staff's dual responsibility to both the division management and the financial staff, I chose not to send this rather frank memo directly, but to rely on 'underground delivery' via Mr. Gossett's obligation to the financial staff. Thus, I assume a copy was delivered to you and, of course, I did not expect an answer since it was unofficial.

Now that I am no longer a part of GM (my heart is still with her) I feel I can be more objective in my views. Even from this standpoint, it is obvious to me that this memo is more pertinent than ever (while some parts of it were included in my January 1973 letter of resignation to Mr. Terrell), that it indeed portrays a road map for GM future success.

The recent IBM ruling would seem to indicate that anti-trust action against GM is coming soon and that it is mandatory that GM improve her business and management practices before this fully competitive era descends on her.

> *Sincerely,*
> *John Z. De Lorean*

I did not hear back from Gerstenberg, formally or informally. I never really expected to. And as far as I can tell there has been little meaningful progress made on the problems at General Motors as I perceived and presented them to management in the memo.

CHAPTER SIXTEEN

Epilogue

Some see danger in bigness. They fear the concentration of economic power that it brings with it. That is in a degree true. It simply means, however, that industrial management must expand its horizons of responsibility. It must recognize that it can no longer confine its activities to the mere production of goods and services. It must consider the impact of its operation on the economy as a whole in relation to the social and economic welfare of the entire community. For years I have preached this philosophy. Those charged with great industrial responsibility must become industrial statesmen. . . .

   —ALFRED P. SLOAN, JR.,
     Adventures of a White Collar Man (1941)

. . . (and) I hold that if companies are attacked simply because they are big then an attack on efficiency must be a corollary of that attack. If we penalize efficiency, how can we as a nation compete in the economy of the world at large? . . ."

   —ALFRED P. SLOAN, JR.,
     My Years With General Motors (1964)

American business, especially big business, today suffers from an immense credibility gap. Whenever people in the U.S. are polled on their attitudes toward the institutions of our land, business ranks close to the bottom. It is ironic because some of the businesses and industries most responsible for the boom and growth of this country's economic system, and for providing the ingredients of a lifestyle unparalleled in any other part of the world, are now among the most severely criticized.

They are criticized not just because they are powerful and big, but because they have not responsibly used the franchise of power and the size given to them by the public. In such an atmosphere bigness becomes identified with badness. One reason is that once business success is achieved it is often used to isolate executives from the very source of their success—the customer and the marketplace. Executives who are isolated often misconstrue their franchise from the public as being a virtual mandate for the assumption of omnipotence. In a highly competitive marketplace such an attitude would not last long. After a short time, the isolated executives would find their markets taken away by competitors who were attuned to the wants and needs of the public and who were exercising their franchises to operate responsibly.

The domestic automobile industry is not such a highly competitive industry. At best it is an oligopoly dominated by one company, General Motors, which accounts for more than half of the domestic industry sales each year. At worst it is an outright monopoly with GM being the monopolist. Erosion of power in such an atmosphere occurs slowly if at all, although the deepening of foreign car penetration in the past two decades indicates that it might happen. It develops slowly because of simple economics. The competitors do not have the resources or the firepower to attack the dominant company. Customers, therefore, are faced with a limited range of choices as an alternative to the dominant company. Today in the auto industry the choices are among essentially the same products.

After watching the corporation over a long period of time, I have slowly reached the conclusion that, in reality, General Motors' competitors in America exist by reason of GM's sufferance. GM has the potential to eliminate Ford,

Chrysler and American Motors any time it desires. This could be done in a short time, as little as one year, by simply lowering prices or not raising them to the point where GM forced the competition out of business.

There is no question that General Motors sets the prices for the automobile industry. There isn't an executive with any competitor who will not privately admit this to be true. Some even admit it publicly. In 1968 Chrysler, in a bold move, announced a price boost of an average $89 per car on its 1969 models. Those in the industry felt that the maneuver was adopted by Chrysler to signal to GM that it needed this kind of a price lift to make a good return on the new models.

But GM announced its prices a short while later and they averaged only $52, or $37 less than the Chrysler boost. Chrysler was embarrassed. It had no alternative but to roll back its prices to an average of $55 a car. GM was hailed as a public-spirited company for forcing the Chrysler rollback and, in a sense, I suppose it was. But I also remember several top GM executives taking gleeful pleasure in a show of brute power, from the fact that they'd made Chrysler management back down. This incident served as a notice to everyone that GM could pull away the price supports from competitors and force them all out of business any time it wished. A similar incident occurred in 1966 when Ford was also forced to roll back an earlier price hike on its 1967 models from $107 to $66 per car, because GM came out with lower prices. The reverse has not been true. When the Ford Pinto was introduced in 1969 with a price that was $172 less than the Chevy Vega, there was no GM rollback. Though the Vega often sold fewer units than the Pinto, it did turn a profit at times, and when it lost money the losses were easily absorbed by GM's other highly profitable lines.

General Motors' dominance was best evidenced during the long auto sales slump, which began in late 1973, when executives from Ford and Chrysler admitted that they could no longer compete across-the-board with GM in the marketplace. They simply did not have the financial strength. These two multi-multi-billion dollar companies, ranking among the largest in the world, were actually admitting they did not have the money to compete. So the other domestic auto companies are following a policy of hunting and picking niches between GM's product lines, while tackling the giant in a few selected areas.

Considering their size, both Ford and Chrysler could dominate just about any other industry in the world. But in the American automobile industry they must play second and third fiddle. Even though Ford was superior to General Motors in product innovation during the time I was with GM and Chrysler surpassed it in technical innovation, neither firm made substantial cuts into GM's half of the market. General Motors is so gigantic and power-laden that the miracles of free enterprise can no longer operate, rewarding innovation and imagination and punishing lethargy and unresponsiveness. Today General Motors is partially surviving on the momentum created by its founders and shapers, plus the muscle provided by its massive dealer network. And yet it still is able to totally dominate the American automobile scene.

Such size and power is not bad in itself, if it is used responsibly, as Sloan indicated. Bigness, theoretically, can be good if it functions responsibly. When it does not, the results are always bad.

The insensitivity I witnessed at GM concerning the effect of its operations on its many publics told me that there was no industrial statesmanship accompanying its bigness. Generally, consideration of the impact of its decisions on the economy and society was not an input in the GM decision-making process, as the following example indicates.

In the early 1970s, the corporation decided it wanted to build two new assembly facilities because of the anticipated growth in the market. The GM Assembly Division proposed that the plants be located in Memphis, Tennessee, and Oklahoma City. Pontiac and Chevrolet Divisions got into the discussion by suggesting that the new facilities be located in their hometowns—Pontiac and Detroit, Michigan. I was managing Chevrolet at the time. Our proposal was prepared and backed by Bill Gossett, the Finance director, who had compiled compelling financial reasons for locating a new plant in the heart of Detroit and the auto industry: We could obtain urban renewal land at a fraction of the cost of land elsewhere; Detroit had a ready pool of skilled workers; and shipping costs were such that it actually cost less to ship a whole car around the country than it did to ship the components to make it.

To these financial reasons we added a moral dimension: The mushrooming domestic problems in the city of Detroit were, in part, related to the auto industry. The ranks of those unemployed and on welfare were filled with people drawn to Detroit by the lure of automotive jobs and the high wages those jobs paid. When they arrived here, from the South primarily, there were often no jobs available. As a result, the newcomers frequently chose street crime to get money they could not earn in an auto plant.

The 1967 riots were partially created by this climate. The fact that Detroit, the home of the automobile and mass assembly lines, was also called the Murder Capital of the World was an embarrassment to the industry. We had a responsibility to these people and the city. By providing jobs for the unemployed we would be helping to trim the city's roaring crime rate. To us, locating a plant in Detroit made social and economic sense.

Pontiac Division was promoting a similar program for locating an assembly plant in Pontiac which, though smaller than Detroit, had social and crime problems of similar proportions. Pontiac Division had picked up the city of Pontiac in the early 1960s, and it now had to do the same thing in the 1970s.

With Gossett's proposal in hand I dispatched an aide to talk informally with the planning department of the city of Detroit. These were informal, clandestine talks. I had learned from my attempts to try to prevent the 1970 UAW strike that the corporation didn't want me to get involved in what it viewed as corporate areas of responsibility.

The people in City Hall couldn't have been more receptive and enthusiastic. They were concerned because as the crime rate rose the tax base went down. Businesses abandoned their inner-city sites in favor of the new locations in suburbs or in the South. Therefore, vacant land was available in Detroit. We told them how much land we needed for a modern assembly plant and they responded: "You almost can't name too much. Whatever you want is going to be available. If we have to knock down some old buildings, we'll do so."

They also indicated that a favorable price could be

271

worked out, adding that GM would qualify for tax relief under a program designed to bring new business into the city. The Pontiac Division was getting the same kind of reception from its governmental officials who wanted the jobs offered by a new assembly plant and the fresh income that they would bring into the community.

With our ducks in a row we made our formal proposal to Terrell, and Pontiac followed the same procedure. At the time, Gossett carried the program informally up through the financial ranks. But the programs were not given serious consideration by either Terrell or the financial people. They were rejected out of hand. Memphis and Oklahoma City were chosen as the sites for the new assembly plants in the face of compelling economic and social reasons for locating in Detroit. We were told by top level management that it was more economical to build in the cities selected. But we were never shown the figures supporting that contention, or given the opportunity to compare that proposal to ours.

Although it is starting to change under the pressure of federal affirmative action programs, the corporate insensitivity to the plight of minorities in America is in part reflected in the attitude regarding the troubles of the cities in which they do business. I witnessed this insensitivity firsthand on many occasions. When I ran Pontiac I sought several programs to put more minorities into the ranks of the better jobs. The city of Pontiac has a very large black population.

When I walked into the plant there were plenty of blacks at work, but they were all at the lower jobs. There were no black executives, no black managers and damn few black foremen. I remember one exception was a guy in the Pontiac foundry who was such a big, rough, son-of-a-gun, that he was made foreman and a part of management.

We tried to set up several programs at Pontiac to develop blacks for promotion to better jobs. I pressured the corporation and they said, "Well if you send us a good, capable, black executive, we'll hire him."

I said, "How the hell can you do that? The black has no chance. He's educated in schools that are inferior, he can't go to college. If he does go to college, it is many times a bad college, or he's sent to a college where he is given no chance to compete." But the corporation just said, "Find us a qualified black and we'll hire him."

To my way of thinking the responsibility ran deeper than that. So at Pontiac we took promising high school graduates and sent them to a nearby college, paid their tuition and set up a work schedule so they could go to school, work in their off hours and during the summer.

Trouble was that many of these kids couldn't pass the college entrance exam. So we set up a pre-education program to give them the qualifications necessary for college work. Eventually, some became satisfactory employees and began to rise in the management ranks. In another program we discovered a number of dedicated employees, blacks, whites and Chicanos, who were illiterate. Since the medium of communication in business is often writing, they couldn't advance from their jobs, even though many were basically intelligent. We set up a program to teach them to read and write. I will never forget the first graduation class, and the looks of these employees, some with tears in their eyes, because a whole new world of communication was opened for them. They could read and write.

One of the most demanding challenges we had at Pontiac was called "Operation Opportunity." It was an outgrowth of the unrest in the cities in the mid-1960s. The idea came from Pontiac's Personnel Manager, Theodore B. Bloom, who was very sensitive to the problems of the community. In this program we worked with the local chapter of the Urban League to hire the so-called hardcore unemployed of Pontiac. We took these people, who had never worked a regular job for any lengthy period, and tried to get them accustomed to the regimentation of the American way. It was hard. These were people accustomed to sleeping until four or five in the afternoon, then getting up and making the rounds at night, perhaps committing crimes. We were trying to get them into the system and tell them, somewhat ironically, that it was better to get up at 6:00 a.m. and stand in a hot, smokey foundry and work their fannies off for eight hours.

The truth was we had a helluva time keeping these people on the job, until we sought more help from the Urban

League. The League assigned people to guide the new workers. Their responsibility was to go to the workers' houses and drag them out of bed, if necessary, to get them to work on time. After they had done this for about 90 days or so, the workers started to get accustomed to a regular income. It was more money than they'd been able to get off the street and it was regular. Pretty soon they started renting houses or apartments, buying color TVs or cars and new clothes, and getting locked into the payments necessary to keep these nice things—like the rest of the working world. They got so hooked by the system that they couldn't afford to quit. They didn't want to go back to their previous life. They became part of the American system. We ended up with a retention rate of about 55% which I think was phenomenal considering the depth of the problem.

We got no corporate help or encouragement when we put these programs in at Pontiac. GM tolerated them because the division was doing well. They were not given corporate visibility until minority hiring programs became a fashionable trend or were dictated by the government. Then General Motors started citing our programs as the major efforts in the corporation for the advancement of blacks and other minorities.

About the time these Pontiac programs were reaching fruition, I was asked by Columbia University to do a chapter in a book being written on black economic development. It was part of the popular American Assembly series at Columbia which focuses on major American problems. I wrote the chapter which I felt accurately depicted the condition of blacks in America; how they didn't really have a chance unless the whites took compensatory action and gave them an opportunity. My chapter was pretty hard hitting but in no way demeaning to General Motors or its business system.

The word got back to the corporation that I did this and I was told that I was not allowed to put my name on the article. First they wanted me to withdraw entirely. When I said that was impossible, they wanted me to have my by-line taken off of it.

A Columbia official called someone in top management

and told him that the things that I was saying were exactly the kinds of things GM should be standing for. In essence, management was being told that GM should be proud to be calling national attention to severe social problems and recommending that they be cured. It had no choice but to leave the chapter and book alone.

When I got to Chevy, the corporation was still complaining that there were no hireable blacks when the pressure was put on them to bring minorities into the corporate fold. So I proposed that the corporation turn its home-grown college—General Motors Institute—into an all black institution. I said: "If you bring in nothing but minority kids, the best minority kids in the country, for about six or eight or ten years, eventually you will have an infusion of bright, well-trained, intelligent minorities in the organization. In ten or twelve years you will start seeing some junior executives and eventually some senior executives who are minorities. That's the only way that GM will ever be a truly integrated organization. And if you don't make it all minorities then you should make it half minorities.

To back up my feelings I told the Chevrolet personnel people:

"All I want you to sponsor at GMI is black students. Chevrolet is going to sponsor nothing but black students."

Well, GM management went right through the roof. I was told I was going to destroy the school's standards.

When word of my order got to The Fourteenth Floor I was called into Terrell's office and he said, "Mr. Roche says that you are discriminating against whites. You are trying to keep nothing but blacks in there. You're discriminating against whites and, by God, we're not going to stand for that."

By the time I got all through with the corporate hassle over my plan, about half of Chevy's sponsorees at GMI were minorities, which I considered a victory over the system.

To me these actions of failing to recognize the broad corporate responsibilities to social problems were in direct opposition to what Sloan was talking about when he stressed that businesses had duties beyond the mere commercial aspects of their work.

The best interests of the country were certainly not being considered when General Motors announced an average price hike of almost 10 percent per car in the summer of 1974, for inflation was already eating away at the average American family's income. It became a cold and calloused decision in my mind after people on the financial staff told me that the size of the increase was raised when it learned that the pricing announcement would come at the time President Nixon resigned from office. The corporate bet was that all of the publicity given to the historic events taking place in Washington would overshadow and diminish the attention given to the GM price hike. And that is precisely what happened.

In addition to its failings in the area of industrial statesmanship, General Motors is not the efficient well-run company that it was under the guidance of its founders. This is so, in large measure, because it has lost sight of the formula for success and the long-range goals set for it by those men.

In the time since I left active management, I have often been asked, "What would you do if you were running General Motors?"

Part of the answer to this question is quite simple: Return to some of the basic principles of management promulgated by Sloan. General Motors' strength comes from its diversity within the confines of one industry. This offers many different approaches to the demands of one marketplace for wheeled, motorized vehicles. That diversity is severely diminished today. As GM centralized, management moved to combine, consolidate, and intertwine the operating arms of the corporation. The Detroit Diesel and Allison Divisions were combined; parts operations were likewise blended; and the manufacturing-assembly capability of the car divisions was all but taken away and given to an entirely new entity, GM Assembly Division.

Each of the car divisions was given the design and manufacturing responsibility for parts of all GM's cars. The rationale was that these moves made good financial sense. I suspect, however, and no one told me this, that these moves were made primarily to thwart or complicate federal government antitrust action. A closely knit and intricately interwoven General Motors would be much more difficult to break up than a distinctly diverse operation.

These moves destroyed the heart of General Motors' decentralized operations. So the answer to curing the company's ills today includes a rapid move back to the point where the divisions are easily distinguishable entities, responsible, to a large degree, for the success and/or failure of their own operations. Such a move would include giving the divisions back much of their assembly responsibility and cutting back the program of standardization to the point where it makes economic sense. GMAD could be maintained, in part, to assemble cars for the smaller divisions, but it should be obliged to report to those divisions and not to corporate management.

Such a shift back to decentralization also would require that corporate management on The Fourteenth Floor relinquish its role in formulating operating decisions. It must be returned to its traditional function of forming corporate policy and planning the company's future. This is a very difficult thing to do because it would require taking the reins of the corporation out of the hands of the financial managers and putting them into the hands of competent operating executives capable of a broad understanding of the business. That type of executive rarely exists in upper management today. To solve this I would redirect the management development system to produce the wide-ranging, well-experienced executives needed for the top slots. This can only come from the cross-pollenization of an executive's job experience at a level where he can see and feel the operations and make the various facets of the company work.

In the mid-1960's the financial people in control recognized that their own backgrounds were insufficient for understanding and running the operations of the company. They sought to give operating experience to the financial segment by putting executives who'd worked their way up through the financial ranks into group vice-president spots. This did not work. The group vice-president job was too far up the management ladder to provide experience that would actually help the executive. You don't teach a guy how to play football by making him coach. Instead, put him on the team, on the third or fourth string, then teach him the basics and let him move up to the first team as his ability and performance improve.

So, too, with management experience. An executive really learns the business in the low- and middle-management areas. Under this kind of management development system I would take an assistant chief engineer, and make him an assistant regional sales manager, or even a regional sales manager for a couple of years. Then I'd put him at a similar level in manufacturing. Eventually, he might manage a plant. This could be followed by a stint in the overseas operations. He would learn all the facets of the business at the level where the work is actually done. This type of training could be accomplished with bright executive talent in all segments of the business. Thus, an executive on the finance staff could be switched to manufacturing or sales in a similar manner. As I noted earlier, the reason Harlow Curtice was such a seasoned and well-rounded executive is that his operating experience was backed up by a solid financial understanding which he had acquired while he was controller of a division.

This type of system would eventually produce executives who understood the wide ramifications of the business. Those who were successful would rise to a point where they would be managing one of the divisions. The success with which they ran these divisions would determine their ability to one day manage the whole business. Former GM President Charles Wilson used to say that the purpose of the GM management system was not to weed out candidates for the top spot of the corporation but instead to produce many well-qualified candidates for the top, any one of whom could run General Motors.

By putting the day-to-day control of the business back into the hands of the divisional managers we would eliminate the need for the huge central staffs of the corporation. These staffs grew as decision-making became centralized. When it centralized, GM became one giant division and these staffs now perform the same function as their counterparts in the divisions in areas such as marketing, engineering, finance and manufacturing. With decentralization these staffs could be dismantled and trimmed to a size and shape more befitting their traditional role in the corporation as advisors and specialists on call by the divisions.

As a matter of overall corporate policy I would abandon the low-profile, defensive, almost head-in-the-sand public image which the corporation maintained. This posture comes from a misunderstanding of the role of business in America and the reasons behind its poor image. General Motors management, as far as I can determine, does not believe that its poor public image comes from an inability to discharge its broad industrial responsibility to GM customers, shareholders, employees, and the public in general. Management feels that it is under attack from all sides today because there is a growing fire of unrest with American institutions which is intensified by liberal thinkers and fanned by the press. As the biggest factor in one of America's most prominent institutions—the automobile industry —General Motors management feels that the corporation simply draws the lion's share of criticism. The best way to reduce this inevitable criticism, as top management sees it, is to keep a low, faceless profile.

I believe that industrial statesmanship in the Sloan sense requires just the opposite approach. The responsibilities of bigness demand leadership. Leadership by its very nature is highly visible. In February of 1974, then Chairman Richard C. Gerstenberg told an audience of investors, educators and the press: "We must do well before we can do good." The gist of his message was that the corporation had to make money—profit—before it could exercise its public responsibilities. This may sound naive to many but the opposite is true. That by doing good, exercising a role of leadership and public responsibility, General Motors, or any American business, will do well and promote its long-term health and viability. The ability of General Motors to understand its responsibilities can be obtained only if the corporation breaks away from its formal management mold which shapes and demands a homogeneity of personality among its managers. The stiff corporate structure should be replaced by one that will accommodate those who are not easily categorized, who do not fit into the current mold, but who can make enduring and substantial contributions to the success of the company.

The system is so rigid now that I do not think an innovative thinker like Alfred P. Sloan, Jr. could qualify for a job in the upper ranks of General Motors. Even if he did, he wouldn't have the freedom necessary to operate effectively there. I do think that my fall from favor and subsequent departure from General Motors posits the inability of the system of management to blend and accommodate. The rigidity of the system would not tolerate my successful alternative to the standard way of doing business. Even though I was working for the ultimate good of the corporation, I was not permitted to make a contribution.

In today's atmosphere there is virtually no likelihood of outsiders taking over the management of General Motors. The system stresses longevity and loyalty. And as long as the sheer size of the corporation continues to ring up acceptable profits, there will never be pressure from the outside members of the board of directors to bring in fresh management blood. Therefore, the vehicle for internal change does not exist in the corporation today. This situation leads to the conclusion that General Motors is incapable of changing. If so, in the end, change may be forced on GM from the outside. It is well known that several government agencies, such as the Justice Department and the Federal Trade Commission, have compiled volumes of data and evidence to support antitrust suits designed to break up this giant automaker. Court actions against IBM and AT&T indicate a growing mood to harness the power of the largest American businesses on the assumption that smaller businesses will create a more competitive climate which will work to the ultimate good of the consumer and the country. The thought of antitrust action against General Motors produces white-knuckled fear on The Fourteenth Floor.

I hope that the dismemberment of General Motors does not take place. But I know that the men who made GM great would be seriously concerned with the course that this company has taken today.

And while there is certainly time to redirect the company back to the road plotted by those founding fathers, I doubt that it will be done from inside.

In making these assessments of my career with General

Motors, I realize that my heart and spirit are still with her. My life at GM was a personal Horatio Alger dream with a sad ending. In the ending to this dream the company I so revered was no longer the company I was working for. There was no room for me at GM. And so I left.

Conclusion

On September 3, 1975 in a letter, John Z. De Lorean forbade publication of our book, *On a Clear Day You Can See General Motors.* Nevertheless, any concern that I had that the book just delivered to Playboy Press was anything other than the book he asked me to write with him was dispelled in a second letter from him five days later on September 8, 1975.

He first indicated his overall approval of the manuscript and then said that there were some changes and deletions he wanted to make with an eye toward expanding the manuscript to make the book harder hitting. He explained: "In place of these deletions, I want to expand greatly on the future of American business and my own future plans to build an 'ethical car'—and my chances of making it with GM hassling me at every turn.

"I want also to expand on which ways I was like my counterparts and in which ways I was different. We do not get very far into my essential motivations and how they helped me at one stage in my career and killed me at another."

He then listed eight areas for expanding the book which included:

"—Much more emphasis on monopoly aspects, examples of crushing competition. NDH machine tool bearings. (NDH is GM's New Departure Hyatt division).

"—Salaries uncalled for (among GM management).

"—Discuss how Curtice, Knudsen and now Cole were and are being blamed for every problem.

"—When I was having a problem, no one ever bothered to ask me about it.

"—Kiplinger PR survey—GM the worst review."

The letter proposed to "end on a discussion of free enterprise and saving our economic system—not just GM.

"Go into detail on my future plans for an 'ethical car' company:

"—Can it survive? Detail manner in which GM has hassled me through bankers, suppliers, woody wagon, bad-mouthing.

"—Cover in detail the destruction of all of Pontiac correspondence on the airbag and the morality of a public company destroying records.

"—To reinforce the monopoly aspect—discuss some of GM's giant fiascos which would have killed most other companies:

1. Fuel injection
2. Air ride
3. Turbo Glide and Buick counterpart
4. Wankel Engine
5. Monolithic Convertor—billions wasted

"—Expand corporation attitude toward consumer and dealer.

"—Cover a few of the methods used to bribe NATO buyers of Allison engines and bribes paid in locomotive business."

It was signed: "Sincerely yours, John Z. De Lorean."

Index

THE BIG BESTSELLER
THAT UNVEILS A WORLD
WHERE SEX IS A WORK OF ART . . .
AND ART IS THE ULTIMATE SEDUCTION

PROVENANCE

BY FRANK McDONALD

"LONG, RACY, FAST-MOVING . . .
STRETCHES FROM THE
STEEL-AND-GLASS CANYONS OF
MANHATTAN TO THE
DARK CATACOMBS OF ROME,
WITH STOPS IN THE
DELUXE HOTELS OF
LONDON, PARIS, ZURICH."
The New York Times Book Review

"FASCINATING . . . INTRIGUING . . .
A GLITTERING WORLD
TO WHICH FEW OF US
HAVE ACCESS . . . A GREAT STORY."
Los Angeles Herald Examiner

"STUNNING . . . SHEER DYNAMITE . . .
A COLOSSAL JOB OF
STORYTELLING IN THE
GRAND MANNER."
West Coast Review of Books

 AVON 50120/$2.75   Prov 9-80

A STUNNING AND PROPHETIC THRILLER
OF INNOCENT PEOPLE CAUGHT IN A
WEB OF INTERNATIONAL SUSPENSE

CANNIBALS AND MISSIONARIES

MARY McCARTHY

author of THE GROUP

"PURE PLEASURE . . .
A TENSE, INTELLIGENT ENTERTAINMENT."
Chicago Tribune

"FASCINATING . . . A KIND OF
CANTERBURY PILGRIMAGE WITH MACHINE GUNS."
Mary Gordon, The New York Times Book Review

"Mary McCarthy turns her keen mind and brilliant
style to the subject of terrorism and an airplane
hijacking . . . a tale psychologically astute, ironic
and ultimately heartbreaking . . . superb."
Publishers Weekly

"A return to the wicked brilliance of her early
work . . . sheer pleasure to read."
Quest

 AVON   50690/$2.75

CAN 9-80